AFRICAN EMBRACE

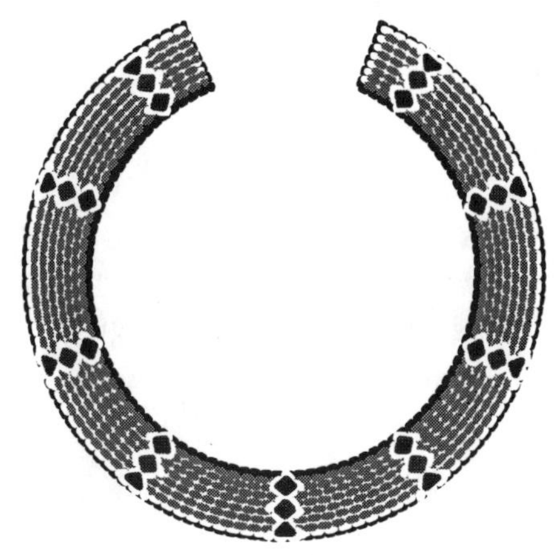

L. Dalton Casto

Published by:
African Ways Publishing
33 Hansen Court
Moraga, CA 94556

ISBN: 0-9659830-1-3
Library of Congress Catalog Number: 99-94706

Printed in the United States of America
9 8 7 6 5 4 3 2 1

To my family—Myrtle, Carol, Kent and Lynnanne—whose willingness to accompany me to darkest Africa at the cost of pet disposal, leaving friends and the abandoment of education programs, made the trip feasible.

Acknowledgment

I am most appreciative of the skills and enthusiasm of a number of people whose contibutions brought this book to fruition. My daughter Lynnanne Lang merits most of the credit for identifying the photos used and for obtaining publishing permission. My daughter Carol Fishel, upon her return to the U.S., served admirably as earth anchor ala NASA. My son Kent Casto undertook the task of escorting our daughters and friends for a visit to our home in Kenya and then provided assistance for the family's memorable African park Safari.

Betty Gardner continues to earn my gratitude for inducing a modicum of sophistication in my writing and Pamela Newacheck for converting my rough typing into useful script.

TABLE OF CONTENTS

INTRODUCTION

Certainly I had no intention of turning the lives of my wife and three teenagers upside down by switching careers in my late forties, especially with the upheavals incident to relocating. But that is what happened. We accepted a two-year assignment with the Peace Corps Family Volunteer Program in West Africa—Ghana—formerly the Gold Coast.

In effect, once I entered into service through African development assistance programs, I psychologically never returned home again. From Ghana, I worked in Uganda and then in Kenya for a nonprofit enterprise, a development assistance organization dedicated to providing assistance to low-income groups, tribes, and other associations. Thereafter, I traveled and lived in many other African countries, studying their development programs, conducting research, and writing.

Living and working in Africa to better the condition of low-income people is fascinating and at times terrifying. I was beset with experiences both pleasant and otherwise—often flatly incredible. These experiences warrant inclusion in this book for two reasons: first, for the expansive information about the African setting they provide, promoting a better understanding of the problems of our work; and second, for their entertainment value.

Of course, I never plunged headlong into a protracted stay in Africa to experience only a tourist's pleasure. To help develop food production, jobs, or other possibilities for improving the lot of a low-income people was a worthy and fascinating goal. In the beginning, I could not have envisioned how difficult it would be to achieve these results. Eventually, I came to understand some of the reasons for the failure of Western assistance projects. I delineate these fatal errors in assumptions and techniques through an analysis of actual projects: those for which I was personally responsible, as well as those of the larger professional organizations with which I was familiar.

The results of such an investigation are important because they have a beneficial effect on Western assistance planning. After all, the steadily worsening conditions of many African countries herald the need for more productive assistance efforts. However, the soundest of programs cannot completely contain the deterioration caused by the African governments' own fallacious policies.

The number one disastrous policy is the drive to Africanize their economies. The purpose is to replace with black citizens the Lebanese, Asians, and other non-blacks that held the skilled jobs and businesses during colonization. The process appears cheap and easy to the governments. They see no need to protect or remunerate the non-blacks for their loss of wealth and property. A mere refusal to renew business licenses and work permits eliminates the non-blacks' reason for staying in the country. The various governments have different approaches; some are selective, some vary the timetable. However, the inevitable result is the same in the long run. With the exodus of these non-blacks, the skills, administrative ability, and technology they possessed go with them. Critical as this is in understanding the sorry state in which the African countries find themselves, it is not adequately reported to any substantial extent.

A primary reason for writing this book is to share my opinions on this important consideration. I gained my expertise from personal involvement in three African countries plus Tanzania and from observations of the results of policies in others, like Zaire and Nigeria. In Ghana my objective was to help set up a facility to enable the unsophisticated black people to replace the departing Lebanese. Here I watched the destruction of the socio-economic structure when the Asians were forced to leave within ninety days. Kenya's destructive policy was on a slower schedule and its effects were less immediate.

Life and work were engrossing at all times, and we lived on the continent during a period of outstanding historical importance. A discussion of some of these events provides the theater of operations, the working rules, the restrictions, and the conditions governing our efforts at development. Just five years before our arrival, Dr. Kwame Nkrumah, Ghana's first president, who was also a rising star in Pan-African and U.N. politics, found he could not return home again from his China trip. In his absence, the army had taken away his throne along with an economy in disarray.

In Uganda we saw the end of that country as an organized, administered nation. Brigadier General Idi Amin, President for Life, had his infamous dream that directed him to Africanize his country. This resulted in the expulsion of fifty thousand Asians (Indians). By the end of the ninety day period allotted for this "cleansing of the country's exploiters," Uganda lay in economic and social ruin. The soldier-bandits killed and looted at will while the general applied his program of genocide to any tribes and individuals he dreamed might be disloyal.

We departed the bloody, disorganized land of Uganda and arrived in Kenya during the celebration of Jomo Kenyatta's acceptance of a third five-year term as president. Kenyatta, affectionately called "Mzee" (Swahili for "honorable old man"), could hardly have been more beloved by his people. Aside from his credentials as an imprisoned victim of the colonial British, he was a canny politician. No one disputed the validity of the accolade "father of the nation."

Kenya was also in the throes of Africanization. We saw the last of the white-owned ranches, dairies, and farms pass to black nationals. The Kenyan Asians were being slowly, but systematically, squeezed out of retail and other businesses. Skilled people—repairmen, electricians, and such—became increasingly rare. The quality of life declined, with no compensating improvement either in black unemployment or opportunities for advancement in the business world.

My wife and I were chagrined that we hadn't made a measurable difference, but we at least gave it a good try. Certainly we improved our own knowledge of black Africa. Moreover, during our travels and one-on-one experiences in providing assistance and in establishing a consulting service, we had unique opportunities to judge the problems caused by the incompatibilities of Western assistance policies with the different cultures and values.

We hope this narration will provide an insight into some of the reasons for the difficulties and declines that have occurred in African socio-economies.

The Talking Drums

One of the wonders of Africa are the drums—no celebration is complete without them…but the 'talking drums' are in a league of their own. The 'talking drum' is carved from the kyendur tree and is covered in elephant skin. It is so large that it must be supported by props.

Fascinated with this unique part of their culture, I was given a demonstration while in Ghana and found the drums' acclaimed effectiveness to be no exaggeration The talking drum was used as the Ghanaian telephone system of both yesterday and still to some degree today. Clever drummers have in the far past been able to incite entire states to fight against one another.

Section I

WEST AFRICA

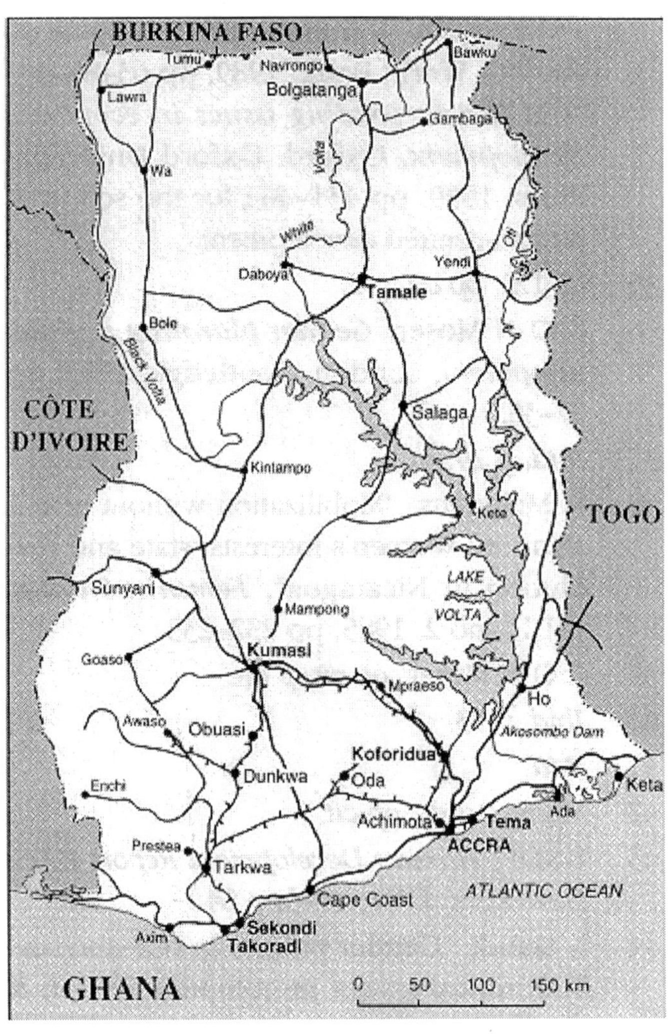
BURKINA FASO
Tumu
Navrongo
Bawku
Bolgatanga
Lawra
Gambaga
Volta
Wa
White
Oti
Yendi
Daboya
Tamale
Bole
Black Volta
Salaga
CÔTE
D'IVOIRE
Kintampo
Kete
TOGO
LAKE
VOLTA
Sunyani
Mampong
Goaso
Kumasi
Mpraeso
Ho
Awaso
Obuasi
Akosombo Dam
Koforidua
Dunkwa
Oda
Keta
Enchi
Achimota
Tema
Ada
ACCRA
Prestea
Tarkwa
ATLANTIC OCEAN
Cape Coast
Sekondi
Axim
Takoradi
GHANA
0 50 100 150 km

Arrival in Ghana

Our African adventure began in January 1971 when we—myself, my wife, Myrtle, a registered nurse, our daughters, Lynnanne and Carol, and our son, Kent—boarded a Pan American flight whose destination was Accra, Ghana, a West African coastal city near the equator. Our plane stopped in Senegal and again in Liberia; in both places we were met by an incredibly humid blast of furnace heat as we stepped off the plane. It catalyzed our sweat glands, inducing an instant saturation of clothes and left us gasping for breath. We became limp and apprehensive.

We lost some of our trepidation with the warm welcome we received at the Accra airport. George Harlley met us and introduced us to the press. He headed the Ghanaian agency responsible for the project on which we came to work. That night he and his attractive wife, Emily, hosted a lawn party at which we met dozens of government officials and people with whom we would work.

Our orientation period began soon after. The instruction focused on the ways of this strange environment: the necessary haggling in markets, the new foods and fruits, the bewildering number of customs. We quickly learned one important necessity for life in Ghana related to their all-important beer. Since bottles for the excellent, locally-produced Star Beer required scarce foreign exchange, customers could seldom purchase a supply without exchanging bottles. To satisfy his thirst, a consumer needed to hang on to his bottle inventory. We failed to include a case of bottles in our luggage, but we gradually built a starter set through gifts and exchanges of personal items.

Our preparation committee provided a bit of culture shock for us that took some getting used to: A cook-houseboy had been recruited for us and was ready for service. Having managed all our lives without servants, our immediate reaction was to "pay him off." More than that, we had a built-in antipathy toward the stereotypical white person living in an undeveloped country, lolling about and being attended by a gang of exploited natives. Still, neither we nor those we were working with lived up to this image of native exploiter; under the circumstances, we decided against voicing any rash objections.

As is usual with stereotypes, individual situations seldom fit. In Ghana, virtually all food has to be purchased daily in the market and prepared from scratch (no Cuisinarts). Dishes must be washed by hand as well as all cleaning (no vacuums). The tropical climate means great quantities of laundry that all had to be ironed, especially underclothes, to escape an egg laying, airborne, skin irritating, parasite. This chore was accomplished with a charcoal fueled flat iron. The expatriate finds servants virtually indispensable.

Having help around the house is not the only reason for engaging a local. From the hour an expatriate moves in, he is confronted by men knocking at the door wanting to be steward, yard boy, gardener, chauffeur or guard. Until you hire whom you need, you can answer the door a dozen times a day. No one believes that an expatriate doesn't require help; rather, the locals assume that Madam or Mister merely wants to do more screening. Furthermore, to be made aware of how important even a steward's job is in the eyes of the huge unemployed population, one soon loses any sense of guilt, low wages notwithstanding.

During this period, we became aware of the role reversal prevalent in Africa domestic service. Why is it, we wondered, those who do the cleaning, ironing and shopping (everything Westerners regard as part of the female domain) are one hundred percent male? The answer: Women remain at home in the traditional villages, raising the children, growing the food, looking after the old folks and assorted relatives as they always have done. Conversely, because the traditional male practices of raiding and defending against raids have become obsolete, they have time to do work away from the village, and domestic work is the most available.

We did experience an unexpected and delightful bonus as a consequence of employing "servants." We came to know their wives, children and a plethora of relatives, several of whom seemed always to be coming in from the country for a visit. We were often invited to their home villages for various celebrations. We learned their traditional methods of cooking and the native foods, although they preferred to bring a wife or mother around to our quarters to give us cooking instructions.

Finding the pluses in hiring natives can make huge cultural and living adjustments much easier. In any event, we soon settled into domestic routines. The stewards did the marketing, prepared and served the food, cleaned up, did the washing and ironing, made the beds and managed the housework. There is no question theirs was a full-time job. Certainly Myrtle could not have kept up with her nursing activities without such help.

The motivations leading to the decision to take a break from our good life in America to go to Africa related to Myrtle's and my belief—the family would benefit from the adventure. She was eager to offer her professional nursing skills where needed. Experience with another culture would add to the children's education. For me, a down-to-earth reason was the pleasures I had found in promoting good workmanship. Some of my most satisfying achievements had been in business salvage; that is, turning around potentially worthwhile but mismanaged businesses and helping to promote new endeavors.

The Ghanaian challenge offered unlimited opportunities for putting my particular skills to work, with rewards measured not in profits but in the gratification of directly participating in improving the wealth of an aspiring nation. In short, I was content in believing that I could make a difference in the economic training supporting twenty years of wide practical experience. How could I not be of help?

Ghana specifically had particular attraction. As one of the first African colonies to win independence, she had become a laboratory for nation building. I could look forward to observing first hand, the unraveling of the colonial system.

Moreover, the leading personality of Ghana's move into independence, Kwame Nkrumah, epitomized the phenomenon of an emerging personality equal to leadership in an important world event. No more charismatic, traditional leader existed in the entire political structure of post-colonial Africa. His avowed ambition to become Pan-African leader of the entire continent was regarded as a heroic vision in international liberal circles. It appeared believable that he might succeed in fashioning the dark continent into a coherent whole, suitable for entry into the family of civilized nations. This trip and the assignment in Ghana, seemed to be a once-in-a-lifetime historical opportunity.

The Assignment

All sorts of assistance-giver agencies find their way to Africa. The World Bank and its sister, the International Monetary Fund (IMF), together with the Agency for International Development (USAID), are the best known. The U.N. has myriad specialized organizations that address issues of health, food production, education and such. Other volunteer agencies have a presence: the Peace Corps, church-supported programs and a variety of others. These workers have short-term commitments and usually volunteer on an expense-only basis. In fact my two-year contract was also expense-only.

Our program was a Peace Corps anomaly, never tried before nor subsequently. The idea was to field experienced people who could tackle large projects. To recruit such talent, they recognized that families had to be part of the program. Actually, the Peace Corps' function was primarily one of recruitment, delivery and financing. An agency of the Ghanaian government furnished housing, transportation and activity direction.

The family program, being new, was carried primarily on the basic administration devised for the single, young, college student volunteer. For instance, our expense-only living allowance per person was based on the basic Peace Corps program for a college student—the same baggage weight, vacation time, etc.

In contrast, the officials of the major agencies are careerists. They expect to spend their working years in development and assistance pursuits. They send their children to school in Switzerland, Spain or elsewhere, and they aspire to earn promotions and retirement pensions. These folks live well in their "European" enclaves. As a generalization, they prefer associating with other expatriates and the elite of the governments with which they work. Most are content in their chosen occupation, are not particularly adventurous and prefer to take their vacations at home or in Europe.

While this description is not to denigrate these professionals, it does suggest their inclination to adopt the bureaucratic wisdom of their working world: to ensure their budgeted funds are exhausted each year (as other governmental departments are required to do) and under no circumstances criticize the organizations and programs that pay their salaries.

Other groups of volunteers, some with different levels of expertise, made a commitment to spend varying lengths of time in their contract area. My family and I met the criterion for this group. As did four other businessmen (with MBA degrees or the equivalent) and their families, we agreed to spend two years assisting the government of Ghana in implementing its Africanization policy (Ghanaian Business Promotion Act). The objective of this policy was to replace non-black businessmen with black citizens. Although these aspirants were expected to acquire already organized businesses and were given the opportunity to exploit present and future commercial prospects, they had no skill or experience to bring this task to fruition. Consequently, the need for our consultant service was total. My associates and I undertook to organize this assistance.

We enjoyed interviewing and selecting the eager-to-learn candidates which we hoped could succeed us as a well trained staff of national consultants. To our dismay, we found our training sessions became largely theoretical. Although the government had discontinued Lebanese work and business permits, very few black citizens stepped forth to be entrepreneurs, even though the program gave them the opportunity to take over a proven business situation.

This program of Ghanaization, or Africanization, turned out to be based in emotion and pride, and perhaps a modicum of greed. But, without belaboring the motivation, it had little foundation in economic principles. The framers of the policy simply did not understand the concept of entrepreneurship: ability to take risks, management skills, the amount of dedication necessary and all the rest of the elements that make up a successful proprietor.

Beyond the abstract characteristics of successful individual owners, an existing business community is the product of a long period of natural selection. For many reasons, countless businesses have failed and fallen by the wayside, leaving the successful ones standing. In Ghana the chances for these ex-colonial citizens, who had no business experience, credit, banking connections, nor record-keeping skills, to be successful even in continuing the operation of established businesses turned out to be near zero.

The results of such misguided programs were inevitable. When a business license failed to be renewed, the Lebanese or other non-black sold out his inventory and departed. Doors closed and stayed closed, never to reopen. For two years we watched the dissolution of these businesses to the detriment of the country as departing non-blacks took away their business expertise, administrative ability and capital, intellectual and otherwise.

Even though we came to Africa to help the black citizens seize an opportunity to become businessmen in their newly independent country, it did not happen. Taxi drivers, retired civil servants, school teachers and other citizens did not seize the grand opportunity, as expected, to acquire these deserted Lebanese businesses. No one anticipated this lack of citizen interest.

In the absence of eager entrepreneurs, we concentrated our effort on building an ongoing (we hoped) small business consulting service that could handle whatever existing business clients came by and could grow in usefulness as the service became better known. Various government agencies sought our advice. We also made suggestions for prospective new enterprises that would create jobs, produce food or husband foreign exchange. Naturally, these objectives were of extreme governmental concern.

Although we lost a great deal of our initial enthusiasm for the project and some confidence in our ability to effect a big change in the welfare of these African people, the experience was a sociological education. We could watch closely the actions of political leaders, traditional chiefs, businessmen and others, and observe how these leaders and citizens manipulated, or adjusted to, new laws and regulations. We saw how their attitudes reflected their freedom from their colonial masters and how all these elements worked, each in its own way, to create a nation.

Kwame Nkrumah: Africa's Shooting Star

Together with the cultural briefing necessary for our daily living needs, we undertook a study of the political structures that had evolved in the post-independence period. The socialistic, central planning system differed greatly from the free market system to which we had always been accustomed. This research involved a narrow focus: a study of the short and heartbreaking reign of Kwame Nkrumah, Ghana's first prime minister.[1]

In the first place, it was Nkrumah who basically fashioned Ghana's socio-economy as well as setting up a large number of its manufacturing facilities. As a result, our management-consulting project had to contend with his embedded policies and innovations. Moreover, as I became drawn into African development beyond Ghana, I found that he was a role model, or at least a pioneer, in the establishment of the antithesis of the colonial free market system. This Marxist innovation, called "Scientific Socialism," became the pattern for most of the African countries after their independence.

1 Kwame Nkrumah wrote ten books: the first, *Towards Colonial Freedom* (1946); the last, *Handbook of Revolutionary Warfare* (1969). They all related to anti-capitalism and recommended revolutionary tactics necessary to the pursuit of freedom. book titles and the references and quoted materials reveal that the Lenin-Stalin philosophy heavily influenced his thinking.

While Nkrumah was beholden to Marx and Russia for his economic systems, of far more importance was his pivotal role in the development of the international assistance policies for Africa. Moreover, as one of the first black post-colonial leaders, he carried the hope of both the Eastern and Western world for the advancement of the new order of independence. The liberal West could not do enough for him and his country. Certainly, Nkrumah seemed to have an auspicious future.

Our study of Ghana started with the state of the would-be nation at the time the British conferred independence. Since this was a voluntary and planned relinquishing of control, there was every motivation to provide for an efficiently functioning socio-economy. Accordingly, when the British lowered the Union Jack and sailed away, they left competent administration of the most prosperous state in West Africa in the hands of well-educated and professionally experienced people and a well-trained civil service.

The country had a built-up infrastructure, an adequate foreign exchange fund and exploitable resources, including an excellent potential for food production. The colonial system had created a *lingua franca* that allowed the various tribes to participate in a central government. It had a workable free market system, an independent legal establishment and a democratic political system.

Moreover, it enjoyed world support and had virtually unlimited economic resources from well-wishing nations at its disposal. Support was also available from many assistance agencies—USAID, the U.N., the Peace Corps, churches and many others—who broke new ground in generating well-intentioned policies to help the new African state.

With this foundation, along with worldwide interest and support, Nkrumah needed only to pick up the reins turned over to him. But none of this existing socio-economic organization had his stamp. Certainly, he could not just maintain or carry on a colonial system; it wasn't his nature. So, in 1961, his government introduced measures to free the Ghanaian economy from the colonial mold. The innovations coalesced into an agendum called "Nkrumahism," essentially a combination of African Socialism and Pan-Africanism. Nkrumah claimed non-alignment, although Russia was his mentor. This amalgam of pragmatism and diverse ideas, tainted by the inclusion of ego indulgence, left little room for mundane democracy. But it was a major step on the road to complete power.

None of Nkrumah's radical ideas about government bothered his worldwide supporters, who were largely liberals and none too antagonistic toward leftist politics anyway. Nkrumah had a free hand to design the foundation for the new state, unhindered by enemies (which eventually became many) or the plethora of money lenders, supporters and would-be advisors who would not admit his policies could only lead to disaster.

Kwame Nkrumah

The Nkrumah government discouraged imports by imposing high tariffs and introducing price controls. Since Nkrumah never trusted foreign investors, he established many new manufacturing industries as state corporations. A large-scale mechanized farming policy was also initiated as a public enterprise.[2]

In 1963, Nkrumah inaugurated a seven-year national plan which envisioned the speedy emergence of Ghana as a socialist industrial power. By 1964, Ghana had been transformed into a legalized "Socialist-single-party state" dominated by Nkrumah, who had hundreds of opponents detained or imprisoned without trial.

2 This was an ill-conceived idea of the USAID. It totally failed because of diseased crops.

During these early post-colonial years, the humanist, liberal philosophy underlying the good intentions of Western assistance givers could hardly have been less realistic. Apart from the assumption that it could tailor a future design for the state, the West erred in attempting to impute virtues, characteristics and motivations to these "down-trodden" victims of colonialism that they neither understood nor possessed. Under these circumstances, it is understandable that the assistance efforts not only failed to realize their objectives, but, in part, actually contributed to the worsening conditions of the people.

One of the basic misconceptions about the post-colonial states related to empathy. Colonialism had a very bad name, often justified, but the effects could hardly be understood from afar. Western well-wishers imagined how they would feel under the yoke of the white man. Once freed of this domination, they assumed that age-old tribal loyalties would automatically be given over to the concept of "state." Surely under the direction of unselfish leaders, the people would unite to focus their energies into nation building.

That these charismatic new black leaders, who had won their government positions under colonial-sponsored elections, would use the various assistance donations to buttress their own political power rather than to build the nation was beyond belief. Loading the civil service with their extended families and tribal members indicated their choice of loyalties. Unfortunately, the predominance of tribal loyalties continues to prevail throughout much of Africa.[3]

Nkrumah happily fostered these attitudes, which advanced his own aspirations. He especially fancied the presumption that tribal loyalties would be given over to the state since he perceived loyalty to the state as loyalty to him.

Nkrumah filled perfectly the role of a black leader charged with the responsibility of leading an emerging country into the world of independent nations. Had the liberals opened a casting office they

3 Nigeria is a prime example. Each of the several state sections threatened secession in the past. But the coup incident to the Ibo-attempted secession in 1967 resulted in a full-blown Ibo-Yoruba civil war with enormous loss of life.

could not have chosen a more appealing player. Nkurmah's hatred of capitalism, especially the multinational type, and any vestige of neo-colonialism, coupled with his affection for socialism, made him the darling of those who thrilled at the liberation of the black people. They wished him Godspeed into the world of free nations.

Not only did he fit this particular image nicely, but his towering ambition to eventually rise above the leaders of other small, tropical ex-colonies to create a Pan-Africa added much luster to his appeal. Accordingly, while he vigorously pursued the power being transferred from Great Britain, he viewed the office of Ghana's first prime minister, and later president, as stepping stones to his major goal: emperor of a Pan-African state.

To this end, he was a principal founder of the Organization of African Unity (OAU).[4] Through this alliance of the African states, except South Africa, Nkrumah could seek to dominate a united Africa. Such an organization needed a suitable headquarters building. Nkrumah especially wanted to provide this home, but so did Haile Selassie, the king of Ethiopia. Despite prodigious Ghanaian efforts, Selassie completed his project first. Nkrumah's multi-story building, with its dozens of detached villas overlooking the capital city of Accra, was a big waste. For what's the value of a second headquarters layout to a continental organization or a palace without an emperor? Even the prestige of such a grand undertaking was lost because of its failure to be completed on time. While its formal title is the "State House," it is lugubriously referred to as the "Elephant House."

Despite suffering a major disappointment in losing this competition to be home to the OAU, Nkrumah's international activities continued. Along with India's Prime Minister Jawaharlal Nehru, he dominated the U.N. for years, particularly during the time Belgium sought to free her colony in the Congo. Although Nkrumah never

4 The charter of the Organization of African Unity was signed on May 26, 1963, in Addis Ababa, Ethiopia, by 32 independent nations. Since then, all but Rhodesia and South Africa have joined upon gaining independence. The aims of the OAU are: 1) To intensify and co-ordinate efforts to improve living standards in Africa; 2) To defend sovereignty, territorial integrity and independence in African States; 3) To eradicate all forms of colonialism from Africa; 4) To promote international co-operation in keeping with the Charter of the United Nations.

achieved his ambition to preside over a Pan-Africa, during a span of nine years, from the formation of Ghana's first independent government in 1957 until being toppled by a military coup in 1966, his career was a brilliance in the international sky.

In considering his career, there are many unanswered questions. Did Nkrumah throw his energies into building Ghana into a mighty nation after accepting the impossibility of organizing a Pan-African state? Or did his manic energies permit simultaneous pursuit of both objectives? Whatever the answer, he committed tremendous resources to a grandiose program he called "jet-propelled development."

Nkrumah rationalized this approach by comparing his situation to that of the developed European countries who had had 300 years to evolve and develop. He didn't have so much time. And with the subsidies, donations and indulgence of the assisting agencies, as well as commercial lending institutions, he now had the means to try. Beyond that, he must have viewed the combination of Western and Eastern interest as a stimulating and implied support of his ambitions. In any event, nothing served to put a brake to his frenzied spending schemes.

In 1988, Douglas Rimmer, a visiting research fellow at the Africa Institute, related how much had been written supporting the argument that developing countries should disassociate themselves from international capitalism.[5] Nkrumah supported this thesis in the ten books he wrote from 1946 to 1969. *In Neo-Colonialism: The Last Stage of Imperialism* (1965), he presented an encyclopedic record of the investments in Africa by international companies and their exercise of a continuing imperialistic power.

As for Ghana, Nkrumah's policy of business development was accomplished almost exclusively through state agencies, the major exception being the Valco aluminum smelter which was financed largely by American Kaiser and Reynolds corporations.Of course, by eschewing outside financing on the rest of his constructions, he maintained total control by using these factories as political resources. Still,

5 Douglas Rimmer, "Ghana's Economic Decline," *Africa Insight,* vol. 18, no. 3 (1988).

regardless of Nkrumah's or his successors' views, Ghana was, in practice, disassociated from international capitalism, and until 1988, Ghana received no major investments by foreign firms.

With this control and credit, Nkrumah built mansions for himself and acquired a huge yacht. Other large-scale projects followed, such as an international airport and a state airline. At the same time, he built more factories.[6] Regrettably, the basic planning for his many projects had little grounding in an analysis of economic feasibility—quite the opposite. His objectives focused on enhancing the grandeur of the state and himself (he seemed to regard the two entities as one).

In addition, he had political considerations. These state projects served to create a patronage. They generated high-level management positions and other jobs for those who would be grateful. Of course, this policy contributed to ineffective management and monumental economic losses. (An anti-government paper in 1971 claimed 150 stewardesses held jobs in the state-run airline that had only one weekly international flight.)

Nkrumah's giant Volta River Project at Akosombo was in a class by itself. The dam was 370 feet from bedrock to crest and backed up the river for 250 miles creating, reputedly, the largest man-made lake in the world. Its 3,275 square miles would provide cheap lake transportation for an enormous area. But the primary purpose was to meet the power needs of the Kaiser Aluminum smelter being built in conjunction with the dam at Tema.

Kaiser's five-potline reduction plant, reaching an annual capacity of 220,000 tons, needed enormous power sources. The massive complex of power generators exceeded the output of any other generating unit on the continent and easily provided this requirement. Even after supplying Kaiser's contract for sixty percent of the

6 He built factories with terrazzo floors, modern machinery, nice architecture. He built them without market study or located sources of materials. He had no skilled management nor work force in mind. A huge packing plant, for instance, was built with no ranches to supply the beef; a soap factory with no mutton tallow source. These monuments gave a great appearance of successful development if one did not look too closely.

power and the needs of Ghana itself, there was still surplus power available for sale to the neighboring countries of Togo and Benin.

The industrial park designed for the aluminum plant and other industrial projects to come, seemed adequate to any need. But plans change. The first program involved the use of Ghana's own enormous bauxite deposits. But the designers found it would be more costly to develop and transport the local ore than to import it from abroad. Consequently, a substantial harbor was required to service the ships importing millions of tons of ore and taking out the finished product. Tema had no natural harbors. So undaunted, Ghana built an artificial one. It took some doing. A reported forty million tons of granite were torn from a mountain ten miles away and trucked to the site of the breakwater. The harbor became operational in 1961. By 1971, it handled nearly three million tons. Of course, a giant complex like this required ties to Accra. Accordingly, the construction of a four-lane freeway spanning the sixteen miles to the capital seemed adequate for the purpose. One curious thing happened during President Clinton's 1988 Ghanaian visit, papers reported power shortages. In view of the earlier lavish production, one is left wondering what happened.

The value of this complex to the Ghanaian economy cannot be questioned. Moreover, its financing was easily arranged. Kaiser furnished a large part. Of course, such undertakings involve tradeoffs and the ecological and sociological costs were staggering. Ten thousand families—80,000 individuals—became refugees. Ten years after the evacuation, they still had not been remunerated for the loss of their homes and farms. The Peace Corps failed in an assignment, at one time, to work out a means of paying them. Health hazards increased as well, particularly waterborne diseases such as bilharzia and malaria. Because of the desire to realize the project's hasty completion, a forest containing some of the world's most valuable timber was submerged—to the distress of the carving industry, since this region included the only source of ebony in the country. Also, drowned trees in the shallower parts of the lake created a navigation hazard and an impediment to net fishermen.

The Volta River Project certainly qualifies as a monument to Nkrumah's economic dreams. Whether or not it can be justified on a socio-economic basis, it will live forever.[7] The state house is a monument of a different kind. It serves to represent Nkrumah's broken dreams of a Pan-Africa, for not only is it a symbol of his failure to secure the headquarters location of the OAU for Ghana, but it symbolizes that the OAU organization itself had virtually no potential for the creation of a united Africa. Actually, the member nations have never agreed on any policy. The only consensus they have reached is their virulent hatred of the white South African government.

What went wrong with the modernization drive of this new independent state, considering all the advantages it had for success? During Nkrumah's nine-year stewardship, he led the country into bankruptcy with his unfettered borrowing. By relying on an unworkable system of government regulation of commerce, he demoralized the market-controlled economy left by the British. In an attempt to provide unrealistically cheap food for the urban voters, he destroyed the farmers' incentive to produce more than needed for their own use. His single-party political system stymied all elements of democracy.

All sorts of character defects, including paranoia and megalomania, are suggested explanations for Nkrumah's overreaching ambition and his never-ending quest for security and power. But what about the international assistance policies and tolerance that permitted these indulgences? A more constructive channeling of the loans and donations would have insured economic results instead of grandeur and political objectives.

The justification for the hands-off policy of the donors and lenders seems to be if they regard a country like Ghana as independent, then it has to take responsibility for its own mistakes—good intentions but simple-minded logic. A new government is given the

7 Douglas Rimmer made an assessment of the project I had not heard before. The indirect benefits—encouragement of other power-using industries, household electrification, irrigation of agriculture through control of the waters of the Volta and others—greatly disappointed expectations. After weighing the external diseconomies inflicted by the dam, he concluded that the overall effect of the Volta project has been negative (Ghana's Economic Decline, *Africa Insight*, vol. 18, no. 3 [1988]).

bank and army, with draw-down privileges from the donor agencies and mandated to go forth to build a nation. Ghana, as well as a number of other African countries, have suffered catastrophic results from the bestowing of such "trust."

Whatever conclusions these speculations engender, the facts are that economic devastation, together with social and political restrictions, meant that Nkrumah had to go. On the evening of February 24, 1966, the army, supported by some elements of the police, took advantage of Nkrumah's visit to Peking and put an end to his reign and his Convention People's Party.

Thus ended the career of sub-Sahara's first black modern head of state. He had acquired international acclaim and dreamed impossible dreams; but, like a shooting star, his fall from power abruptly eclipsed his luminosity. He atrophied into a plaintive voice broadcasting from his friend Sekou Toure's Guinea and later died of cancer in Romania. A photo of his toppled statue lying in the street on the morning after the coup was captioned "The Fallen Idol."

Nkrumah—"The Fallen Idol"

Post-Nkrumah

Following the unseating of Nkrumah, the coup's leaders managed the country by a committee of generals and police until they experienced some civilian opposition. Gwynne Dyer described this opposition: "What happened in Ghana recently was not a revolution, but potentially something far more revolutionary. The professional classes—doctors, lawyers, professors, engineers and so on—went on strike and forced the military government to set a date for handing power back to civilians."[8]

In 1969, they peacefully handed over power to the elected civilian government of Dr. Kofi Busia. The Busia administration managed to avoid any reform or improvement, such as recommitting to an economic free market instead of central planning or eschewing state ownership when such policy was inimical to the health of the economy. Neither did he recognize how the policy of state ownership was acting as a dead hand on the economy. Nor was there any attempt to correct the coup's endemic mismanagement and corruption.

Dr. Kofi Busia

Busia seemed more concerned with the perquisites of the office rather than seeking ways to slow the slide of the economy into penury. One of his obvious pleasures was to roar around town in his white Cadillac, accompanied by an entourage of large cars and motorcycle outriders, sirens screaming. (It was commonly alleged that even a coffee break could instigate the "outing.") Certainly, his efforts to celebrate his position never excluded enjoying the perks of power. In keeping with the traditions of successful Africans, he undertook to build a home in his ancestral village that would reflect

8 Gwynne Dyer, "A 'Civilian Power' Victory," *San Francisco Chronicle*, December 11, 1977.

his status as president of the nation. He fenced in a whole section of land as a setting for the mansion. The legislature accommodated him by suspending the tariff due on his European furniture purchase, along with the air-conditioning equipment necessary to preserve it from the tropical 70 x 70 climate (referring to temperature and humidity).

An irresponsible politician living extravagantly on the back of a deteriorating economy is of less consequence than the insidious policy his administration unleashed. While Nkrumah created an unworkable economy, Busia's Africanization policy deprived the country of the skills and administrative ability of the non-black citizens. Both plagues—irresponsible politicians and Africanization—were spreading across Africa.

The government's attempt to deal with the ever-mounting shortages and general deterioration took the form of lofty declarations: "We are declaring war on the economy and on the food shortage." After a short time, an announcement would herald victory: "We have won the war."

In 1972, Commander-in-Chief of the Armed Forces, General Ignatius K. Acheampong, overthrew the Busia government and became Ghana's military ruler. We looked forward to some improvement. It did not happen. The economic conditions grew even worse and he was forced to resign in 1978. By then, because of conflict with the army officers in charge, the better-trained manpower and three-fourths of the skilled professionals had left the country, leaving it even more denuded than after the debacle of Africanization.

The following year, in June 1979, junior officers, led by wild man Flight Lieutenant Jerry Rawlings, assumed control of the government. His Armed Forces Revolutionary Council executed Generals Acheampong, Arifa and Fred W. K. Akuffo, Chief of the Defense Staff. Rawlings' band of managed-economy ideologues revealed their attitude toward a free-market economy by bulldozing the Accra market to the ground. Three months later, Rawlings placed the country under the civilian rule of Dr. Hilla Limann, whose government had no means of halting the economic decline. His administration's effort to revive food and cash crops production was a total failure.

Flight Lt. Jerry Rawlings

The senior army officers who governed Ghana from 1972 to 1979 were unable to comprehend the conflict between market forces and government economic controls and stipulations. The junior officers and students who ran the country after Jerry Rawlings' second return to power in December 1981 had no better insight. Leon Dash, writing for the *Washington Post*, expressed his opinions of the 35-year-old Flight Lieutenant Rawlings' idealism:

> *The six-week-old government's leftist swerve has pushed beyond the socialist visions of the late Kwame Nkrumah, Ghana's first president, and borrowed from Libyan leader Muammar Qaddafi's eclectic model of "direct democracy" through "popular committees" that theoretically will manage all aspects of the lives of Ghana's 14 million people. Later in a radio broadcast he reported a statement: I ask nothing less than a revolution, something that will transform the social and economic order of this country.*[9]

By January 1982, the regime was almost devoid of resources, had an inordinate budget deficit, no foreign monetary reserves, a debt of $348 million and was confronted with a Nigerian oil boycott caused by a debt of $150 million.[10] In 1983, to compound the misery, one million of the one and a half million Ghanaians who had migrated to Nigeria, incident to the oil boom, were summarily expelled back

9 Leon Dash, "New Rulers in Ghana Return to Leftist Path to Cure Nation's Ills," *Washington Post*. February 17, 1982.

10 *Journal of Contemporary African Studies,* 1989-90, p. 50.

to Ghana. In Ghana's lush, agriculturally productive land, inadequate nutrition and starvation were common.

Such grim conditions finally forced some action. "In April 1983 there occurred a remarkable turn-around in policy...The PNDC (People's National Defense Committee) was somehow persuaded to undertake an economic recovery program under the tutelage of the IMF and World Bank with the support of bilateral aid donors."[11]

Some of the improvements involved a reduction of government spending and provision to encourage agriculture and food production. "The approach to a realistic exchange rate, along with the removal of domestic price controls and liberalization of the import regime, have recreated producer incentives."

At a time when Ghana's population of over 12 million was ill nourished, with actual starvation not uncommon, she had to somehow accommodate a million refugees dumped on her. But the unconscionable reality of all this hunger was that it needn't have existed. Prior to the event of colonization, hunger occurred due to natural calamities or war. Each tribe produced its own food or had a well-proven system of trading. The colonial system of specialization allowed the development of cities and dependency of large parts of the population on the surplus production of the subsistent farmers. But with the breakdown of the political system, Ghana was unable to find a way to produce and distribute food.

The attention to agriculture was a simple change in policy that could have been effected at any time. The farmers had always been ready to produce if they could make a profit. The policy also applied to the cocoa farmers, who now were to get three-fifths of the on-board value instead of the traditional one- or two-fifths.[12]

11 Quoted in Rimmer, "Ghana's Economic Decline," *Africa Insight,* vol. 18, no. 3 (1988).

12 Cocoa has been Ghana's chief export. In the average of the years 1972-74, cocoa beans and products accounted by 60.8 percent of the total exports of domestic products. The tonnage ranges from 390 to 450 tons. The Cocoa Marketing Board has had a statutory monopoly of export buying through agents at a producer price fixed by the government at each season far below the price being reached in world markets (*Africa South of the Sahara* [London: Europa Publications Ltd., 1978-79], p. 408).

Breaking of cocoa pods on a typical farm in Ghana

The system of purchasing cocoa beans through agents was unbelievably corrupt. These agents had absolute power over the revenue of the growers. Although the price was set by the government, negotiations still took place to the disadvantage of the farmers. Furthermore, the agents sometimes paid in script; farmers never knew when they would get cash.

Cocoa was exported illegally across borders. The army was ruthless in attempting to suppress this. On occasion, according to an independent investigative newspaper in Accra, a farmer living close to the border could have his crop seized on just the suspicion that he intended to smuggle it. This paper further revealed that the government was a year behind in the collection of the cocoa revenue from the agents. *Africa South of the Sahara* refers to this problem: "The inability of the Board to secure proper accounting procedures from these agents led them in May 1977 to restore the so called unitary buying system."[13] It still was not a free market.

13 *Africa South of the Sahara*, p. 408.

Post-Ghana

Over the years, we have looked back on our stay in Ghana as our gateway to the continent. We always intended to revisit this vanguard country of the post-independence African nations. The idea never went further, killed by the unending reports of continuing travail: coups, brutality and the desolation of those fine people. Their leaders made a mockery of what could have been a glorious entrance into the family of free nations.

In learning about these years, I have relied heavily on articles by Douglas Rimmer in *Africa Insight*, in which he analyzes the reasons for Ghana's precipitous decline since independence. Other analyses by Rimmer are contained in the reference book *Africa South of the Sahara*.

Rimmer reported the observations of Emil Rado, a colleague with whom he had worked in the Department of Economics at the University of Ghana in 1950. Rado wrote of his 1986 visit to Ghana, his first since 1960:

> *I saw an economy and society in a state of near collapse. Water ran in the taps for five to six hours a day and there were two days during the month with no water at all. Electricity was liable to break down any day and did so five or six times a week. Perhaps five per cent of the telephones worked in Accra (none in Kumasi as far as I could see). A letter posted in Kumasi took three to four weeks to reach Accra. Public transport within the main cities was non-existent... Inter-city "state transport" coaches were the only public transport I saw. There was no refuse collection; I saw smoldering piles of rubbish everywhere... Bad as conditions were in 1986, it must be added that they had been much worse. The nadir was 1983, when corpses lay in the streets of the cities.*[14]

14 Rimmer, "Ghana's Economic Decline," *Africa Insight,* vol. 18, no. 3 (1988.)

Ghana's Jerry Rawlings, out of what must have been pure desperation, called in the World Bank and the IMF; with that collaboration, he has not only salvaged the country but set it on the socio-economic course the West had envisioned for it at independence. *New York Times* writer Howard W. French records this African country's monumental turnaround in his article, "Ghana Shucks Socialism."

French sets the stage by citing 1957, when the newly independent Ghana "became a pioneer in an ultimately suffocating African brand of socialism." Certainly a true indictment, for virtually all the black sub-Saharan countries have suffered economic disaster with their statist policies. A Ghana watcher can rejoice over his observation that "Ghana is showing the way to recovery based on free market economics." He points to the fruits of this reform in the way the traditional industries (cocoa farming, gold and diamond mining) are "booming" after years of neglect. He notes the economic improvements since the country's currency is now "freely traded on the local currency market."

"Diplomats and analysts here," French reports, "credit the turnaround to Ghana's current president, Jerry Rawlings, and Kwesi Botchway, the finance minister he appointed in 1983." The article provides profound proof of Rawlings' break with past ideology: "The most remarkable reform efforts have been in selling off state companies and opening the door to foreign investors who want to buy them or invest elsewhere in this once nearly closed economy." He quotes World Bank economist Ravi Kambur's evaluation: "'After 10 years of reforms, Ghana faces many more years of difficult choices... But for once the problems are those of explosive growth, not of stagnation.'" Kambur modestly avoids acknowledging the World Bank's hand in this triumph.

Flight Lieutenant Jerry Rawlings, President of Ghana, and Yoweri Museveni, President of Uganda, are two remarkable men. Both shed their socialist convictions and initiated programs inimical to their ideology. Consequent to this wholehearted embrace of a free market system, they are rehabilitating their shambled countries.

The two presidents have vastly different backgrounds. Rawlings inherited (after a coup) a deadly incompatible system, which he managed to drive to the hopelessness of a refugee camp before being forced to seek an alternate course. The guerrilla leader Museveni managed to win power from other guerrilla groups to take control of a country which had been a killing field for decades and whose economy was little more than a barter system. If accolades for such turnarounds are passed out, the World Bank and other donors are clearly entitled to their share. But changes would not have happened had not the donors recognized a potential both in the leaders and in the resources of the countries.

Upon reflection, I would have been overjoyed by news that the bulldozed Accra market was alive again, teeming with thousands of market women selling everything from the clay balls pregnant women seem to regard as a pre-natal necessity, to the Java prints specially loomed for Ghanaian women. Current changes make it possible for such a market to be revived.

PROJECTS IN WEST AFRICA

I came to Africa a highly qualified businessman-economist and possessed a good deal of consulting and promotional experience involving American small businesses. Initially, I was confident! How could I fail to not provide a highly beneficial service to these unsophisticated African businessmen? But, after much chagrin and frustration, I soon found lots of reasons why this wouldn't be such a cinch.

On the basis of my own experience and my observations of the failed efforts of others, I have developed some postulates addressing the difficulties involved in the integration of Western technologies with those of the so-called "primitive" economies. The following list of projects may yield some insight on the nature of the misunderstanding.

Bad Advice

This episode illustrates the care needed to avoid providing inappropriate ideas or advice. In this instance merely thinking out loud set a program in motion that resulted in a business catastrophe.

"Hello, Mr. Owusu? Yes, I am Lynn Casto; glad to see you. What can I do for you?"

"The pastor of my church says you have a small business service to advise people with businesses," Mr. Owusu replied.

"That is correct," I said. "Yes, your government has arranged for us to give that help to you businessmen in Ghana."

"Well, I have a small business," he informed me. "I make enough to pay for my food, but I do not prosper at all. You show me a way to make more profit?"

"Well, sure. We'll try. Tell me about your business," I inquired.

"I am a stockist. I sell children's clothes, scarves, handkerchiefs, blouses, oh so many things. I sell wholesale."

"You sell to the market women who carry the goods around on their heads?" I asked.

"Yes. Also to those who sell in the kiosks and off the sidewalk. I have *plenty* customers," he said boastfully.

"How do you see your problem?" I continued.

"My stock is small—very small. I run out of things. I then have to close up the shop and go to the Lebanese for more goods. My customers go other places while I am gone. Maybe I send the small boy, but he gets cheated. Sometimes he loses the money," Mr. Owusu complained.

"You have such little space? You cannot keep more stock on hand?" I asked.

"No. I have plenty space. My money is too small," he admitted.

I sympathized, "Yes, you have trouble—much the same as many people have. I suppose you cannot borrow from the bank. You have no collateral?"

"Oh, I borrowed from the bank to get started," he said. "I owe them five thousand dollars."

"Five thousand dollars!" I was amazed. "You bought no building. Why could there not be more money for stock?"

"I bought a lease that has very low rent. It is a lease that started a long time ago, when rents were cheap. It cost four thousand dollars," he advised me.

"I see. Then you bought stock with the remaining thousand?" I continued to probe.

"No. I paid the loan officer a thousand for making the loan."

"Then you used the money on hand to buy your present stock?"

"Yes."

"And the bank will give you no more money?"

"That is so."

"I know in your country there is very little credit. You sell for cash and have to pay cash for your stock. That is too bad. It would be good if you could get credit from the Lebanese."

"Yes. But they only give credit to other Lebanese and people with big stores," he said.

⁂

I saw Mr. Owusu a week later.

"Hello, Mr. Owusu," I greeted. "You have a happy, smiling face today. Did you acquire another wife?"

"No, but I think you helped me solve my problem." He went on. "I went to my pastor. He told the Indian who has the knitting mill that I am a very honest man and that he should give me some credit. The Indian told those oh-so-smart machines to make blouses with a pattern only for me. No one else can have such a pattern. Now I have plenty blouses. He gave me credit for six hundred dollars."

"Good for you. That is a lot of blouses. You must sell hard."

"Now that I have credit, I can give credit to my customers. I will have plenty sales."

His remark shocked me to my toes. I knew that by a careless observation the credit genie I had freed would destroy his business.

"My friend, I advise you to be very careful. Everyone is not as honest as you are. Your customers are not used to credit. But if you must, I suggest you give credit to no one for more than fifty dollars. Don't let anyone owe you more. Those market women are very shrewd."

The next time I saw Mr. Owusu, I needed only one glance to know something was wrong.

"Hello, Mr. Owusu. What happened to your smiling face? You look so sad."

"I had to sell my lease. Only that way could I pay my debts. You were right about the market women. I gave credit to them, but no more than fifty dollars to each as you advised. Then I would give them no more."

"Well, you were cautious. What happened?"

"When I would give them no more credit, they wouldn't come back to me even to buy for cash. They go to another stockist. So I no longer have even a cash business. And none of them will pay me. Do you know of another business I can get into?"

The Tortilla Monopoly

This project illustrates how an adviser can suffer an unpleasant surprise if he becomes personally involved in the goals of a project and fails to assure himself that his associates are also working toward the same objectives.

I like Mexican food: tortillas, tacos and enchiladas. Maize, the main ingredient of tortillas, is an important crop in Ghana. It occurred to me that if tortillas, a Mexican staple, could catch on in Ghana, their popularity might counter the growing dependency on imported wheat. And I might be able to get a Mexican meal once in a while.

Some benefactor had donated to the Ghanaian government, a gleaming modern food laboratory equipped with all sorts of scientific devices. The benefactor even had the foresight to train a cadre of technicians to operate the lab and to recruit a world-famous food scientist as director. Obviously, this organization needed only the idea. The Ghanaian government could take it from there.

The lab people were enchanted. They were saying, "At last, a project!" They would get to work immediately on the preparation of a budget and a detailed experimental program for my approval. That stopped the program in its tracks. I had no funds for such activities.

This is a situation that can be found throughout Africa, if my widely scattered observations can serve as a basis for such a generalization. Well-meaning Westerners will sometimes provide highly technical tools or facilities—perhaps a modern factory—with the expectation that the government will be duly grateful and will have the expertise and interest to put it to work for the greater good.

However, if the largess is not designed to address the actual needs, or isn't within the capability of the people, the gift, however beneficial in the abstract, will never become operational. Why the obvious can't be anticipated is a source of wonder.

I once observed crates of palm oil machinery moldering at the site of the plantation. They had been delivered, placed under guard and no one knew anything about their purpose, value or any plans for their use.

Since the government lab seemed unable to get started on research, I undertook to see if I could organize something. I learned the Mexican embassy had an African cook who, not surprisingly, had been trained to cook Mexican cuisine. On becoming acquainted with Olita—she even had, or had acquired, a Spanish name—I learned that she made tortillas every day. She would grind the corn for masa and fashion the tortillas from the dough. She agreed to do some experimenting in support of my plan to introduce tortillas into the Ghanaian food channels.

We began our market research phase by setting up a booth in an expatriate school's fund-raising fair. The school catered to the Western enclave: USAID, U.N. personnel, missionaries and others. While this group had few native Ghanaians in the mix, at least it offered a chance to prove part of a potential market.

I believed that since I had a tortilla-making expert, and if the market tests were favorable, I would have a project that might interest the food development section of the U.N. or some other agency.

I purchased the supplies out of personal funds, and on the evening before the fair, we enlisted the aid of our families in preparing the sale goods. I had a carpenter fashion a tortilla press based on designs I found in an old *Sunset* magazine. This would be necessary for a large production, since the patty-pat, hand-fashioning method would be far too slow.

We entered the fair loaded down with tortillas and taco fillings. What we didn't sell could be given away as samples. Too bad we hadn't doubled our inventory. When the filling ran out, the individual tortillas sold like proverbial hotcakes. People lined up to request future deliveries, for which we unfortunately were unequipped to handle.

Olita giggled and clapped her hands in excitement. One could almost visualize the lightbulb of an idea switching on over her head. She saw a proven market and had a valuable trade secret. No one else knew how to soak the corn kernels in a lime solution, grind the corn into masa and manufacture the tortillas. She no longer needed me. And, since I had never thought it necessary to learn the source of the lime or the skills for preparing the stuff, she had a monopoly. She intended to put her father into a Mexican food business—on a strictly commercial basis—and closely guard the secret technology.

Oh well. I had planted the seed. And perhaps a commercial approach was the best way to promote interest in this new food. However, for the rest of my stay in the country, I saw no evidence of the technology leaving the Mexican embassy kitchen.

Writing Checks For Fame and Fortune

I never did fathom the nature of the bank loan officers and the deliberations that led them to refuse loans or to accept proposals. I knew that bribes and family or tribal affiliations could smooth the way. However, clients with successful business experience, who seemed to me eminently qualified, failed to obtain money for well-planned expansion objectives, while others could obtain loans with no identifiable rationale.

I had two clients who were brothers. Each owned his own auto repair shop. Kojo Opuko, with whom I dealt, had been trained in a Mercedes factory in Germany. He had acquired a Mercedes, but had little money when it came time to return home. But a Mercedes is a sign of affluence and success in Africa. He wanted this car back in Accra. So he drove it home.

That's how he described it. However, it could hardly have been that easy. After getting off the Mediterranean ferry, he was faced with driving the entire depth of the Sahara, perhaps two thousand miles as the crow flies (an unreliable method of measuring distances, to be sure). But this he did.

When I came to know him, he no longer owned the Mercedes. He and his brother struggled to make a living in their shops. And they were desperate to promote some working capital.

I naturally assumed the need was for the expansion of facilities and procurement of tools. I regarded the brothers as first-class craftsmen—ambitious and reliable. Even so, they drew a total blank at the bank. After a while, I learned the true purpose of their need for a loan.

They had a dream—capitalism in its purest form. Their aspirations centered on acquiring enough money to buy a taxi, preferably a nine-passenger Peugeot. It wasn't because they hankered to be cab jockeys; the idea was to rent the vehicle for ten dollars per day to a working driver. The absolute beauty of this scheme, as they perceived it, was how the vehicles would pay for themselves, with the owners (capitalists) having little to do.

I could see no way to help these men in this type of endeavor, nor was I interested. I sought to increase wealth in some way, not merely to assist in distribution. However, they solved the problem in a way which I would never have dreamed. One day, one of the brothers excitedly informed me of a tip he had received from a friend in the bank. Since the friend held an advanced degree from a London university, I could hardly dismiss the bit of information out of hand, as I might have been inclined to do.

The information related to how loan officers determine the soundness of a loan applicant. They examine the activity of his account. If it is active, soundness is indicated. So the brothers proceeded to introduce some activity. In view of their limited resources, the solution had to be simple and direct. And so it was.

Every day, each brother drew a check payable to the other for deposit. In this manner, the same small sum transferred back and forth, had generated "activity" in both accounts. I expressed amusement at their plan and elicited a hilarious response with my suggestion that a witch could move them along toward their goal more expeditiously. But what did I know?

I left soon after this failure of my expertise to help this client achieve his aspiration. After a time, I received a letter from the brothers. It read: "We have accomplished our fondest dreams, just what you and I worked so hard for. We now own a taxi and rent it out, and we see how we can get more. We did just as you suggested. Each day, my brother and I deposited a check in each other's account. The same checks went back and forth for three months. Then we applied for a loan—and got it."

How I became a participant in such a dream—and especially how the idea, although highly successful, became mine—was mind-boggling. While the brothers wanted to share their good fortune with me, I didn't feel they were being gratuitously complimentary for some minor imaginary participation. The alternative explanation was that they regarded my attention and desire for their commercial success as a beneficial force. Why not? The belief that malicious thoughts directed toward a particular person can result in his misfortune is a commonly held one. Why not the reverse?

This same, strange, banker logic occurred in a situation in East Africa in which I attempted to help a sugar cane farmer salvage his crop. His previous bank loan had proven to be inadequate and he was searching for money to pay for the labor required to get the crop up to the harvesting stage.

I offered his bank an opportunity to salvage its defaulted loan. I advanced the proposition that my organization would make a direct loan to the farmer adequate to his purpose. As a consideration for our financial assistance, we would expect the bank to allow us a primary claim on the crop proceeds for our reimbursement. The bank's counteroffer provided for us to pay off the farmer's defaulted bank loan and then the bank would advance further funds. The counteroffer came too late to save the crop.

Since our interests were in bailing out the farmer, not the bank, I declined the belated offer. The crop never matured, the bank lost all chance for loan repayment, and the farmer went broke.

The Auto Mechanic Park

The following experience typifies the way Western-trained, Third World people can misapply the exquisite technology they learned abroad to home problems.

Auto repair is a major industry in Accra, thanks to the chaotic automobile situation in that city. The traffic is unbelievable. The city is awash with taxis, lorries and buses rushing around in a cacophony of sound that is devastating to the ears and exceedingly risky to life and limb. Drivers' only concession to responsibility is to honk the horn with obvious delight. Everyone, pedestrian as well as driver, attends to his own safety. And since there are no discernible restrictions as to speed, parking or much of anything else, this maelstrom spawns a cottage industry for mechanics of all kinds.

In addition to the high incidence of collision damage, automobiles take a terrific beating from the poor roads. In addition, the exuberant driving habits of the drivers add greatly to the woes of the cars. The highest possible speed is deemed appropriate on the straight-aways, regardless of the distance. Full power is thrown on, slow for curves, speed, slow and more speed. Furthermore, maintenance isn't a discipline that has widely caught on. There is plenty of work for mechanics.

Of course, there are the formal, well-capitalized, modern garages. Inevitably, they swarm with apprentices. It is common for three of these little men to be perched on each side of an engine while the master mechanic performs his examination and repairs the malfunction. Eventually, these apprentices become mechanics. Since they have no capital, they fall into the classification of roadside mechanics.

They ply their trade under trees, in shacks, on vacant lots—wherever they can find a secluded spot. Even by Accra standards, they create an eyesore in various parts of the city. The city council decided to do something about this situation. It acquired a piece of land and developed a program. First, the area had to be cleared, homeowners bought out and squatters forced off the land. Thereafter, streets could be laid out, utilities brought in and an orderly arrangement of stalls made available for the gypsy mechanics.

This splendid idea to rid the city of a nuisance and provide better service for customers either ran into snags or else the town just lost interest, for it abandoned the program. Nevertheless, while the city lost interest, the homeless mechanics did not. Very shortly, mechanics of all types flooded the mostly-cleared area. They set up operations in a hodge podge of tin-roofed shacks and shelters made of palm fronds, scrap lumber or whatever material could be obtained. The government program thus came into being—after a fashion. The arrangement suited the mechanics—after a fashion.

Some of my clients had staked out space. It came to pass that I initiated a proposal for completion of the original plan. The bright young men of the Ghanaian development agency responded with enthusiasm, desperate for a project. They came up with a beautiful design—albeit staggeringly inappropriate—as a solution.

The plan provided for showers, a cooking hall and lounges for the customers. Each mechanic would have a suitable building for his trade. "Marvelous!" I told the designers. "Oh, by the way, what are your cost estimates for this fully, thought-out plan?" I casually inquired. "Well, it's high," they agreed. But they hastened to add that the rent of twenty to thirty dollars per month they intended to charge the mechanics would return the capital outlay.

"Theoretically, that's true," I agreed. Then I realistically pointed out how difficult it would be to find a sponsor to finance such an elaborate installation. Moreover, mechanics now paying no rent, and only earning a dollar or two a day, are poor candidates for bringing in much revenue.

I had nothing more in mind than to revive the foundered government program. It had provided the land for any relocation that actually did take place. It needed only a basic design for bringing in utilities, a layout of streets and business locations to bring some order out of the chaos of the original project. But these designers, eager for a chance to put their education to work, were too chagrined over the non-acceptability of their original creation to start over on the more rudimentary plan I envisioned.

I often wondered about the value of highly sophisticated Western technology to Third World people. Not only is there little reason for applying this technology, it sometimes replaces common sense when it comes to seeking solutions. I interviewed an applicant for a consulting position in the MDPI. To test his approach to a problem, I presented the hypothetical case of a small businessman. With the pleased expression of a man with an instant solution, he said, "First we must prepare a model."

I don't remember where he trained, but Harvard business school graduates often use computer models to solve complex problems. To my candidate, an abstract model might obviate the need for individual analysis of the small businessman's skills, background, experience or any other personal characteristic that would determine his fitness for a business project.

The Reluctant Farmer

An assistance person can suffer almost terminal chagrin over the way a client can immerse him in his project through exuberant enthusiasm and a facade of total dedication. Then, after both parties have spent much time forging a program that appears to predict a good chance for success, the client has lost interest and returned to his village or he has become equally enthusiastic over an entirely different scheme.

This behavior is not unique to Africa of course, but in a land of little opportunity an assistance person can be excused for expecting that a client would seize probably his only chance to succeed in something he claims is of the utmost importance and follow through.

A person came to me seeking assistance for a plan he had to develop a plantation. Although he was a city fellow, he claimed agricultural expertise. Actually, he showed me the remains of a lost crop that had failed because he ran out of money before harvest time. He had located the area he wanted, not too far from Accra, on a major road, fertile and flat enough. It had several small natural ponds, indicating a high water table. He believed he could hire women to transport water to the higher ground. It was Fanti tribal land, so he would require permission from the chief before he could gain possession, but since my client was a member of that tribe, we foresaw no problem.

We called formally on the highly regarded chief, whose esteem by the community was derived, curiously, from his direct decent from an important historical figure. His ancestor had been the rear-guard commander of the column of the migrating Fanti people on their travels from their inland home to the coast. Since the danger from attack is as great from the rear as it is from the front, his ancestor's prestige matched that of the column leader.

Calling on the chief

He and his staff received us. The *okyeame*, the spokesman or chief linguist, is a most important assistant. He advises the chief on traditional law, custom and protocol. The danger of a chief speaking too hastily, speaking in anger or just saying something stupid is obviated by the practice of speaking through the *okyeame*. This arrangement corresponds with the Western practice of employing an "explainer" who interprets what politicians really mean.

Then, of course, he had his drummer. Every chief of any importance has a household drummer. The days when the huge talking drums actually sent messages are over, but they still herald praises of kings, chiefs and other individuals on festival occasions. The drummers claim the pounding is a literal paean to the chief. But major social, military or political occasions are quite often dressed up with drummers.

It is a curious thing about these talking drums. With the proper technique they can convey the most intricate messages. This is possible because of the tonal nature of the language. That is their mystery as explained to me by a drummer.

A large, simple, white, concrete building served as the castle. The chief turned out in a multicolored, hand-loomed silk kente cloth, the Ghanaian costume, draped like a toga, leaving one shoulder exposed. Then, he incongruously topped off his exquisitely fashioned costume with a rimless, felt, Western style hat.

After the courtesies, we got down to business using the stylized procedures. In Fanti, my client made his request to the spokesman, who relayed the message to the chief. Then, I would receive a translation. Both sides enjoyed the ornate prose.

The chief, speaking through the talker, would say: "Mr. Opoko is indeed fortunate to have the interest of the distinguished visitor from far-away America to assist him in this undertaking."

I sought to match his rhetoric: "Mr. Opoko is indeed blessed with the understanding and support of such an illustrious chief and wise tribal elders." After we tired of this game playing, the chief graciously conferred the use of the land on my client.

Following the agreement, the chief ordered a full-dress libation-pouring ceremony as a means of insuring the success of the farming venture, which could now move forward. We moved to another area, where a sort of altar had been constructed. The person conducting the ritual invoked the attention of the gods with an imploring chant, while intermittently sprinkling drops of schnapps (which we had thoughtfully brought with us) on the altar. He advised the spirits of the necessity and worth of the venture and urged them to provide all possible assistance to the project.

The Ghanaian use of the celestial spirits is no joke. Routinely, whenever a bottle is opened, a few courtesy drops are sprinkled on the ground. Even drinkers at a bar can often be observed pouring a dollop on the floor from time to time.

Well, now we had the interest of the spirits and the tribal blessings for the use of the land. With such heavy sponsorship, how could my client fail to prosper? In Africa, it can happen.

The next step was to assist my enthusiastic client to draw up an agricultural plan. Over the next few days we estimated prospective income, labor costs, planting schedules and the rest of the details necessary for a bank loan application.

We submitted the application to a loan officer, who seemed quite willing to have the loan processed. Around the time I thought there should be some news on the loan application, I called on the loan officer. I didn't enjoy this experience.

The banker led with: "Where is Mr. Opoko? We looked favorably on the loan application and so informed him. But he sought to increase the loan amount to include the cost of a Peugeot! And then he admitted he was searching for a farm manager! Of course, we can't finance such a change of plans. We agreed to discuss the original proposal in a meeting the following Tuesday. We haven't seen him since."

I had no answer to this staggering question. When I tracked Mr. Opoko down and demanded to know what had happened, he offered the laconic explanation, "I changed my mind."

Pity the Peasant (Commercial Agricultural Handicaps)

Food production and distribution is a historical and major problem in Ghana, as well as in dozens of other sub-Saharan African countries. It needn't be, at least in some of these countries that have the fertile soil and the daily twelve hours of equatorial sunshine and usually sufficient rain. Moreover, it was not until post-independence that their subsistence farming system began to fail them. No one dumped surplus grain on them prior to that time, either for humanitarian reasons or surplus disposal. (Many farming communities, especially those near the coast, have been permanently damaged by their own government's action of smothering the market with free grain dumped from abroad at prices substantially below the farmers' cost. Once the farmers are forced to leave the land in their search for a livelihood, they are not eager to return.)

I worked with organizations engaged in agricultural projects in three different countries. The experience allowed me to acquire knowledge of a good cross section of African agricultural handicaps. And while no fundamental solutions resulted, it did wipe from my mind some current Western explanations (myths) for the African governments' inability to meet post-independence challenges.

Myth 1: The colonial powers forced an agricultural shift away from food crops into exportable cash crops. To accept that explanation, one must wonder what the farmers were eating while growing cotton, for instance. They never imported food to any noticeable extent. Further, if that was an unsound practice, why do the independent governments continue to export peanuts, palm oil, bananas and other agricultural products?

Myth 2: Per capita food production is declining because of lack of capital. Increased capital resources can only be a requisite if a solution to the myriad problems of commercial farming can be found first. While lack of capital is a chronic handicap to the subsistence farmer, this disadvantage can be overcome with the development of sound credit.

As a consequence of the attitude of Western assistance associates and my own studies, we felt we could at least pinpoint the problem areas relating to poor food production. We decided it could neither be laid at the door of colonial administration nor inadequate assistance programs. The primary fault certainly lies with the governments' own political and administrative procedures. However valid that contention, the reality is per capita food production has been declining since independence. The void left by this growing shortage is being filled by the ever-increasing purchase of imports and the charitable largess of the West.

But the potential is there. These countries can grow bananas, cocoa, yams, pineapples, grain, citrus, peanuts, the staple cassava and more. Ghana can grow them all. Furthermore, most have a solid potential for expanded production. The requirement, basically, is for the development of the applicable commercial techniques that will bridge the gap between potential and need. This need is expanding rapidly due to vast population growth and massive rural migration to cities.

The obvious explanation for the agricultural failure is that since independence the new governments took a wrong turn. They committed themselves to allowing a planned, regulatory economy to supplant the colonial free market system. While the intent was to correct the inequities of the market system, the approach called for government involvement in functions previously handled by the market system. Thus the government established price controls, purchasing agencies and warehousing, and distribution policies, and oversaw the ordering and selling of supplies, seeds, fertilizers, machinery and such.

Leaving aside any warranted criticism of the philosophy behind this approach, the governments lack the administrative skills to coordinate the needs of both producers and consumers. The farmers can't depend on the government monopolies to supply the seeds, fertilizer and machinery when they are needed.

For example, Kenya has large flat tracts of fertile soil that, prior to independence, yielded huge amounts of cotton and maize. No longer. The British had mechanized their own farms and dependable rental organizations furnished a service to those native farms that had the size and terrain to benefit. This technique was lost with independence. The government made an effort to provide a plowing service. Although the machinery was improperly maintained, that was not the problem. The problem was with the administration. The farmers soon learned that the tractor managers wouldn't hold to an agreement, even if the service was prepaid. Consequently, the custom plowing service didn't replace the traditional land-softening method—the women with the hoe—to any great extent.

Although this particular government service failed to provide any important benefit, the farmers themselves could have supplanted their oxen and women, except for the government's greed and unfairness. Generally, the government bows to urban demands for cheap food. This policy comes at the expense of the farmer. Although he will strive to evade price controls, this ploy is difficult for the farmer producing crops such as cocoa since he has no market other than the government purchasing agents.

In another instance, the Ghanaian government agents' greed permanently destroyed cooperation with the farmers. They forged an agreement with the farmers to supply tomatoes for a processing plant they were building. When harvest time came, the plant managers used the opportunity to take advantage of the farmers' vulnerability. They slashed the price agreed on and the farmers were faced with either dumping the crop or accepting what was offered. That was the first and last crop produced.

The major disadvantage for the subsistence farmer is lack of credit, especially if he sees an opportunity to expand production beyond family needs. Unfortunately, credit systems supportive of subsistence farmers are not widespread. Essentially, a credit system must depend on collateral and/or trust. An urban house is a readily acceptable form of collateral, but the farmer is not often the property owner. A crop could be a potential basis for a loan, except for the virtually nonexistent element of trust. In its absence, the bank will have no assurance that the loan money will actually be used for the intended purpose or that the sale of the crop will be used to repay the loan.

My involvement in the chronic food shortage issues began when a would-be entrepreneur brought a proposal to our organization seeking assistance for a trucking scheme. On the surface, it seemed eminently practical—one wondered why it hadn't been done before. The gist of the idea was to save the market women the onerous task of individually transporting from the rural areas the produce they sold each day in the markets.

These hardy souls travel early each morning, in *tro tros* (Datsun trucks with benches and a cover) or other passenger vehicles, to the highlands to make their purchases. They return with bulging baskets of pineapples, citrus, bananas or whatever is in season and sell it at the formal market, out of a kiosk or directly from their head loads. The train also provides transportation to some areas, but the risk of frequent breakdowns is high.

It is an inefficient way and so limited in application! But this simple, traditional system moves a tremendous amount of food from the rural areas to urban consumers. It works so well, within its limits, because it continues a traditional practice. No one need learn any new laws and it escapes regulation because of its unconcentrated nature. Custom has formalized the routine. The farmer knows what the women will take. The women know that a load will be available. Since it is strictly cash at every stage, there is little risk for anyone. But soldiers nag and punish the women retailers, from time to time, in an attempt to enforce some arbitrary, irrational, price-fixing policy. It's a pity government policy makers can't learn what a market-controlled system can accomplish.

Certainly, there existed a theoretical need for truck transportation. We discussed the project with both farmers and market women. We got their interest at first because, as outsiders,we conceivably had something new to offer. The farmers' response indicated plenty of potential for expansion in the short run and much more if they could ever be convinced that the trucker-wholesaler could be counted on to show up as scheduled—*with cash*—to absorb their expanded production. But they saw no possibility of that happening. Furthermore, how could they arrive at a fair price when there was no competition among the buyers? Under the present arrangement, they explained, a throng of market women show up. They dicker with a number of competitive producers until a satisfactory price is established (a classic example of a free market system). Then the clinching argument against the truck idea: it was felt such a concentration of commercial activity would be sure to put the buyers at the mercy of the government price fixers.

ALFAMA—USAID Mechanization Project

Mechanization is often the West's magic solution to the inadequacies of primitive agriculture; never mind its irrelevance to the tiny shambas or farms, lack of capital and know how, as well as a myriad of other handicaps involved in replacing manual labor—women—with machinery. Still, anyone observing a woman working the soil with her all-purpose agricultural tool—the hoe—wonders about better ways.

Accordingly, I hoped I was wrong. I withheld judgment about the chances for success when USAID (U.S. Agency for International Development) undertook a giant mechanism scheme on the plains of Accra, Ghana. The nature of the project was a Kansas-type corn plantation. Since neither I nor my associates had anything to do with this project, we lacked knowledge of the program's strategy. Unfortunately, the resultant, awful failure became known to everyone. It illustrates how the West can make colossal blunders when attempting to introduce an inappropriate system into a country where climatic conditions, culture and every other aspect are incompatible with it.

The project managers increased their eventual anxiety by prejudging the project's success. They had issued calendars and other public relations materials trumpeting their big breakthrough in commercial farming approaches.

The failure wasn't just a setback, such as poor yield, it was a complete loss. A blight killed every would-be ear of corn. Critics of the program claimed the AID people had introduced a new disease. Unfortunately, it also spread to the surrounding farms.

I was unable to procure a copy of the cause analysis. If one indeed exists, it has not been made public.

In an interview with Robert S. Loomis, a professor of agronomy at the University of California at Davis, he explained to me how Western agricultural assistance people often fail to appreciate the reasons for the low yields of seed used by subsistence farmers. They can hardly wait to provide the farmers with the high-yield seed that does so well in temperate climates. It is a question of evolution guided toward special needs, he explained. The seed of the subsistence farmer hosts a broad spectrum of genetic defenses to cope with disease, weeds, pests and drought. Accordingly, crops sown with the traditional seed will always produce some return, sometimes enough to avoid complete starvation, while the narrow-gene spread that concentrated on yield can be a complete wipeout.

Obviously, the failure of ALFAM doesn't exclude mechanization or other Western solutions. Commercial farms have succeeded in various African countries, usually after having surmounted problems a Kansas farmer could hardly fathom. It does suggest, however, that mechanization should not attempt to broadly supplant subsistence techniques. Apart from the good chance that Western technology will fail, traditional farming methods have evolved to address the peculiar needs and circumstances of the people in ways that mechanization could not, even in theory.

Still, despite the mistakes both of Western assistance efforts and the disastrous results of African government experiments, a summary in the *1989 USAID HIGHLIGHTS,* reveals that African food production is improving. African farmers have increased production for each of the last four years by about four percent, compared with one and a quarter percent in the years preceding. Agriculture production grew twice as fast in countries practicing policy reform.

The contention is that this improvement will grow as more countries turn their back on old approaches to economic management by reducing government controls over the economy and allowing the price of agricultural produce to change with market demands.

The Dilemma

The divergence of different cultures can affect the participants in a variety of ways. It can be amusing in the abstract. On a more personal basis, it can cause confusion and misunderstanding. In certain situations, the results can be downright dangerous. The following reflects some of these aspects.

"Do you know about the rest houses here in Accra?" The question was asked by a most lovely young African girl who had just arrived that evening from her village. She had accompanied her boyfriend, a young Peace Corps volunteer, into Accra for his flight out the following morning. He had completed his tour and was returning home.

It was a startling question, asked with the seriousness one would associate with an inquiry about the location of a particular church or shrine. But a rest house has no connection with the function of rest and even less with the business of worship.

However, her eyes left no doubt that she expected an answer to the question. It was also obvious that she knew what rest houses were, whether she thought I did or not. Of course, I did know, as did everyone else who lived in the city of Accra.

A rest house is not the "Tea House of the August Moon." The designation is euphemism at its extreme. They are usually concrete structures, possessing all the charm and ambiance of a bomb shelter. Although stark, the design fulfills its purpose. Each room contains a bed that is a work bench for sexual intercourse. The rent for an hour is low, but clean sheets are extra. You furnish the girl.

The measure of activity can be determined, one is told, by the number of condoms (called "birth controls") discarded under the bed. The kindest description one can give of these places is that, while they are no more subtle as to purpose than a public toilet, they are also as straight forwardly functional.

It might even be called a growth industry. The large modern hotels, and the occasional motel, cater to the tourists and the affluent. Africans, generally, have no need for the luxurious commercial overnight accommodations when they travel. There is always a member of their extended family to put them up wherever they may wish to spend the night. But the sleeping arrangements are most likely too crowded and uncomfortable. Hence the rest house provides a private place to while away an hour or two.

The setting for the young woman's question was a table on the outside of the popular Star Hotel. Her escort, whom I knew somewhat, had invited me to join them.

They were a charming couple. He had been stationed in his girl friend's village, at the site of the giant Akosombo Dam fifty miles from Accra. They had become fast friends. It is difficult to be more specific; they were certainly not lovers. He appeared to be the epitome of the straight-arrow, the all-American, small-town boy. She was a gorgeous woman, dressed in the splendor of traditional Accra fashion. Her neck-to-ankle dress, a cacophony of vivid colors, was matched by a turban of infinite folds and tucks, an architecture that would do justice to a rose. Although she was an example of Africa's most lovely girls, a high standard indeed and exquisitely feminine, she appeared no more lascivious than a young Marie Osmond. It seemed inconceivable that her boyfriend had changed her maidenly status (if that had indeed been her initial category). Still, one can never know for sure.

I don't recall her name. It was probably Ayama, if her parents followed the Akan practice of naming children for the day of the week on which they were born—Ayama or one of the other six possible day names. Of course, it may have been Marie or Emily, if her parents favored Christian names.

The volunteer's two-year contract was over and life had to move on to the next phase. He wouldn't return. There was no big emotional problem; they were sweet kids who had no intention of complicating their lives. She accompanied him to town as a farewell gesture.

After a bit of desultory conversation, he wandered away. Immediately, Ayama came alive, as if she had been waiting for this moment all year. She again quickly whispered the question relating to my knowledge of a rest house. "Of course," I said. With her eyes shining, breathless with expectation, she leaned toward me. "Will you take me to one?"

Perhaps she interpreted as acquiescence the strangling noises I made as a result of my shock. Or, perhaps she never considered the possibility of my refusal. In view of her loveliness, this would be perfectly understandable. She went on, half to herself, and somewhat exultantly it seemed to me; "None of the girls in my village have ever been to one." She hurried on: "I stay with relatives tonight. John's plane leaves at nine tomorrow morning. You can meet me at the airport, after his plane leaves."

John returned to the table. I suppose part of my consternation with the situation arose from my initial image of two innocents: he from America and she from a village still (supposedly) immersed in the traditional style of rural life.

The exotic episode of a beautiful native girl initiating a romantic encounter cries out for an appropriate tropical setting. The grounds of the Star Hotel eminently serve this purpose. I sat back and studied the scene.

The dance floor is at the bottom of a series of terraces. Each terrace had a table and chairs all open to the stars. The hot, sticky air of the day and the cooled on-shore night breezes still laden with moisture are almost palpable. The set decorations, alá Mother Nature, are really overblown. Even Trader Vic would have sought to tone it down.

Bougainvillea crawls everywhere—up buildings, across roof ridges, snaking along utility wires—flashing all the colors of a controlled Fourth of July fireworks. Some flame trees, solid with heavy blood-red blossoms, grow alongside some preposterous banana trees. And there is jacaranda—lots of jacaranda.

In this setting, the young Ghanaian women glide down the terraces to the dance hall. Their flamboyant costumes dramatically highlight the kaleidoscope of intense natural colors common in this tropical tableau.

On the dance floor, they and their partners begin the slow, swaying shuffle of the misnamed "high life" dance; perhaps Ngumiel and his band from Nigeria will be playing this West Coast music, emphasizing the heavy beat of African drums. There may be sixty couples shuffling in a manner easily recognized as a possible source of dancing trends in the U.S. At the end of the set, new couples will form, since many of these women come as singles.

Obviously, Marie's village was not of the traditional sort. After I shifted mental gears and recognized her kinship with the modern women of Accra, I adjusted my attitude.

At this point, an explanation of my recently-acquired anthropological knowledge of the more sophisticated Ghanaian women can reflect the change of understanding required of me. Urban women (more accurately, the emancipated women, as distinct from those in the Moslem and rural areas) are a separate population and have a detachment from men that is hard for a Westerner to picture. They don't shun men; their prodigious production of babies establishes that fact. In urban areas, their domination of the small-scale retail trade in the local markets allows them to support themselves. With this independence they appear to be as free and uninhibited as the trade winds. Their pursuit of being their own person has expanded to the more traditional areas.

In the heavily concentrated market areas, you see women almost exclusively, a flowing mass of color conducting their trading business or just visiting. The teeth displayed in their frequent smiles remind one of the surf breaking on a nearby beach. They swathe themselves in yards and yards of the brightest Java prints, printed especially for Ghana. And unless their heads are laden with baskets of trade goods, they will probably be wearing their intricate headdresses of matching material.

As much of an identifying feature of the female body as her breasts is a small black face peering over his mother's shoulder. The child rides astride her back, supported by a section of cloth looped around his buttocks and tied in her front.

Is the enjoyment of this abundant freedom a reaction to the constraints of the traditional life of women back on the farm? Or are they just doing what comes naturally following the shedding of tribal shackles? If they had been born in the village and remained there, they most likely would have married at a young age and engaged in carrying out the duties of married women, whose purpose in life was defined long ago by her ancestors. She must grow the food for the family: children, husband, grandparents and assorted relatives, while ensuring a flow of children.

Of course, her husband does not receive her valuable service resource for nothing. It requires a negotiation ceremony wherein the husband-to-be's family has to accumulate a packet of wealth sufficient to induce the bride's father to part with his daughter. This bride's price may be a combination of cattle, camels, goats, money or whatever moves the father. (It is easier for some humanists to regard this payment as a mere token incident to some mystical sealing of the families, rather than the merchandising of a daughter.)

I became painfully aware of this bride-purchase custom early on while traveling in rural areas with my two daughters. A uniformed official at a government checkpoint began eyeing my girls with a rather disconcerting interest. Although their beauty customarily attracted attention, this man seemed to be making a studied appraisal. Since he held the gate, we had to wait him out.

I had been in the country long enough to know the status of rural African wives, their perceived purpose and the characteristics that determined their value. With this background knowledge, I could see through the official's game playing. I assumed he was merely practicing his "stock judging" expertise. And he did have access to good practice models, if I may immodestly say so.

Lynnanne, my blond, buxom fourteen-year-old stood out as pretty in any crowd. And as a potential wife-package, she obviously had nursing capacity and a body that could work all day at agricultural chores. Nevertheless my older daughter, less endowed with those features, had her own style of beauty.

But it never occurred to me to regard these traits as salable merchandise. In my naiveté, I treated the official's offer to negotiate a sale of one or both of my daughters as a joke, without realizing his deadly seriousness. My would-be son-in-law regarded my laughing response as an insult to his bona fide proposal. It took some apologizing and explanations to extract myself from this nasty situation. I never again treated lightly what seemed like outlandish propositions.

In view of the aforementioned independent lifestyle and attitudes, the concepts of virginity, bastardy and prostitution have no significance. Accordingly, a straightforward expression of sexual interest initiated by either sex is perfectly acceptable. Prostitution, at least our meaning, would not translate and the idea of a pimp would be regarded as ludicrous; the girls do expect a "present"—a sum of money. Of course, this is prostitution by definition and some girls do live on this income. But even girls who have no need for such economic support also expect a—gift. It's expected—it's the custom.

From casual observation, without trying to delve into any psychological explanations, it appears that the women we might call prostitutes carry with them no observable stigma. In any event, however this unfettered sex is regarded, it is not associated with the commercial and impersonal sex for pay in the Western world.

Although this discussion can explain a lack of inhibition and offers a candid treatment of the subject, it fails to address her motive, for I pooh-poohed any illusion of her having a crazy attraction for my body. No, she sought adventure and the status as the only one of her peers to be entertained in a mysterious big city rest house. Perhaps, similarly, a Western girl might dream of a tryst on a luxury yacht.

What to do? It was too late for a fatherly response, such as, "While I know of them (the rest houses), I have never been there and I don't think you should either." It was obvious from her nervousness, that she did not share her secret desire with her friend and would not welcome any further discussion in his presence. I had to either sublimate some of my attitudes and let this gorgeous woman make the decision or walk away and not look back. But the message in her eyes, which locked on mine when I got up to go, was as clear as if spelled out in neon: "You promised."

I found myself in a box. I had not considered this comely young woman in sexual terms. Perhaps in other circumstances, I would have had a regard for her akin to that I would have for my daughters' friends. At an estimated eighteen years, she was fully developed. My cultural attitudes were in turmoil. I had early conditioning and inhibitions about deflowering maidens. Besides, it seemed a bit incestuous, she being the same age as my eighteen-year-old daughter. And wrestling with my conscience, I could not shrug off the fact I was a married man.

What to do? How could I justify rejecting her and breaking her heart? I could have run like hell when she asked me. But I didn't. However passive my acceptance, I didn't refuse. I can't caddishly fail to show up. I owe her an appearance. Yes or no.

The next morning I arrived at the airport at a quarter to nine, still undecided. It later occurred to me that I was in an O'Henry type of dilemma. While the narrator, of course, recognizes he is being used, is that so terrible? And is he confined to the Western prohibitions against older men lusting after young women and all the rest of the restrictions concerning extramarital sexual involvements? Or will he "think" African and joyously accept the lovely present of the gods? Surely they would be unforgiving of a rejection.

We'll never know. For at a quarter past nine, the loudspeaker rustled its vocal cords: "TWA flight 680 to Monrovia, Dakar and Paris will be delayed one hour." Time to draw up a litre of beer. One kills time in the tropics, whatever time it is, in that manner. But it didn't seem good form to sit down with the girl and her soon-to-be-airborne boyfriend. It was a bit embarrassing somehow, and surely would spoil the magic moment of departure.

At ten o'clock another throat clearing from the speaker, and then: "Flight... will be delayed until noon."

This solved my dilemma. There was no way I could miss my previously-committed noon appointment and I had no confidence that an actual noon take-off would occur.

I had to leave. I walked by her and caught her eye. With all the subtle body language I could manage, I said, "Sorry, it was not meant to be!"

L. Dalton Casto in West Africa

Some of the men I worked with...

Section II

CENTRAL AFRICAN TRIP

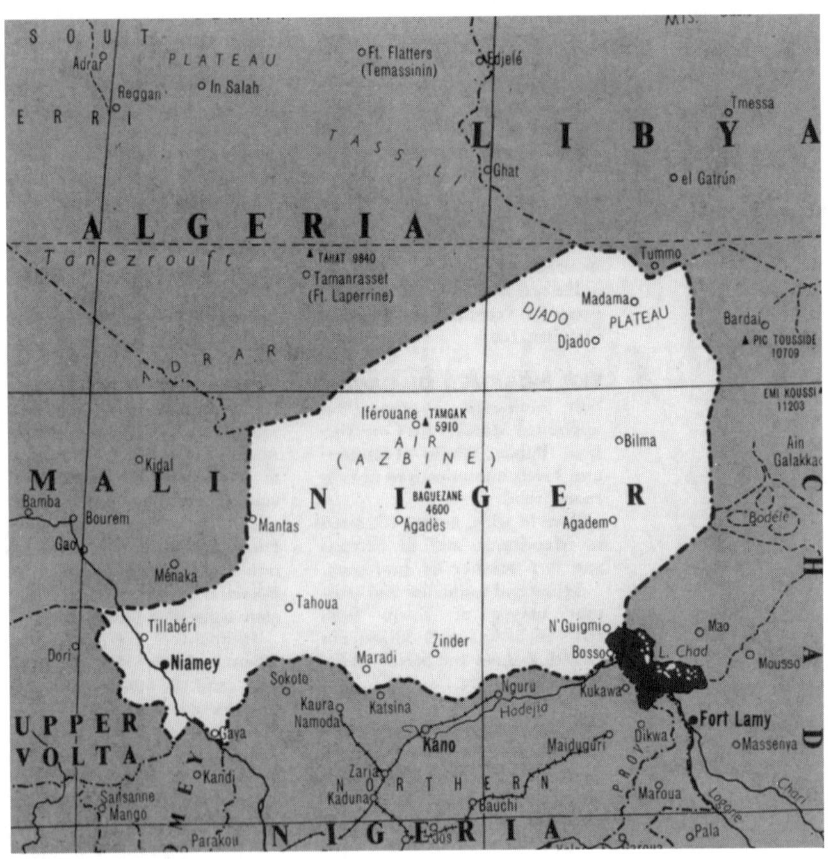
ALGERIA
LIBYA
MALI
NIGER
UPPER VOLTA
NIGERIA
Niamey
Agadès
Zinder
Maradi
Tahoua
Tillabéri
Bilma
Agadem
N'Guigmi
Bosso
L. Chad
Fort Lamy
Kano
Sokoto
Katsina
Tamanrasset
(Ft. Laperrine)
Djado
Madama
DJADO PLATEAU
AIR
(AZBINE)
Iférouane
Ghat
In Salah
Tummo
Bardai
Gao
Ménaka
Kidal
Bourem
Niamey

CENTRAL AFRICA TRIP

Outward Bound

After a year of working in the humid heat of Accra, and beset with myriad frustrations, I decided a good place to spend my two weeks' vacation was the desert. In view of the exploratory nature of the safari I had in mind, it had to be solo, so I chose to leave the family behind. To use native transportation and to sleep on a catch-as-catch-can basis wouldn't have thrilled my wife.

Not only would the desert afford some respite from the cacophony of auto horns and the generally incredible noise level of the city, it was also the right location for a visit to the Hausa, intriguing desert-dwellers who would show up in Accra from time to time. These tall people had mahogany complexions and were decidedly different physically from the small, dark West Africans and culturally they were worlds apart. Their Islamic religion and observances contrasted sharply with the predominantly Christian Accran blacks. And while many Ghanaians wore European-style clothes, the Hausa preferred robes and the distinguishing cap denoting their religion or headdresses reminiscent of the old Folger coffee trademark—a tall fellow in a yellow star stuck robe. A cloth headdress completed his costume. These desert people stood out in any crowd. I was exceedingly interested to see how they lived when they were at home.[1]

1 Although the Hausa speakers may be regarded as a distinct tribe, the word denotes a *lingua franca* spoken mostly in Northern Nigeria and on the Western edge of the Sahara by a host of tribes.

Another ethnic group I had hoped to encounter were the Tuaregs, a tribe I first heard about in my boyhood reading of P. C. Wren's *Beau Geste* and the stories of other writers as Byron Khun de Porok. Porok describes them in his book, *The Mysterious Sahara,* published in 1929:

> ***The people of the veil—noble, yet savage, brave, yet heartless, whose origins no man knoweth and who walk proudly in their fierce and fearless majesty* (p. 116).**

In another reference he presents this image:

> ***To me the Tuareg always appeared like strange apparitions riding on white camels, their faces hidden behind their veils and seeming to glide down the gloomy canyons in a manner that makes them ghost-like and utterly unreal* (p. 148).**[2]

A trip to the northeast offered a fascinating number of choices of things to see and experience. And besides the people, there was that geographical improbability, the Niger River.

I planned to travel north through Ghana to the capital city of Upper Volta (now Bourkina Fasso), Ouagadougou (affectionately referred to as Wogo) and then, east to Niamey, located in the southwestern tip of Niger. On the return leg, I planned to travel south through Dahomey (now the People's Republic of Benin) to coastal Cotonou, the capital city. From there, a pleasant journey back to Ghana along the coast road through Togo. At least I planned it that way.

The preparations for such a journey involved obtaining visas for each country. As each embassy holds your passport for two or three days, one does not go rushing into a trip that crosses so many boundaries.

It was easy to figure the route, but the means of transportation left some questions to ponder. Airlines linked capital cities, but that

2 Byron Khun de Prorok, F.R.G.S., *The Mysterious Sahara*, (Chicago: The Reilly & Lee Company), 1929.

was not the kind of trip I had in mind. As for a private automobile, which I did not have, the problem centered mostly on the atrocious condition of most roads. That left the only other alternative: to travel, as the mass of people do, by what is loosely referred to as public transportation. This offered a number of choices.

The nine-passenger Peugeot (the French estimate of capacity, not the African) is the fastest, most expensive. The most dangerous characteristics that arise depend on the type of arrangement agreed to by the owner of this expensive machinery and the driver. The driver usually pays the owner a fixed, daily rental. In order for him to make a profit, he flattens the springs with the size of his load and floorboards it all the way. Safety considerations are superseded by economics.

Essentially, any vehicle having space will look for and take fares. The most usual, however, in the populous states of Ghana and Nigeria, is the Datsun pickup truck outfitted with benches on each side of the truck bed, which is covered by a low canopy. These are called “mammy wagons,” “tro tros,” “bush taxis,” and other colorful names. Vans are also common and in some areas there are regular passenger busses. The fares are modest. However, for the less affluent, space can be purchased on top of the load of virtually any freight-carrying truck. In fact, the drivers vigorously solicit passengers. In many places there is little other public transportation. Thus do African people travel.

Providing lodging for transient non-natives in this touristless land is not high on anyone’s list of priorities. Peace Corps hostels were scattered across this vast, sparsely populated area. Peace Corps volunteers could provide hospitality. I carried a light goatskin pack, a specialty of the Ghanaian town of Takoradi. It contained a light blanket, a windbreaker jacket and a few other necessities.

I had no particular problem with the native fare, although the stew laced with red peppers could distress a Mexican. This lethal concoction, poured over rice, provided a good meal once I got used to eating with tears rolling down my face. But with the excellent bread and dirt-cheap bananas, I lost no weight.

Heading north, I hitched a ride in a Peugeot driven by a cowboy who liked to make time. By evening we had reached the border town of Bolgatonga—the end of his line. I decided to look for a hostel and stay the night. Two lads joined me, wanting to sign on as bearers. This seemed appropriate for a white African explorer, so I turned over my goatskin pack. They took me to a hostel of sorts, but it was clean and cheap. After I checked in, they guided me to a large hotel fashioned from the damp crumbling concrete that seems to be the West African building material of choice. The hotel Le Bull had a bar.

In the bar lounge I noticed two petite American girls playing cards and, though it was March, listening to a medley of Christmas carols on the jukebox. It turned out they were Peace Corps volunteers on vacation from their teaching jobs in Liberia and were headed for Ouagadougou, my destination as well. Our itinerary diverged at that point. They intended to swing through Mali, hoping to reach Timbuctu before returning south to Liberia. Barely old enough to vote and neither one weighing over a hundred pounds, these young women didn't appear daunted by a trip of 2,500 miles over some of the world's most arid land, using native transportation all the way. Only one of them spoke French in these mostly French-speaking areas.

I spent much of the next day waiting for a Peugeot driver to collect a passenger load for Wogo. He failed, but I negotiated a ride in a Beetle with two Hausa traders. This car made a stop at every police station for "understanding" relative to the cargo it carried. A little friendly discussion and some gifts made it unnecessary to search the car for prohibited or dutiable material. Toward evening I became aware of a certain urgency in the schedule. They explained their haste as a desire to reach a friend's house in time to join him in evening prayers. We arrived in time.

The charming wife greeted us, brought out the prayer rug for the men and settled down for a chat with me. (Women and Christians are excluded from this prayer routine; I suppose on the assumption they are not going anywhere anyway.) Meanwhile, the men proceeded with the ritual washing of feet and the proper positioning of the rugs in relation to Mecca. The ceremony then began. While chanting an acknowledgment of his belief in Allah as the true God, the worshiper rhythmically touches his forehead to the ground by lowering and raising his upper body. The whole ritual takes a while.

Meanwhile, the wife and I, with our limited mutual vocabulary, were enjoying our attempts at conversation. From time to time we had a communication impasse. Every time this happened, the praying would be suspended for translation help, then resumed. Finally, our conversation problems required too much attention. The praying got postponed. I wondered what consequences could result from a short-changed Moslem prayer—but no punishment rained from the sky.

Upon arriving in Wogo, Upper Volta, I transferred to a taxi whose driver proudly assured me he could take me to the Peace Corps hostel. With a rush and flourish, he deposited me at what he believed was my destination and sped off. It was Peace Corps all right—the Peace Corps office, closed for the night. I went trudging off looking for a restaurant, a hotel and a place to change money.

I found a nice restaurant with an exquisite Vietnamese hostess. She had long black hair and was wearing a brilliantly-colored, high-necked *cheong sam*. She was an exotic creature. She opened the kitchen, prepared a sandwich and exchanged some money for me, proving she could be accommodating as well as beautiful. Interestingly, I later learned that a church group used this restaurant as a rehabilitation project for ex-prostitutes.

I needed a place to sleep. Since I had not found anyone who knew the location of the Peace Corps hostel, I settled on a French-run public hotel with swimming pool—nice, not in keeping with my economic constraints, but, what the hell—live.

Later, about midnight, as I walked along the street, I heard a feminine cry: "Mr. Casto—Lynn—hey!" My school teacher friends had arrived earlier, had located the Corps hostel, came downtown but were now unable to direct the taxi back to the hostel. "Did I know where it was?" they asked. I did not, but I grandly offered to share my comparatively luxurious quarters.

This offer was declined, tentatively and regretfully, in view of the difference in class between my place and theirs. But they were worried about their gear and had already checked in and paid. “Will you hold the offer open in the event we cannot find our place in one more try?” they asked as we parted. I never saw them again.

Wogo is a pleasant contrast to the snarling, noisy, auto-infested cities of Ghana and Nigeria. The French colonized for glory. Upper Volta, Mali and Niger, for instance, are without any particular economic resources except for subsistence farming and stock raising. They head most lists of the world’s poorest countries.

Even in the capital cities, it is quiet and peaceful enough to hear the slap of sandals, the whisper of bicycles and the subdued put-putting of mopeds. There is wine and cheese available, as well as food prepared by French-trained chefs. Altogether, the amenities and atmosphere of French Africa are delightful. But there was no question about my having reached the desert. Upper Volta *is* desert.

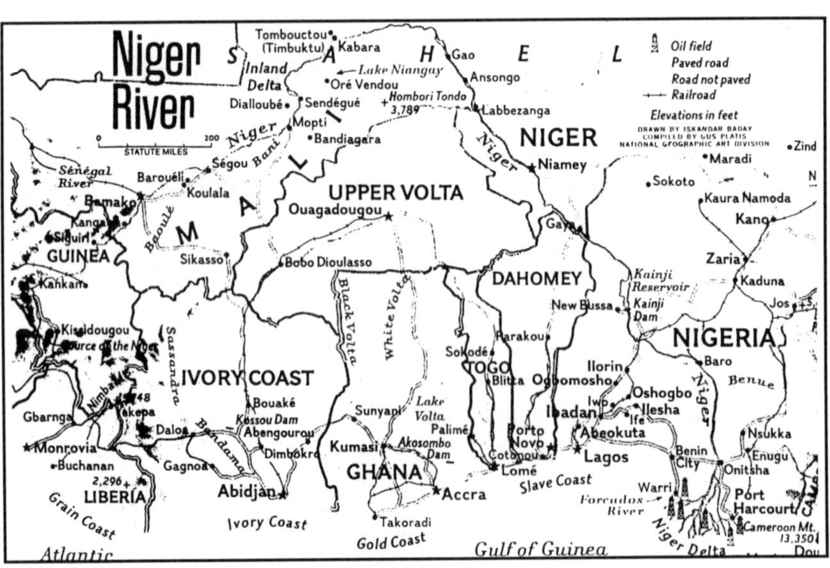

The Upper Volta region

I began to have doubts about going farther. Why leave this delightful town? Moreover, I learned that Niamey was on the other end of a moonscape. I checked the available transportation service from Wogo to Niamey. Although air service between the two cities existed, land transportation was scarce. Only hardy souls elected to make a living by hauling passengers over that forbidding stretch, but I found one. The beat-up condition of his vehicle, however, gave me a definite pause.

Its redeeming feature was the air-cooled Volkswagen engine. I would have been loath to compete with a regular engine for water. Originally a van, it appeared to have gone through a number of metamorphoses, judging from the makeshift parts, special wheels, tires, roof rack and such.

Still, I placed my fate in the hands of the weather-worn driver as did some other hardy souls who undoubtedly had a far greater need than I to tackle the journey. Although it wasn't easy to wrench myself away from the tranquillity of Wogo, I did have a schedule.

In any event, the trip proved to be rugged, incredibly hot and dusty, but suffering such conditions was profoundly preferable to a breakdown. I learned to appreciate the skill of the veteran driver, who coaxed his vehicle through such bad stretches as sand by whispering what I presumed to be entreaties under his breath.

Niamey is a modern, clean, attractive city that reflects the French influence on the heavily preponderant Moslem culture. The population at the time of my visit was about 150,000. Business is conducted at a relaxed pace, as if to the rhythm of the Niger, which bisects the city in the manner of the Seine in that other French city. Camels, burros and trucks share the load in distributing the cargoes of river grass, wood, animals and other material brought in by the large river barges that dock in the center of town.

I watched a camel-and-burro team, loaded high with wood and grass, shamble up from the barge docks unattended. These workers knew their destination. Later, I saw the same two sharing fodder in an alley, indifferent to the gas-powered vehicles that had so far failed to render their jobs obsolete.

I recall another picture of the amalgamation of old and new, framed in the setting of Niamey's super-modern airport. While satisfying my curiosity about this showplace of which the people in Niamey were so proud, I could observe desert families dressed in all their tribal accouterments—there were old folks, babies and all between, squatting on the gleaming terrazzo floor brewing tea.

Tuareg man and his family

I wondered what male member of the family would be traveling to where and why. Would the traveler be a favored son, educated abroad with little feel for the desert? Or would he be a person old enough to recall memories of when the same distance he travels by plane took weeks on the back of a swaying camel?

As I had moved inland toward the desert, I could observe a gradual shift in demographics. The predominant smaller coastal blacks began to give way to the taller, robed, cinnamon-colored desert people. In Niamey the change was almost complete. Blacks had become a minority.

In Niamey, it is possible to see a cross-section of all the desert groups, particularly since the nomadic Peul and Tuareg tribes have been forced south by drought. The government also maintains an outdoor museum that depicts the way of life of each of the major Niger tribes.[3] The distinctive habitations, furnishings, tools, clothes and such, are realistically presented. It is the finest museum of its kind that I know.

My modest initial itinerary had established Niamey as the eastern limit of my travels. From there it would be an easy return journey—south through Dahomey, crossing the eastern border of Togo to her capital city, Lome, with the final leg to Accra only 100 miles up the coast to the west.

Why depart from such a simple, easy plan? The only reason: the lure of the city of Zinder, 600 miles east, near the center of the continent. This city fascinated me ever since a youthful reading of its history. Unfortunately, this destination was at the end of the highway and offered no alternative return. Every mile east would necessitate back tracking that mile (except, that is, if it were possible to dip south for a return through Nigeria, but unfortunately, that country had long been hazardous for tourist travel.)

But everything I had seen of Niger fascinated me. I wanted to sample the lives of these interesting Moslem people; to see their farming, stock raising and methods of travel. Although an outsider with limited time, I could at least obtain glimpses. I decided to travel to the end of the road, hoping it would be worthwhile enough to negate the inconvenience of retracing my steps.

As it turned out, it was a good decision to travel deeper into Niger, although the drought that had begun three years earlier was to worsen and become a calamity. As it was, the acute phase of its killing effect began in the last quarter of the year of my journey, 1972. Nearly all the animals of the nomads would die and these independent people would become starving refugees, their traditional life

3 Most of the 4.5 million people who inhabit this huge country (larger than the African state of Nigeria and close to twice the size of Texas), belong to one of four ethnic groups. They are either Hausa or Djerma farmers or Peul or Tuareg herders.

cycles forever lost. In some places the Niger River would become little more than a rivulet, reaching the lowest flow in history.

With the decision to change my itinerary, I had to apply for a Nigerian visa. Perhaps the rulers had become less paranoid or, more likely, new rulers had taken over. On Friday I approached a girl at the reception desk at the Nigerian embassy. The young African girl exhibited a monumental disinterest in my quest for a visa. "Impossible," seemed to be the extent of her desire to converse. However, I piqued her interest when I began to consult a small French-English dictionary for some persuasive phrases.

In response to her question about the nature of the interesting little book, I made a quick offer. "This valuable book—obtained in faraway America—is my gift to you when you so kindly arrange a visa for me."

"Come back this afternoon with two pictures," she answered.

So, with pictures in hand, back I returned to the embassy girl. Within five minutes, I had my visa and she had begun studying the dictionary. I believe she probably signed and stamped the visa herself. Why bother the consul?

Now I could make a radical alteration of my travel plans. I could traverse the Niger desert 600 miles east to where the road ends—at Zinder. From there, I could cross the border into Nigeria, specifically to Kano, the unofficial capital of Hausa land and then travel 700 miles or so to the Nigerian capital city of Lagos on the coast of the Gulf of Guinea.

But first I had to reach Zinder. Since I was versed in non-animal land travel, I went to the market to find out what kind of conveyance might be heading my way. There wasn't much, but I found a freight-carrying lorry with a driver eager to round out his revenue by selling space on top of his cargo of millet.

I bargained for a ride as far as Birni-n-Konni, where I planned to visit a couple of women Peace Corps volunteers. The first price demanded by the driver seemed about right for an airline ticket, had such a thing existed. But after the first week in Africa, one learns to bargain. Arranging a price, however, proved to be only a small part of getting on the road.

"When do you leave?" I inquired.

"Wait small," the driver responded.

"Will I have time to buy some bread and sardines?"

"Yes," he said reluctantly, as if I were jeopardizing a demanding schedule. I hastened back and climbed on top, one of a half-dozen people, and commenced to wait. Gradually, more passengers joined our growing group. After many hours, the vast truck body became solid with passengers. What is that jockey waiting for now? I wondered aloud. A passenger observing my impatience, explained the routine: "He not go less no more riders anywhere."

I had long since become cognizant of the African attitude regarding space—that there is always room for more—but since the load was already completely obscured by the blanket of bodies, I suggested to the driver that we might roll about now.

This caused a hearty laugh all around and drew the response, "Not enough, not enough."[4]

Finally, at dusk we got underway, not because we were "loaded," but only because no more passengers seemed interested in traveling with us. Of course we stopped at every knot of people along the road that looked as though they might have a fare-paying ability. Obviously, the driver's primary concern was passenger revenue. By hustling passengers, he could gain a bonus for himself over his fixed salary or income from freight.

At last we were on the open road, racing the moon across the desert. I had become one with the people of Niger, men and women, old and young—and everyone but me dressed in Moslem robes, wraparounds, headdresses and sandals. Although packed solidly on

4 This forced, hearty laugh is a curious but seemingly widespread African behavior. It appears to be a stylized part of the ceremony connected with friendly but tough bits of negation. For instance, a landlord and tenant may have an interchange such as this:
"We will require burglar bars on all the windows—ha ha ha."
"You will only need them on the lower floor —ha ha ha."
The point of this laughter may be a way of softening the interchange.

the load of millet, we swayed fluidly with the movement of the truck, adjusting to the pull of gravity and inertia.

The exhilaration generated by this huge Mercedes lorry plunging through the night inspired me to wonder what a magnificent sound these fifty voices could make if they joined me in a rendition of "The Desert Song," "The rifts came riding..." But the chill soon overwhelmed such thoughts. God, how cold was the dry wind caused by this hurtling monster, fleeing wide open over one of the few paved highways in the country. We all huddled together, happily sharing our warmth.

Hundreds of miles later, as the first streaks of dawn appeared, the truck slowed down. A passenger informed me that the two stone buildings we now approached was the town of Birni-n-Konni. I extracted a pair of legs and arms, hoping they were mine and clambered to the ground before the truck got up too much speed.

I sat under a tree, wrapped in my lightweight blanket, too cold to sleep, and watched the dawn approach this oasis. The area was level and large, scattered trees gave the area a park-like appearance. The mud-constructed houses, widely dispersed, appeared massive in the dawn light.

As the light became brighter, I could observe the beginning of activity along the track. First, the burros pegged along on some personal errand—probably a visit to a water hole. Then the goats came mincing by. Two groups of different kinds of guinea hens were the next to appear in the early morning parade. Although one group outweighed the other, they were equal in ferocity—squabbling and threatening each other.

I could see a man rounding up a herd of perhaps fifty camels from the surrounding hills. They came shuffling and trotting into town. The scene took me back to my youth and early morning horse roundups on a ranch.

Women began to float by like wraiths. Each with a head load, they glided along, graceful as swans on a lake, presumably going to the fields. They dressed according to tribal tradition, sporting a wraparound arrangement in black that hung from just below the armpits, a white top and a head wrap. It was drab, but it seemed suitable.

I could hear the thunk-thunk of a woman grinding millet for the morning meal. While the vigorous pounding of a pestle into a hollowed section of a stump will eventually pulverize the tiny, extremely hard seeds, the cost in calories expended, compared to the calories gained from the process, must result in a poor payoff.

The two women volunteers I stopped to visit administered a health program for pregnant women. They relied on horses to reach their clients in this remote area. In spite of what had to be a lonely life, they seemed enthusiastic about their jobs and anxious for news of the rest of the African Peace Corps domain.

After a leisurely Sunday breakfast and a bit of rest, they gave me trail information and the names of other volunteers I might want to visit. They suggested if I could reach Maradi by the next day, I could observe market day, which was well worth seeing. After traveling on several vehicles, I arrived in Maradi at dusk.

I walked into a French-owned hotel and signified my intention of staying the night. It soon became evident that the African room clerk understood neither English nor my mimed message—a language impasse. I imagined I could read his bafflement: "Man, don't you know any French or Hausa words, even dirty ones?"

Incredible! I stood in the hotel lobby, baggage-laden and road-stained—unable to put across my need for a room.

What the hell did he think I came for? I marched behind the counter, took a key off the rack and headed for a room.

The next morning at breakfast, I found out why I had not been recognized as a patron: I couldn't be "evaluated." I was an anomaly, a word loved by African journalists. Madam, upon being informed of this intrusion on her guest list, found an interpreter, who was a Belgian tobacco buyer.

Curiously, he had the accent of the American deep south. He explained this oddity with, "That's the kind of English you learn in South Carolina." He then explained the reason for Madam's curiosity. For a white man, with gray in his hair, to arrive in an area remote from trains, planes or busses has no alternative but a private vehicle. You have no vehicle.

"How did you get here?" I was asked.

"Why, I came on top of a lorry. How else?" I didn't seem to be believed.

It was market day. The people began streaming in from outer villages, heading for the town square. The women carried the usual head loads. Burros, camels, carts and light trucks were laden with anything that might attract a buyer or a trade. Calves, goats, horses and camels destined to be sold trailed along. Altogether, the offerings appeared to be a cross-section of everything these people consumed or used.

This entire migration came to rest at the town square. Each trader found space to offer his wares. Mothers prepared meals. Children played games. Women chatted and visited. The men examined the various stock and pointed out the excellence of their animals. The scene was much more serene and peaceful than the razzle-dazzle of big city markets which are characterized by their shouting, haggling and crowding.

Observing the riders and horses was one of the high points of the day for me. The ponies danced and postured, not trying to escape restraint, just exercising their grace. The riders, proud and indulgent, had decorated their mounts and equipment with embroidered cloths, bangles and various pretties. Perhaps this dolling up of their horses is an outlet for Islamic frivolity that cannot be applied to their women.

What a fascinating country—the people, the customs, the attitudes. Even the names of places have the kiss of poetry: Maradi, Birni-n-Konni, Zinder, Niamey and Agadez. Jeweled cities they are not, but the names seem apropos to the living places of this land and its people.

On the next leg of the road to Zinger, I decided to go first class. I paid for a seat in the *cab* of a lorry. As usual, this driver was attempting to top off his load with passengers, but this time I wasn't one of them. This truck had a crew, not just the sole operator. The driver, dressed in the usual Haas robe, clearly seemed born to command—lots of presence and authority of ship-captain caliber. The chief engineer had a different image—aloof, a bit above it all; young and aristocratic were adjectives that seemed to fit. No robe for him. He favored a blue safari suit: a short-sleeved jacket with matching slacks, set off with a blue, US. Air Force-type cap.

The other two men in the crew were clad in grease-stained clothes and obviously drew the dirty jobs. Whether required by their function or out of curiosity, they invariably came scampering down over the windshield, across the hood and onto the ground when the truck stopped, which was often.

We got under way, stopping at every point where passengers might be found, as well as for any other reason that could be used as an excuse. This captain couldn't stand high gear very long.

Then a fuel line broke.

The rough mechanics came tumbling down, got under the hood and removed the offending section of line. Now the chief engineer came on stage. He produced a tool box suitable for storing fine silver. He opened it and selected one of the gleaming tools. Soon, he produced a perfect flange in the end of the tube. With gentle taps, he fitted it in place and then left the clean-up job to the mechanics.

The little circle of onlookers observed this magic in awe. Now, silently, with the air of a surgeon who had just performed a routine heart transplant, he locked up his magical tools and climbed back into the cab. I felt like cheering.

I now digress to explain a personal dilemma founded on cultural differences. In Africa, there is no particular onus against male public urination—in the open sewers, alongside of the road, against a wall—almost anywhere. In fact, one might see an admonitory sign requesting, "No urination against this wall." However, in Arabic countries there is a peculiar twist.

A legendary remark of Richard Button, Arabs, explorer, translator of the *Perfumed Garden*, graphically described this difference. An English lady once gushingly asked him, "What are Arabs like?" His classic response to this banal question was, "Well, Milady, the men squat to urinate, just as you do."

This knowledge, tucked away in my dim subconscious, came rapidly to the fore when we made a comfort stop. I use the word "comfort" advisedly, it being a mere open space. I found that Button was right. But what about me? My toilet training instructions were specific. Girls handled this function one way, boys another. Furthermore, when I was growing up, the cruelest jibe boys could fling at someone they regarded as a sissy was the claim that he probably urinated like a girl. I instinctively felt that I couldn't manage this squatting method. I would probably bungle it. In pondering this dilemma, I also wondered about the possibility of breaching some taboo. Perhaps the Koran treated the subject. In what circumstances could one depart from local customs with impunity? A decision had to be made. I elected to be Mr. I. P. Standing. Happily, no one threw stones at me.

Another custom not observed in Christian countries is the standing provision for prayer. Periodically the driver stopped. The men piled out and washed their feet in water they carried in a kettle-type container. They spread a rug on the sand, faced Mecca and gave their allegiance to Allah—the only God. Then everyone loaded up and off we went—a prayer break, you might say.

We reached Zinger at sundown. It was the end of the road, fabled and storied; the location of the Sultan's palace, seat of rebellion against the French. For me, it marked the easternmost limit of my trip, coming to within a couple hundred miles of the widest part of the continent (save the Horn) of Africa. It had been a hard won fifteen hundred miles since Accra.

Although we on the "bridge" had a mutual vocabulary not exceeding a dozen words, we had become comfortable with each other, more like companions. My purchase of a round of Fatness had broken some ice. As we climbed down, the engineer picked up my pack, hung it on one of the crew and with a smile, pointed the way to Peace Corps headquarters.

Homeward Bound

Zinger, I fear, has not maintained its historical interest or importance. The huge camel markets are no more and the few camel caravans of those still plying their trade generate only minor traffic. The Sultan's palace seems to have weathered; it probably didn't receive the required annual mud daubing. The entire estate suffered from neglect. I expect this lack of care reflected his long absences. An interesting old colonial hotel still stands, living on its former glory, I suppose. At least it had the accouterrments: ornate furniture, elaborate chandeliers, huge mirrors and rugs of diminished beauty. But it reflected no attempt to cater to demanding guests. There is nothing to suggest that, during the colonial period, this city teemed with the French Foreign Legion-Beau Geste types. Even the legionnaire kepi is no longer part of the everyday costume in Zinder.

After a few days of wandering around town and visiting with the volunteers, it came time to head south. The question was, of course, how? Phillip, a volunteer returning from leave, joined me in seeking transportation. He had a project a hundred miles down the road toward the Nigerian border. We also met Austrians Karl and Bruno, whose ongoing route passed both of our immediate destinations. They agreed to take us along upon completion of repairs to their Volkswagen van.

They had started out in Austria, shipped the Volkswagen van across the Mediterranean and plowed their way across the heart of the Sahara, traversing Algeria and all but a hundred miles of the width of Niger. This 2,000 miles of sand had been uneventful, they said, until the engine threw a rod upon reaching Zinder.

Their courage impressed me. I wondered if a double truck vehicle wouldn't have been more suitable. But the van was eminently practical from their standpoint. In Austria, they operated a natural history tourist attraction. They had come to Africa on a fauna and specimen collecting trip. The van was equipped for the expedition:

cages, tanks, traps, camping gear and an oxygen tank, among other things.

Upon the repair of the van, we headed south. My Peace Corps friend would get off at his oasis station. I would go on to Kano, Nigeria, spend a couple of days and begin the thousand-mile trip south to Lagos on the coast. The Austrians intended to pick up the easterly Kano-Fort Lamy highway en route to the Cameroons.

I puzzled over their choice of an easterly route: starting in the far north of Nigeria to reach what I had always regarded as a small coastal nation, until the geography was explained to me. The Cameroons has a long tongue of territory that extends seven hundred miles north along the eastern boundary of Nigeria and terminates on the south shore of Lake Chad. Their easterly direction would reach this strip.

The trip immediately became an adventure—the Austrians liked to stop at any probable habitat of such collectibles as cobras. Of course, they expected me to help, as we beat through some brushy areas, but I was somewhat unnerved by their admonition: "Be careful, some of them are spitters. They project venom at the eyes." Happy to say, we found no cobras!

We arrived at the volunteer's oasis about noon. My Peace Corps friend offered us lunch and then showed us around his project, in effect a giant truck garden. It didn't produce North American salad vegetables—radishes, lettuce and such—since Africans generally have little use for greens. The produce reflected their staple diet: dates, fruits, maize, potatoes, rice and other crops that could thrive under irrigation and the never-ending sun.

Actually, this was a Garden of Eden, blooming like the proverbial rose. The crops were laid out in orderly manner and gave an overall appearance of lushness in contrast with their sere surroundings.

The absence of internal combustion engines and the presence of burros and cattle contributed to the biblical atmosphere. But no indulgent God provided this agricultural gem. The creation resulted from a whole village working together: women, children and—unusual in Africa—men. Agriculture is generally a woman's domain.

Certainly, the fabulous quality of the crops reflected care and enthusiasm. Emboldened by this observation, I asked myself if the success of the agriculture endeavor was responsible for the things I didn't see: no pitiable beggars, no apparent abject poverty and no evidence of ill health. I did get the impression these folks enjoyed an exuberant life.

I marveled at the cleanliness of the streets. Did they have a system of responsibility for upkeep? I asked my Peace Corps friend the extent of his responsibility for these exceedingly favorable conditions. His smile and remark of "we work together," didn't provide a lot of detail. But somehow the whole village seemed to be doing something right.

It was on this occasion I experienced the elaborate Hausa greeting. Our host, having returned from a month's leave, warranted a proper greeting. Since he was fluent in the language and customs and had lots of friends, this ceremony was enacted often.

He interpreted the verbal exchange—a series of questions, each eliciting an expected answer—something like this: "Greetings, how is your father, mother, wife, children, camels, garden, health?" "Is Allah kind?" The whole sequence is conducted in a rapid-fire manner. I never learned if there was an order, but the routine varies in length. However, the answers must always be favorable. It would be terribly rude to describe a problem or pain. The participants enjoyed this ceremony tremendously. The Hausa were obviously delighted that the American living in their midst had become so adept.

I would have liked to stay a while longer. I wanted to know the history of the project and to pin down the extent of the contribution of this Peace Corps project. But my Austrian wildlife searchers were eager to move on. I had a choice of leaving with them or an indeterminate wait for another ride.

On reaching Kano, we began to look for lodging for the night. According to rumor I had gathered along the way, it seemed three English volunteers, with a large apartment, provided unbounded hospitality to transients passing through Kano. We made contact with one of the youths, who invited us to bed down for the night. I drew the bed with a mosquito net and slept soundly. My companions spent the night battling mosquitoes exceeding in ferocity any I had ever known—and I have been to Alaska in the summer. Unfortunately, these fauna collectors had every kind of equipment for the comfort of their mammals, fish and reptiles, but did not provide insect nets for themselves.

The city of Kano, fourth in population in the country, is the capital of the state of Kano, one of twelve in the federation at the time. (The number of states increased to nineteen in March 1976.) This is the home of Nigeria's Hausa-speaking people. While their fifteen million (in 1972) constitutes only 20 percent of the total Nigerian population, they are more powerful politically than that number would suggest. One reason is that these Moslem, desert-oriented people, who speak a Hamito-Semitic language, have little in common with the black, urban Christians of the coast. They would pull out of the federation to form their own nation if a serious challenge to their autonomy was initiated.

I enjoyed Kano as much as any other city on the trip. It gained historical importance as a terminus for camel caravans freighting salt from the northern salt beds. Camel caravans still come into Kano. I saw one group of loaded camels standing at ease. The appearance of the camel master certainly piqued my curiosity. His skin—whatever his birth color—had been burned to the color of rich cordovan. His once-white head wrap and the robe hanging loosely from his shoulders had become the color of camel hide. His body garment consisted of a smock-like shirt and Moslem-style trousers, whose design had a low-slung crotch hanging well below the body. It is claimed this has some religious significance; even so, a man so clad appears to have grotesquely short, stubby legs.

Seldom have I seen a person who appeared more in tune with his environment and life. I was fascinated by his brotherhood with the camels. While he gave no discernible signal to direct them, they all moved and stopped in concert with his movements. He gave my efforts at communication not the slightest attention. Perhaps he had come to regard himself as more camel than human.

His costume featured a broad leather belt responsible for holding some important equipment, such as the camel driver's regulation leather pouch hanging down in front. This item, tasseled and tooled, contains, one supposes, all manner of tools, amulets, medicine, who knows what else? It would be interesting to take an inventory of the contents.

The traditional blade weapons hung from his belt: a dagger, which I presumed was the standard—a sharply pointed affair about eight inches long—and a distinctive Crusader type sword with a blade long enough to barely clear the ground.

The sword, with a configuration of a cross formed by the handle and guard, was much in evidence. Both mounted men and those on foot carried one. However, it is more common in Mali and Niger, the area of the blue-veiled Tuareg. These mysterious "blue men," so called because their skin is blue from the dye in their garments, regard this sword as the every-day equipment of fighting men.

It is fascinating to speculate why the design of this weapon is so similar to the sword probably carried by the Crusader St. Louis of France, when he died amidst the ruins of Carthage in 1270. Prorok remarked on the strangeness of finding the cross to be such an important decoration among the Muslim Tuaregs living in this remote desert area. "They bear the sign of the cross emblazoned on their shields and weapons: they carry Crusader-like, double-handed swords and their knightly tournaments bear a great resemblance to those held on the Continent ten centuries ago."

But, alas, while Prorok finds it romantic to regard the Tuaregs as descendants of the Crusaders, as some do, he can't support the view. It could be that Crusader equipment was copied because it suited the desert way of life. But even the symbolic cross carried down through the years is not necessarily of Christian origin.

One of the major crops in Niger and northern Nigeria is ground nuts. Great stacks of the sacked nuts appear at various collecting points along the major roads. But this product comes to your attention in Kano—beyond any possibility of ignoring it—through your nose. It is in Kano that the millions of pounds of nuts are processed. The town smells like a giant, toasted, peanut butter sandwich.

Typical open market

I spent some time wandering around the city, which included a visit to a market so vast that guides were available for hire (and needed). I stocked up on interesting articles: brilliantly decorated slippers with the curled, pointed toe and a button on the point, amber jewelry, carvings and a bit more than I could comfortably carry.

I obtained an authentic handmade dagger that had been part of the personal equipment of a retired camel driver. I didn't come by this treasure easily. I couldn't manage the first offering price, so I strolled off through the stalls. Throughout the afternoon, one of the camel driver's sons would track me down with a slightly better price, which I would refuse. Finally, after time had elapsed sufficient for the negotiation of a bride price, the camel driver parted with his knife.

My safari was now behind schedule, and so I decided to pamper my body a bit. No more catch-as-catch-can native transportation. I needed something reliable. A Greyhound bus line ran from Kano to Lagos on the coast. Although Greyhound had originated the service, which still had the colors, the dog logo and the clean-cut, smartly uniformed drivers, it was owned locally. I purchased a one-way ticket to Lagos. This move allowed me some much-needed relaxation. Now I could enjoy the meaning of the "leave the driving to us" slogan.

Foolish, foolish! I had traveled through four countries, shoulder to shoulder, hip to hip, as is the African custom, on a half-dozen different types of native transport. I had experienced virtually complete indifference to schedules and a similar indifference to safety considerations if time meant money. What possessed me to think that this intrusion of a U.S. style of travel on African conditions would insure U.S. results?

We started out in the evening, smoothly and professionally—actually on time. I began reliving my recent experiences, relaxing, dozing and enjoying the luxury of space around me. I sat on a bench parallel to the right side of the bus. Since Nigeria favored driving on the left side of the road, English-style, I had a view of approaching traffic.

And such traffic! Once we got out of town, I was struck how this thundering stream seemed endless. But why be surprised? We were traveling the only north-south highway in the most populous state in Africa. Still, the contrast with the tranquillity of the roads in the four states through which I had recently passed created some anxiety. But it was mitigated by the knowledge that I now rode in a modern bus with U.S.-trained drivers.

For a while I had been aware of a fellow passenger seated forward of me. Remarkable for her beauty, and stylishly dressed in West African attire, she was well-adorned with gold ornaments, earrings and silk scarves.

Her attractiveness was exceeded only by her aloofness. Clearly, none of the passengers fitted into her class. I took her to be perhaps a member of a Yoruba paramount chief's household. Still, through the exigency of travel, she shared my bench, albeit at an appropriate distance.

As the night wore on, sleepiness gradually wore the princess down. She would slowly lean toward me, only to catch herself, straighten up, then start sinking toward me again—sleepily. Finally, this lady failed to recover from one of her droops. Her head, with its intricately coifed Nigerian hairstyle—an elaborate construction of braided strands that formed a geometric scaffolding high above her head—came to rest solidly on my shoulder. She began to slumber the night away.

Although she could sleep, I had developed some anxieties. This north-south highway exhibited certain attributes of a battlefield. The abandoned, burned-out vehicles littering the side of the road told of the existence of a Nigerian malignancy holding sway over the highway. While I contrasted this traffic volume with that of the other states, I could also detect a difference in the behavior of the Nigerian drivers and those of Ghana. Perhaps I had just become used to the Ghanaian drivers after a year in that country. In Ghana, drivers managed to routinely violate most conventions of traffic safety and regarded top speed as the only way to travel straight-aways, but they did seem to have regard for the danger of blind curves. On the other hand, since Ghana's highways lacked the evidence of carnage obvious in Nigeria, they may have enjoyed better protection from their gods.

It crossed my mind that this might be some sort of a demolition derby. These Nigerian jockeys seemed to have little understanding of the dynamics of large objects moving toward each other at high speeds, the probability of collision or the consequences. Even as a passenger in a heavy, well-driven and relatively secure vehicle, I still began to wonder if the driver training program furnished to our driver would overcome my perceived Nigerian propensity to regard driving as a giant game of chicken.

I was experienced enough to realize that the condition of the automobile carcasses was not all due to wrecks. An unguarded, disabled car could, within four hours, resemble the discharge from a chop shop—a stripped and plundered body left to litter the highway.

About 4:00 a.m., we stopped to render assistance to a group of Mecca pilgrims whose bus had crashed. The toll was seven dead and ten injured, some badly. We took the walking injured aboard. This incident did nothing to allay my anxiety.

At about six, I became aware the bus had begun to drift. A glance at the driver confirmed my fears. He was resting his eyes. Before I could react, a crunching, grinding, metal-bending screech jolted everyone awake. Arising above the passenger chatter demanding to know "what happened," was the terrified scream of my seat mate, crying that there was glass in her eyes. I turned my attention to the frantic girl. After blowing off any glass still clinging to her face, I sloshed water from my small canteen over her face and clenched lids. The combination of tears and my ministrations seemed to eliminate the peril. Although still whimpering a little, she confirmed her lack of injury by some experimental opening and closing of her eyes.

Later the thought occurred to me that her lovely body had shielded me. I would have occupied forward position had she not been there—with wide open eyes.

We took stock of the situation. The driver had wandered into the incoming lane and hooked a lorry with the right side of the bus. We stayed upright, but the lorry overturned, its top load of passengers scattered into the night like an exploded crate of chickens.

I never knew what treatment the lorry's injured passengers may have received. When our driver had inspected the damage to our bus and decided we could limp into the next station, that is what we did. Perhaps the driver felt we had no more room for broken bodies.

Upon reaching the next station, we learned how the bus company regarded its responsibility to its passengers. It detailed the relief driver, not the driver responsible for the accident, to escort us onward to the coast, a distance of at least five hundred miles. The "transportation" involved a series of bush taxis—the usual Datsun trucks with benches under canopies. Our escort paid the fares, provided food and booked the hotel accommodations.

He couldn't have been more conscientious or effective given the circumstances.

It was nice to have a guide—someone to take us in tow—but we still had to traverse that nightmare alley and witness the astonishing disregard of any normal highway conduct on the part of the other drivers. Apparently, the idea that one lane might be reserved for a single direction of traffic never caught on. Any unoccupied lane would do. Time after time, we would meet a driver roaring down at us, out of a turn, in our lane. Our drivers sometimes slowed almost to a stop. And still, the incredible clutter of burned-out, twisted wrecks of all kinds continued to appear along the road. My sense of vulnerability was heightened from being huddled under a canopy with limited visibility. How lucky we were to have the series of sensible drivers we had for our own conveyances. Perhaps our bush taxi drivers had learned some lessons. Or maybe they had evolved as survivors.

The bus stop in Lagos looked mighty good. I am sure our gracious Greyhound bus driver felt equally relieved.

I thought about finding some conveyance traveling the coastal road to Accra. This highway hugged the beach all the way and passed through such delightful former French cities as Cotonou in Dahomey, Lome in Toga and other pleasant beach towns.

I had previously traveled the road from the Nigerian border and it would have been a pleasant change from the Nigerian hassle. But reconsidering, I realized I no longer had the time to gamble on that mode of travel. I decided to take advantage of the international airport and fly the remaining 250 miles.

Deciding to complete the trip by air left me the night and most of the following day to explore Lagos, where I learned firsthand about the incredible inflation that existed. (Ten years later it was to become one of the world's costliest cities.) The estimates I received on probable hotel costs indicated a need to shop around. The dilemma was that the cost of a taxi to search for a cheaper hotel was also prohibitive. A taxi driver would hardly start his motor for a Nigerian pound, worth about three dollars.

In a stroke of luck, a young taxi driver took me under his wing. It seems he had a lifetime love affair going with America. When he learned of my genuine American status, I became worthy of his critical interest. Unfortunately, I kept falling short of his concept of how a native of that wonderful country should act.

I had become a bit intolerant of things Nigerian by this time and had a criticism or two about his country. This outraged my new friend. He admonished me in this fashion: "Shame on you, sir! Americans no want to act with such unlevity. You may bring lack of good thoughts on your country." But after sufficient chastening, we became good friends and he helped get me settled for the night.

He introduced me to the manager of a native "hot sheet" hotel, who gave me a special rate of three pounds. While this concession may have been motivated by friendship with the cab driver, he saw in me a chance to help upgrade his hotel. He hoped to increase beds booked for the whole night. Perhaps his "super inn" (pronounced supair) would become known to my "esteemed associates through kindly utterances." Indeed, I did so utter, for I had an enjoyable stay.

The staff regarded me with curiosity. A white man traveling as a Nigerian was not a usual guest. They had many questions about my trip: What was I doing in Africa and where did I come from? They were delighted with my meager ability to speak Twi. While they understood little of the Akan language, which is spoken primarily in Ghana, they were pleased to meet a foreigner proud of an ability to speak an African language, although admittedly "small, small" (a West African colloquialism of indicating minuteness and inadequacy).

Later that evening, I encountered my friendly taxi man. I bought us supper. Apparently, after he had gotten to know me, he changed his mind about my credentials. I had made the grade as a proper (propair) American after all. His farewell, which placed a mighty strain on his English resources, could be summarized as: "Now you make good thoughts for your country." I accepted his compliment with pleasure, since I had no desire to "make bad thoughts for my country."

It had been an interesting two weeks, replete with fantastic experiences, contacts and sights. I had met the mysterious blue men. I had come in contact with many of the ethnic groups that make up the Moslem desert people of Niger and Nigeria. I had enjoyed the kaleidoscopic way these people travel, eat, market, pray and interact.

I encountered no hostility, occasional indifference, but little of the avarice so common in other areas—just friendly and helpful people. I had traced the Accra visitors to their source. Now it was time to fly back.

I had one more obstacle to overcome. I got to the airport early. I had a confirmed ticket and the plane was declared to be on time. But when I presented my passport and medical record to the immigration officer, he said, "Please, sir, your papers are not in order. Come with me." (Did he get his line from watching TV?)

My mind raced back to the casual manner in which I'd obtained my visa. Did the Nigerian clerk double-cross me? Had I entered the country illegally? suddenly I didn't feel well.

The arresting officer presented me to the director—an imposing man. He directed his attention to my International Certification of Vaccination. He shook his head and donned a serious expression: "Sir, this is very bad. Yes, an extremely serious matter." Finally, in a sad, despairing voice he reluctantly told me the bad news: "Your cholera vaccination has expired. You will have to stay over until Monday to get a new vaccination before you can leave the country."

I experienced tremendous relief. This could hardly rate as a capital crime, an espionage charge. I stopped sweating. Then the absurdity of it hit me and I realized it was a shakedown. The whole scenario was built around the West African concept of "dash" (gift).

I am constitutionally opposed to bribery of officials and always resist, within reason. Furthermore, I was at the rock bottom of my finances. In those days and circumstances, you had cash or you were destitute. There were no credit cards, personal checks or credit; nothing much to fall back on. I said, "Man, this is ridiculous. I wasn't checked coming in. How can I endanger your country? I'll be gone in twenty minutes if you don't make me miss my plane. I have been on the road a long time. I am broke. Volunteers don't have much money to start with. I have no money left for a weekend in this city. You are forcing me to sleep under a tree somewhere."

I won out. He released me. I was soon back in Accra.

In the spring of 1972, six months after my trip, the terrible effects of the drought that started in 1971 began to seriously ravage the people of Sahel. Five years later, the six countries in a strip of land south of the Sahara, stretching from Senegal to Chad, had suffered devastating losses: in people, animals and crops. *Africa South of the Sahara* provides estimates of the extent of the loss: Two-thirds of the animals of Niger died, Niger River fishing production fell from 16.3 tons in 1973 to 7.0 tons in 1976 and ground nut harvests fell from 191,000 metric tons shelled in 1973 to 25,563 tons in 1974.[5] And the effects were not confined to the Sahel. The whole waist of the continent suffered in varying degrees.

While the Hausa and Djerma farmers also experienced tremendous losses, they were more readily serviced by relief agencies and could recover without giving up their way of life. But the drought ended forever the wild and free life of the nomadic Peul and Tuareg, who lived according to the needs of their animals that were no longer.

5 *Africa South of the Sahara*, p. 679.

When the weather gods shine, the harvest of millet is a welcome work. Hive-like mud grainaries to the right store future rations

Section III

EAST AFRICA

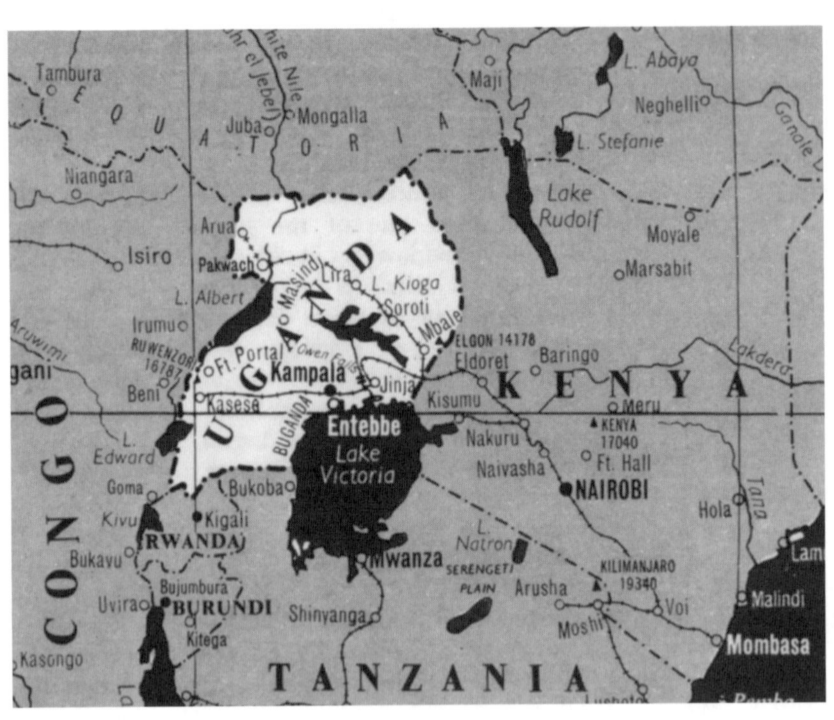
UGANDA
KENYA
TANZANIA
CONGO
RWANDA
BURUNDI
Entebbe
Lake Victoria
Kampala
Jinja
Masindi
Lira
L. Kioga
Soroti
Mbale
Arua
Pakwach
L. Albert
Ft. Portal
Owen Falls
Kasese
BUGANDA
Bukoba
Kigali
Mwanza
Shinyanga
Bujumbura
Kitega
Uvira
Bukavu
Kivu
Goma
L. Edward
Beni
RUWENZORI 16787
Irumu
Isiro
Niangara
Tambura
Juba
Mongalla
White Nile
Maji
L. Abaya
Neghelli
L. Stefanie
Lake Rudolf
Moyale
Marsabit
ELGON 14178
Eldoret
Baringo
Kisumu
Nakuru
Naivasha
NAIROBI
Meru
KENYA 17040
Ft. Hall
Hola
Tana
L. Natron
SERENGETI PLAIN
Arusha
Moshi
KILIMANJARO 19340
Voi
Malindi
Mombasa
Kasongo

MOVE TO EAST AFRICA

As our Ghanaian commitment came to a close, a series of situations and personal concerns caused some serious thinking about our future plans. Primarily, I faced the realization that our acceptance of this responsibility hadn't been worth the toll to anyone both in time and money invested.

The Ghanaian government's ill-conceived program to turn a cross section of Ghanaian citizens into entrepreneurs had proved to be an impracticable dream. The efforts seriously damaged the existing business community. Since the program proved to be unviable, our skills had little basis for application.

As a result, my family and I had two options: search for something to do or pack it up. Neither course was appealing. Fortunately, a non-profit development organization named Technoserve, offered us an opportunity to oversee the company's development operation in Uganda. Since our Ghanaian sponsor had begun to experience budget constraints, we left with good will.

For us this offer was a means of salvaging our African adventure. Technoserve provided much larger food- and job-producing operations compared with the Ghanaian social engineering program. Moreover, it had working arrangements with the USAID organization in place and was well regarded by the Ugandan government.

Still, we had regrets about leaving Ghana. We had made many friends and had built up a reservoir of good will through some successful efforts. The opportunity to observe one of the first African colonies to undertake a transition from colony to independent nation had been enthralling. But now, we looked forward to a term in East Africa.

Uganda

The seeds of the Technoserve organization, which had hired me to come to Uganda, were sown in a rural Ghanaian village. It was here a white man, taking a break from his life in America, had found himself holding a dying child succumbing to hunger. The experience profoundly changed his life forever.

Ed Bullard, scion of an old Connecticut tool manufacturing family, supervised the engineering department of his father's factory until he chanced to travel to Ghana. The misery of that country and his fervent Christian philosophy triggered an overwhelming desire to devote the rest of his life in a search for ways to improve the lives of Third World people. Thus, Technoserve was born.

Ed designed his organization to make a lasting improvement in food production, job opportunities and training in the Third World. The means to reach those ends were flexible. It focused on self-help projects taken on by multiple participants: tribes, villages, credit unions and other associations. Whatever the project, he insisted it be economically sound and eventually self-sustaining. Technoserve was to provide all possible assistance until the project became self-managed and thriving and then withdraw. Of course, the organization is not for profit and non-governmental.

Technoserve relied for funding on grants and contributions and other sources. Eli Lilly, Ford, Rockefeller and numerous other philanthropists are on the list of contributors. USAID and Technoserve developed a long-term relationship whereby projects better handled by a smaller agency were subcontracted to Technoserve.

When I joined Technoserve, it had operations in El Salvador, Honduras, Ghana and Uganda. My first assignment in Uganda was to relieve John and Marion Bates, who had finished their tour and were anxious to return to Omaha.

We were delighted to occupy the Bates' apartment, which sat high on Kololo Hill overlooking the capital city of Kampala. We were amused to note an unusual feature in this concrete-constructed building's second-story apartment. It had the door of a jail house—

heavy duty lock and hinges—and was a most impressive means of controlling ingress, or egress for that matter. "Are thieves such a threat?" we asked John. He answered with a deprecating shrug, "No, it's just some weird idea of the builder."

The idea that someone thought it necessary to spend all that money on such a safety feature was a bit unnerving, but the time came when we respected the builder's judgment in furnishing the apartment with a siege door.

Living in a set of rooms impenetrable to anyone not equipped with a cutting torch could be both comforting and disconcerting. Later, when we learned that danger was an actual possibility, we wondered if John's studied disinterest in discussing this anomalous door reflected an apprehension that we might panic if we knew we might be faced with the need for such safety. This speculation was buttressed by John's anxiety to join his wife in Nairobi, where we learned she had been packed for weeks.

My first reaction to the people of Uganda was disappointment. My experience in Ghana had conditioned me to expect Africans to look as if they belonged on the dark continent. In contrast to the Ghanaian women in their flamboyant costumes and their manner of living, Ugandan folks appeared to be run-of-the-mill Europeans, notwithstanding skin color. Still, if the stereotypical image of African savagery is true, I came to identify Uganda with the real Africa completely.

Captain Speke

Fresh from a brief vacation in the States, we were anxious to explore this profoundly unique country. Uganda gained worldwide attention when Captain Speke located the prize men had sought for thousands of years—the source of the Nile. On July 28, 1862, Speke achieved that objective when he stood on the northern shores of Lake Victoria and watched the lake give birth to the river. He saw the four-hundred-foot, never-ending font of water hurtle down the Ripon Falls, commencing its thirty-four-hundred-mile journey to Egypt.

Not only was discovery of the Nile's source a delight to the geographers of the world, but Uganda, as the cradle of the Nile, was suddenly perceived to have an incredibly strategic importance. It was axiomatic that whoever controlled the headwaters of the Nile held the power to destroy Egypt by merely reducing the flow of the life-giving water. Strangely, the idea of turning off the mighty Nile, as if it were controlled by a faucet, was not new, but how such a thing could have been achieved must not have been given too much consideration.

Nevertheless, this potential for catastrophe provided an impetus for the British takeover of Uganda. With this strategic stroke, they provided a vital protection to Egypt and the route to India.

But, in 1907 the protection of Egypt was not foremost in the mind of Winston Churchill, Parliamentary Under-Secretary of State for the colony, when he recognized the industrial potential of Ripon Falls with the following ecstatic observation: "So much power running to waste, such a coin of vantage unoccupied, such a lever to control the natural forces of Africa ungripped, cannot but vex and stimulate imagination. And what fun to make the immemorial Nile begin its journey by diving through a turbine!"

The climate added to the uniqueness of Uganda. Churchill regarded the country as the "pearl of Africa." Emil Ludwig's ode to Uganda's climate, in his description of the Nile written in the mid-thirties, was even more lavish: "Uganda has been likened to Paradise," he began, "for here eternal summer reigns without mortal heat by day without sultry mist by night; rising from a level of three thousand feet cooled by afternoon thunderstorms, by evening wind, almost without seasons, with an equal daily share of sun and rain it is ever fertile, ever bountiful."[1]

1 Emil Ludwig, *The Nile* (New York: Garden City Publishers, 1939), p. 6.

Our impression of Uganda did not differ materially from these descriptions when we arrived in Kampala in late 1972. While "paradise" would seem a bit overstated, we could at least imagine the folks who frequented the Garden of Eden using the country as a weekend retreat. Yes, after two years of sweltering in Ghana's humidity and heat, we gave Uganda the highest accolade.

That being said, we looked forward to working with the Technoserve organization. Development work requires some homework. A knowledge of the customs, attitudes and values of the prospective clients is an obvious prerequisite. Moreover, any project must conform strictly with government policies.

Beyond that, one must make some assessment of the stability of the government—that is, of the leader's potential longevity. Any substantial threat by a force dedicated to the ideology of state ownership of the capital structure would be of special concern. No competitors for control of the Ugandan government, either past or present, exhibited any Marxist leanings.

What did develop from a study of the post-independence history of Uganda was a feeling of déjá vu. The first rulers of Ghana and Uganda—Ghana's Kwame Nkrumah and Uganda's Dr. Milton Obote—shared a fear of coups, but perhaps to an unwarranted degree. Both leaders manifested this fear in a ceaseless search for greater security, imposing conditions that eliminated most vestiges of democracy and civil rights.

The other similarity between these two countries (both of which had been under British control—Ghana as a colony and Uganda as a protectorate) related to their sanguine promise of a successful and prosperous future. Both countries had lush, ample natural resources. The British had left in place a well-organized civil service, democratic institutions and a functioning market economy in each country. Unfortunately, neither country was blessed with the quality of leadership potential necessary to build on their heritage.

Accordingly, these lands, conditioned so well with the best tutelage that England could provide, fell into a morass of sorrow, destruction and loss of civil rights. Coup followed military coup;

each succeeding ruler devoted his resources and efforts toward his own perpetuation rather than to the construction of a viable economic foundation. Ghana's economy plumbed a nadir of depression by 1983. Uganda declined to a point little more than a notch above the barter system.

Milton Obote

Dr. Milton Obote was Uganda's first prime minister. As head of a multi-party alliance and a coalition of distinct notable and traditional rulers, he led Uganda to independence in October 1962. In January 1971, he left the country to attend a Commonwealth Conference in Singapore. During his absence, the armed forces under Major General Idi Amin seized power. Amin became president a month later. Obote fled to the willing hospitality of Dr. Julius Nyerere's Tanzania.

True to tradition, Obote's loss of power by no means retired him. Unless a deposed ruler is killed, he most likely plots to return to power. Of course, the victor knows this and consequently nurses an unholy fear of this happening some day. In Uganda's case, this did happen eventually. Obote *did* return, carried by Nyerere's invading army. He literally drove Field Marshall Idi Amin Dada, President for Life of Uganda, into the desert. Amin found refuge with Colonel Muammar al-Quaddafi of Libya, who himself had usurped power from a king through a coup.

At the time of our stay, Amin seemed to be firmly in the saddle and the prospect of a coup didn't give us undue worry. We had experienced coups before: a bit of skirmishing, gunfire, fleeing heads of government, broadcasts announcing the formation of a new government, then frenzied dancing in the street by the old and new supporters of the change. Later, we came to thank our lucky stars that we had departed Uganda before Amin fled.

The Mad General's Destruction Of Uganda

General Idi Amin

We arrived in Uganda July 1972, fifteen months into Amin's regime. The environment was a picture of peace. The expatriates were going about their lives, frequenting their clubs and attending social engagements as if they were home. The Indians, mostly dressed in their special clothing, were conducting business, going to church... No cloud of impending disaster hung over this scene.

Many of the English were bound to long-term English civil service contracts, with the usual prerequisites for vacations and retirements. They managed key utilities, the post office and such. Other expatriates managed European businesses—banks, insurance companies and the travel industry. There were many Asians, as well as white judges, lawyers, doctors and professors. Whites also manned many of the skilled trades.

Although from time to time, we heard of certain people turning up dead or missing, these occurrences were largely routine in post-independent Africa. Still, disquieting rumors concerning Amin's army reorganization program kept emerging.

One afternoon, as we enjoyed the view from the balcony of our apartment high on Kololo Hill overlooking the verdant Kampala valley of the capital city, the truth of these rumors came rumbling through the summer air. Heavy rolling sounds, coming in intermittent waves, ruptured the brilliant sunshine for perhaps fifteen minutes. At first, we thought of thunder, but no cloud floated across the blue sky.

We learned later that the sounds were connected with General Amin's army restructuring activities. According to the information of a soldier we knew, Amin mustered out six hundred men that afternoon. Our soldier friend further explained the circumstances surrounding the slaughter. All soldiers had been issued ammunition—except the intended victims. The majority of the dead were of the Lango and Acholi tribes; others died because of their misfortune in being Christians—Amin is Moslem.[2]

At the time of the coup, soldiers from the Acholi and Lango tribes made up, by some estimates, 40 percent of the army. The deposed ex-President, Milton Obote, had been a Lango. That sealed the fate of these soldiers as well as most of the tribal members.

During the year that followed, almost two-thirds of the Lango and Acholi soldiers in the army were systematically killed. Many were taken to Makindye Military Prison and different places to be slaughtered in various ways.[3]

As a result of all this killing, corpse disposal became a growing problem. Macabre references to the fat crocodiles in the Nile were frequently made. Whenever a power failure occurred, the story usually involved a corpse clogging the turbines at the Jinja power plant.

One time, I skidded my car to a halt upon seeing some soldiers unloading bundles from a truck at the banks of the Nile. The wisdom was that these trucks rolled at night. Perhaps this load was left over. In any event, I was told later that had I been seen, my body would have been added to the activity. But even with all the disappearances, Amin denied it all.

Amin's single-minded search for loyalty required a weeding out of the Christian soldiers. His solution was simple: draw a nucleus of fellow Kagwan tribesmen (known as "one elevens" due to the three

2 While there was no way for us to verify the extent of this enormous slaughter, many men were killed in this fashion, according to the book, *A State of Blood*, by Henry Kyemba. He was a minister in Amin's government who had known and worked closely with Amin fo twenty years—until he too fled.

3 Thomas and Andrew McMeel, 1977, p.78

parallel lines of their facial tribal scars) from the West Nile district in the far north; supplement this core with between-wars Sudanese soldiers from over the northern border; complete the troop mix with other Moslems, such as Nubians.

Through this restructuring, Amin created a Moslem army whose fidelity to the concept of a Uganda state was nil. Consequently, a nation with six percent Moslem population came under the occupying control of a foreign army with a tradition of ethnic savagery.

While he concentrated on customizing his army, Amin ignored the economy. We continued to assist the projects that were already underway such as: maize plantations, a cattle ranch and an experimental method of feeding cattle with a mixture of molasses and maize stalks. We had the cooperation of government agencies as well as: USAID and U.N. departments. Our organization seemed destined to fill a niche in this land of immense undeveloped resources. But after a while Amin commenced what he called "a war on the economy." Within months, this policy curtailed any developmental activity in the nation.

Any move on the economy had to take the Asians into account, as they seemed to own most of it. In *Hitler in Africa,* the last ambassador to Uganda, Thomas Melady, described the holdings of two Asian families. The Madhavani and the Mehta families owned and operated Uganda's huge sugar industry. In addition, the Madhavanis owned and controlled an enormous industrial empire of seventy companies running fifty-five factories in Uganda alone and employing twenty-one hundred Ugandans.[4]

Henry Kyemba, in his *A State of Blood,* details the extent of Asian economic participation: "The Asians almost totally controlled Uganda's trade, factories, plantations and industries." Asians were heavily represented in the professions as well as in the skilled trades. They held the best jobs even in the businesses they didn't own, such as banks and insurance companies. [5]

4 Melady, *Hitler in Africa*, p. 78.

5 Henry Kyemba, *A State of Blood: The Inside Story of Idi Amin*, condensed in *Book Digest*, December 1977.

Although these generalizations provide some idea of the Asian position in the economy, the retail sector featured the greatest concentration of ownership. Virtually every family engaged in some sort of transaction with an Asian business each day. It could take place in one of the shops lining solidly along the main street in Kampala or in the rural areas. Small Asian shops serviced the populace throughout the country. From this, one might conclude the vast majority of the Asians lived comfortably, but these small businesses had no real potential for production of great wealth. The Asians were hard workers, employing every member of the household in the trade. They lived on the premises and seemed always open for business. These small-business folks lived economically and saved their money for reinvestment, weddings, funerals and retirement. This was reality for the vast majority. But it was the rich ones who stood out due to their conspicuous consumption. They had nice cars and imposing (actually garish) houses. These habits failed to endear them to the Africans.

In East Africa, the position and status the Asians held was evolutionary. At the turn of the century, the British imported a large contingent of East Indians for construction labor on the Mombassa-Kampala railroad (later extended at both ends). These and others became known collectively as "Asians." The opportunity created by the railroad project attracted many other Asians to East Africa: clerks and traders—both wholesale and retail—as well as the artisans and craftsmen—carpenters and mechanics.

As time passed, the Asians endeavored to establish more grass-roots businesses, creating a firm foundation for expansion of their wholesale-retail endeavors—most everything the British were uninterested in doing. Essentially, the Asians established the customs and techniques of commerce.

Sadly, most African countries reluctantly, if at all, accept the skills and administrative ability of East African Asians or other non-black ethnic people that were holdovers from the colonial population. There is seldom any integration between these minorities and the preponderant blacks. Customs, behavioral patterns, religion and physical appearance set them apart. Imagine these brown-skinned people in this sea of black faces; the straight-haired women swirling along in their highly colored saris; the Sikh men sporting their intricately folded white or pastel turbans (white if head of household).

I puzzled over the attitude of Asians toward the blacks. They were an enclave of fifty thousand nestled in a population of ten million, with no vestige of political protection. While as a group they commanded tremendous wealth, this only increased their vulnerability; yet they comported themselves as an aristocracy. Their behavior toward black nationals could best be described as arrogant, invoking a blatant air of superiority. One might witness, for instance, an Asian bank teller motioning a non-black forward to the head of a line of blacks. In my experience, they had a justified reputation for treating their menials in a demeaning and most ungenerous manner.

While giving the impression they had little concern for vulnerability, many urban folks, in private conversation, were more than aware departing British left them sitting on a volcano that would one day erupt. This basic awareness was evidenced by their propensity to trade goods or local currency for any transportable items having international value. Still, small-business, rural folks appeared to have faith their Ugandan citizenship would protect them. Asians hadn't been seriously molested during the twelve years of independence. Certainly, any anxiety they might have had was dispelled to quite a degree by the time Amin shattered their world.

Amin approached his economic restructuring plan with ill-conceived overzealousness. He could have perceived the tiny enclave of wealthy Asians, glittering with wealth, as a golden apple, presenting no obstruction to his harvest. It was apparently his thinking, when he had eliminated the Asians, Ugandan blacks would succeed them in the businesses; and black faces would replace brown ones in the good jobs. Real estate and other leftover property would be claimed by the state. The Asians had to go.

Amin recognized the need for some justification, an "explanation" for his bold plan. The official line of thinking: "We are recovering the economy from the Asians, who have been milking it for all these years."

His proclamation was brutally succinct. "All Asians, except those specifically excluded, must leave the country within 90 days." This order was repeated again and again in the newspapers, on television and in Amin's speeches. Thus was the Asian Diaspora set in motion.

His campaign of justification and vilification was patterned after Hitler's early treatment of the Jews: Denounce an already-hated minority enough and you can affect and control their future. Amin often referred to Hitler as a great man who was completely justified in his treatment of the Jews. Amin "humanely" improvised on Hitler's final solution. He merely looted the Asians before expelling them.

Prior to the campaign against the Asians, I had little sympathy for them. I didn't appreciate their manners or respect their behavior toward the black citizens. My African driver expressed his opinion of them thus: "They live in my country, but they don't love me." As far as I was concerned, they deserved whatever might happen to them.

Yet, when Amin applied his exploitative tactics, I pitied them as underdogs. The punishment they reaped was not commensurate with the misdemeanor of bad manners. Whatever maldistribution of wealth existed, I felt the country would have been far worse off without them.

I ended up protecting more than one. Sometimes, I would allow a person who had been targeted for kidnapping, ransom or execution, to hide out for a day or two in my apartment. I found ways of assisting certain people to escape with personal valuables and I gained compassion for politically helpless people.

Aside from obvious greed, legends differ as to Amin's motivations for the elimination of the Asians from Uganda. Amin claimed he received his instructions in a dream. He contended that, while on a trip to Mecca, he encountered a rare rainstorm. He regarded this as a sign from above to stand by for an important message. The subsequent dream took the form of a straightforward, divine directive: Get the Asians out of Uganda in three months' time. Amin walked the well-worn path of leaders justifying their acts under the sanction of a dream.

Given Amin's particular type of mentality, he might have interpreted his dream as an authorization for an act he already had in mind to do. Furthermore, other aspects of the same mentality would induce him to frame such an important action with fanciful and extravagant trappings. Nevertheless, he did not make such irreversible and exceedingly significant decisions for purely trivial reasons. Certainly it reflected his love for power, his cruelty and his racial hatred, but he had a more practical reason as well. Conveniently, he used the Asian expulsion as a scapegoat for an already floundering economy. His ever-present urge to maintain the good will of the army must also have played a part.

An intriguing story—one of revenge with a historical precedent—concerned Amin's alleged proposal of marriage to a moneyed Asian woman from one of the sugar families during a social event. She rejected his impertinence in the manner of the aristocratic German woman when Chancellor Hitler made the same mistake: "You peasant! How dare you?" (Many Asians, understandably, favor this version.) If this were in fact the true motivation for his move against the Asians, it would constitute a draconian revenge—with aspects of an Old Testament reaction to wrongs.

A student of Amin's behavior could conclude that any of these theories, or a combination of them, might be valid. Still, whatever the initiating factor, many Africans were gleefully sympathetic with the General's program to "regain control of the economy," especially those whose motivation was to acquire some of that abandoned wealth.

Melady agrees with Amin's boast he had overwhelming support for his economic war. The politically conscious class supported him totally. In Melady's opinion, the economic achievement of the Asians had proved to be their downfall: "Amin capitalized on African mistrust, jealousy and resentment of these achievements. He broke an already festering sore and encouraged the spread of racial animosity."[6]

Many who had been employed by the Asians had serious trepidations about their jobs once the Asians left. Even though the Asians paid no more than they had to, payday could be counted on; not so with African employers.

Mamdani describes how he and his friends got the news the Asians had to depart Uganda. On an evening when friends were sitting around socializing, at the eight o'clock news time, the host suggested, "Let's listen to Amin." He was, addressing a conference. Then it came. "The Asians must leave" in so many words. A thunderbolt out of the blue. The group was staggered; they could not believe what they had heard. Everyone was talking and lamenting. But there was Amin again: "Asians came to Uganda to build the railway. The railway [is] finished. They must leave now."[7] The exodus began within days.

It might be expected that such a massive government program would have been accompanied by an equally massive set of instructions that were the result of substantial planning. Not with this one. The first directive excluded Asians with Ugandan citizenship. Twenty thousand had made this election when offered the choice of British or Ugandan citizenship by the departing British. Nearly all the Ismaili Moslems did so, acting on the advice of their popelike religious leader, the Aga Kahn. Perhaps he foresaw this would add an element of future safety for his subjects. His expressed reasoning revealed his perception that his followers had an implied obligation to their homeland to become citizens. As it turned out, this didn't help in the end. Another directive provided for the exclusion of those with particular skills or professions; agriculturists could also stay.

These confusing regulations and directions changed daily, and it soon became obvious to Amin that all the Asians throughout Uganda would have to assemble in Kampala to be sorted out.

6 Melady, *Hitler in Africa*, p. 135.

7 Mahmood Mamdani, *From Citizen to Refugee* (London: Francis Pinter Publishers Ltd., 1973), p. 12-13.

About fifty thousand people (the number varies widely), the sick, pregnant, unfit, old and young—all began showing up in the city. Families, some who had never before left their small businesses in the interior, came to town confused, frightened, no more aware of their fate than the slaves of an earlier Africa's past had been when they were being assembled for shipment.

The only thing that saved Kampala from becoming a makeshift refugee camp (while Asians were waiting their turn for processing) was the power of the Asian extended family. Along with their strong religious ties, this worked to provide those less fortunate with a place to sleep and the care needed during the travail of awaiting their unknown fate.

The evaluation program began, hoping to complete the task of segregating those who could prove they fell into one of the excluded categories in ninety days—no more. Neither the pope of Rome nor the pleas of the British could dissuade Amin from keeping to his schedule.

New regulations for proof of citizenship came down daily, each more nonsensical than the last. No workable guidelines existed for the evaluation of excluded categories.

But the process, feasible or not, proceeded. As could be expected, the African administrators heaped brutality and plain cussedness onto the conditions of chaos. Ugandan passports could be confiscated or destroyed by officials just for fun. How do you prove Ugandan citizenship without proper papers? Melady also reports on this: "Some officials blithely tore up the papers in front of the desperate Asians."[8] All day Asians stood in long lines in the sun waiting for some sketchily anticipated treatment. The lack of any clear policy caused much anxiety in the thousands of people who had no destination other than a penniless existence in some unknown refugee camp.

8 Melady, *Hitler in Africa*, p. 82.

Asians being forced to leave Uganda

Soon it became obvious the task was doomed from the start. General Amin, with his usual forthright approach to problem solving, ended the ridiculous evaluation program: "Get them all out and hold to the three-month schedule."

Great Britain recognized a responsibility to other Asian subjects and helped, albeit slowly. She did not want to take them in all at once. Accordingly, the British High Commission maintained its normal short office hours, 10:00 a.m. to 12:30 p.m. and 2:00 p.m. to 4:30 p.m. Amin became impatient and ordered the process speeded up, to no avail. Then he ordered the arrest of one hundred Englishmen. This put the High Commission into high gear, 7:00 a.m. to 7:00 p.m. every day of the week.

However reluctantly, England complied with her commitment to British passport holders; around fifteen thousand were accepted. India admitted those holding Indian and Pakistani passports. Canada, Australia and others took quotas. Others slipped into Kenya and Tanzania, although realizing that these could be only temporary havens, since there was a prevailing expectation that Kenya planned a bash-Asian day sooner or later as well. (England in fact did have an ongoing arrangement with Kenya to take out four thousand Asians annually.)

One Asian girl wrote a letter to the editor of a Nairobi paper (the recently nationalized Kampala paper would not have had the temerity to print it) passing her sorrowful judgment that "General Amin's dream is our nightmare." Another schoolgirl's letter asked why the Asians couldn't paint their faces black and continue to live in their homes. A Hindu dairy farmer asked me, "What will happen to my beautiful cows? I don't care about not getting paid; I just want them taken care of." I didn't have the heart to tell him that his productive "children" would soon end up in the slaughterhouse. The best advice I could offer was to turn them out and let them forage for themselves if the government didn't send someone around by the time he expected to leave.

Even if the government had a plan to deal with such contingencies, managers were not available to direct an ongoing dairy operation. And with undisciplined units of the army looking for loot, the cattle never had a chance. The soldiers would only consider the shillings they could obtain from the sale of the meat.

The first contingent of Asian people leaving for the airport could have benefited from some briefing as they would be required to traverse eight different army checkpoints during the twenty-five-mile passage. As it happened, the Asian women—dressed in their silk saris, adorned with their treasured golden bangles and earrings—presented an irresistible target for military souvenir collectors. They were systematically stripped of their jewelry as they passed through the checkpoints.

The harassment and abuse became so excessive that terrorized Asians began balking at running the gauntlet to the airport. In order for Amin to maintain his diaspora schedule, he had to calm their fears. His method was to announce that hereafter, elements of the police would be on duty with the army. The inclusion of the more humanitarian police might have calmed the fears, except that the police were equally terrified of the soldiers. Still, a stream of refugee Asians traveled to the airport, carrying what they could of the pitiful remnants of their once vast possessions.

The soldiers who inspected the trains transporting Indians and Pakistanis enroute to Mombassa, Kenya, were particularly harsh. Some passengers were grossly humiliated. Some were stripped naked; many others were robbed even of the meager thousand shillings that was allowed them. Many rapes were reported.

The Asians became fewer and fewer. Well-known faces would suddenly be gone. The conversations of those remaining reflected their two primary concerns: what country might take them in and who had made it to where. Amin made a macabre threat to ensure compliance with his time limit. He promised to "resettle" those who refused to leave Uganda to the Karamojong country in the arid northeast, the territory of the Hamitic cattle people. They do little farming and exist primarily on the blood and milk of their beloved cattle. The urban-shopkeeper Asians wouldn't have been able to cope among the naked, spear-carrying tribesmen—better to get out of Uganda on time.

They all got out of Uganda—one way or another—mostly under infinite personal distress. The beloved extended-family relationships were broken and Asians were scattered around the world. The Ismaili could no longer enjoy their daily visits to the mosque, and the Hindus and Sikhs suffered similar deprivations.

Also, never to reappear was a delightful Sunday afternoon custom enjoyed by the Asian populace: turning out in their best to parade on the boulevard and around the adjacent park—the elders meeting and talking with friends, the young girls flirting and hoping to be noticed by the young men and vice versa. They created quite a sight—their adorned black hair, honey-colored skin, rainbow saris, brilliant silk scarves and varicolored turbans were very picturesque. The General must have been pleased to see it end, as he had derisively likened the effect to a street in Calcutta.

In only a short time the Ugandans found they had killed the proverbial golden-egg-laying goose. As the mass of Asians moved out and the professionals, the wealthy and those with international connections quietly slipped out too, the commercial sectors either fell into chaos or ceased to exist. Workers would report to a factory only to find it locked up. The best restaurants soon closed.

The tourist industry died with the departure of the Asian tourist managers. Consequently, Amin closed the country to tourists, although he subsequently sought to re-open it. He signaled this change of mind with a ludicrous banner that stretched across the main boulevard. The caption heralded the news: "Welcome tourists." Actually, a few brave souls did venture into this troubled land, but the game lodges could provide little needed by the guests.

Sadly, the magnificent tourist attractions of this country are unlikely to ever recover, even if peace comes to the land. Unrestricted animal slaughter, resultant of the breakdown of game park controls and animal protection, gutted a major enticement. I read an account in which the last terrified band of elephants were machine gunned by soldiers greedy for ivory.

General Amin's understanding of economics didn't include any theoretical concepts. The fundamentals of his thinking could be summarized as, "Take the Asians' money and give their businesses and property to black Ugandans. When the Asians are out of the country, blacks will be rich and will be in control of their own economy."

While these sentiments certainly produced a hard-to-beat slogan, Amin never succeeded in transferring wealth-producing businesses, dairies or plantations to black Ugandans. Of what use is a dairy whose cattle have been slaughtered? Further, a plantation or business without working capital and the necessary expertise produces no wealth? Instead of transferring wealth producers, he created carcasses.

Amin had no idea that, by removing the entrepreneur and manager, he broke up the elements of capital, labor and materials that worked together to provide goods and services to a willing market at a profit. It must not have crossed his mind that no replacement pool of managers existed, particularly those with the family-forged commercial ties so vital in this circumstance, where overseas connections are necessary for material and capital sources. It is said Amin exhibited surprise in finding that it takes more than a button pusher to operate a business.

Henry Kyemba, in *A Path of Blood,* said, "I experienced the death throes of a whole nation as it spiraled down toward mere subsistence, its population cowed by thugs who were bribed with luxury goods and easy money to kill on Amin's orders." He also comments on the massive brain drain. Asian doctors, lawyers, accountants and other professionals fled, but many of the highly educated Africans, such as professors and heads of the university departments, fled as well.

While the administration took some obvious steps to preserve foreign exchange during this unsettled period, it lacked the apparatus and the knowledge to be effective. Amin declared a moratorium on international debt payments. And he sought to prevent automobiles from leaving the country. A departing European could contrive to exchange his worthless shillings for a round-the-world airline ticket, which would become a charge against foreign exchange.

Wealth left the country in the Asian shopkeepers' determination to leave their shelves bare. In this, they succeeded completely. Non-Asian customers, who had ways of departing with their purchases, cleaned out the imported bargain-priced goods—expensive jewelry, books, exotic food, clothing and office equipment. While the Asian businessmen had the means to replenish inventory in normal times, the Africans, who took over the Asian businesses, had no way of acquiring anything not locally produced.

Consequent to all this liquidation of inventory and personal property sales, the Asians developed some heavy concentrations of shillings. They frantically made every effort to convert this Ugandan scrip into any transportable value. Checks drawn on out-of-country banks were the best means. But bales of shillings remained on hand.

The government learned to use these surplus shillings to prop up its propaganda campaign to vilify the Asians. Television programs would show grinning soldiers discovering and confiscating huge bundles of Ugandan shillings in raids on temples and homes. These events supposedly substantiated the government's charges that Asians "milked the economy." "But for the alertness of the soldiers, the iniquitous Asians could have smuggled this wealth out of the country," the announcer would breathlessly explain.

Even in this productive land, food shortages became critical. Milk and cheese became black market items following the slaughter of dairy cattle. Commercial farms no longer operated. Imported necessities could no longer be obtained through normal channels, since the Asians had been taking care of the importing.

One astonishing development concerned the enormous sugar industry. After a while, the wholesalers ran out of sugar. A rumored explanation was the new black managers were unable to produce any sugar at all because of an unfortunate change in their manufacturing methods. The Asians had operated the mills continuously; the blacks adopted a five-day week. When the machinery stopped, the juice and raw sugar permanently solidified in the pipes. Whether or not this explanation correctly described the reason for the end of sugar production, the local paper, after injudiciously reporting the end of sugar production, ceased to exist as a private publication.[9]

The one factor that prevented widespread hunger was the popular reliance on subsistence farming. The south favored a dish called *matoke*, made from steamed plantains. The northerners subsisted on the millet and sorghum raised in their area.

9 Encouraging reports from Uganda indicate that in the 1990s, the sugar plantations are being restored by the Asian Madhvanis family and sugar production will reach pre-Amin levels by 1995 (*Forbes* magazine, July 18, 1994).

The government's lack of policy toward the abandoned businesses and real estate reflected a complete absence of understanding of the situation. It had expected a smooth transition from brown to black ownership, experiencing no great decline in function. At first Ugandans were allowed to purchase the Asian shops. Later, the army decided to assume control until the situation could be sorted out. Typically, it soon became a capital offense to achieve a business transfer. Some would-be entrepreneurs were shot before they could prove they had acted properly under the first policy.

When it was still legal for the populace to acquire and own the Asian shops, Kampala Boulevard was littered with the papers and records of business establishments. The throwing away of the files, as if they were less important confetti, added to the festive occasion. The new African owners had no knowledge of the value of business records, sources of supply and such. These festivities didn't last long. Once the new owners faced the fact that they had no way of obtaining stock, finding skilled help or acquiring any of the myriad skills and know-how they needed, they went out of business. The shops that lined the boulevard soon became empty, gutted.

General Amin enjoyed taking a stroll around the city with his staff and friends, inspecting vacated Asian businesses. In a grand manner, he would make a gift of a particular business or property to one or another of his entourage. I observed his presentation of the pre-independence Speke Hotel, one of the best, to an army officer. Certainly this was the candy shop for many. People who had barely learned to drive might become the proud owners of a nine-passenger Peugeot—the ultimate African concept of wealth.

Amin's sublime ignorance was evidenced by his impulsive decisions and remarks, proving he had no idea whatever for rectification of the situation he had blundered the country into. production of goods and services settled at its lowest discernible level. Amin had plunged the nation into an abyss, where it was to stay. He did make a few shame-faced efforts to get some institutions started up. He advertised for Palestinians, Libyans and Egyptians to immigrate to Uganda. Some did, but they never stayed long. Along with having no stake in the land, they must have taken little comfort in the chaos and danger of the environment.

As discipline in the army continued to decline, the word "army" became synonymous with banditry. Any property could be grabbed. Virtually everyone lived in fear of being robbed or killed, and rape was common. No recourse existed. Since the ethnicity of the occupying force of soldiers differed from that of most of the population, there was, in addition, no mercy.

Thus "Pearl of Africa," "Paradise," and all such extravagant terms of endearment by now applied only to Uganda's geography. The devastation of its people's lives had become complete.

Death of a Uganda Cattle Ranch

The leopard-mauled calf had died—-not an unusual occurrence. The daily log disclosed that leopards killed about fifteen percent of all the calves born on this Uganda cattle ranch. This productive spread could easily bear the loss. Leopards were only one of the unlikely risks a Colorado rancher would have to contend with back home.

Compared with the political risks associated with Ugandan enterprises, Indians, outlaws and rustlers would have been minor irritants.

A cattle ranch startup became my first responsibility in this new Ugandan undertaking. Having been raised on a Utah ranch, I was excited about this new opportunity. Of all the projects the company had going, or that I started, this was the most interesting.

A Uganda credit union with some money to invest had bought a large tract of land and a few hundred head of scrubby cattle. This ranch lay some seventy miles north of Kampala, the capital of Uganda, and midway between the twin sources of the Nile: Lake Victoria and Albert Nyanza. (The presidents of Uganda and Zaire, to amuse themselves, agreed in 1972 that Lake Albert should be renamed Lake Mobutu Seko Seko, while Lake Edward, to the south, should become Lake Idi Amin Dada.) Choke National Park, where the famed Murchison Falls funnels the entire Nile River into a nineteen-foot cut, was a bit farther north.

The new ranch owners approached Technoserve for assistance in obtaining more financing, management expertise and organizational help. Before a decision could be made, the credit union had to endure Tech exceedingly thorough economic and political investigations.

First, the project had to be consistent with the government's development program. After passing this test, it had to propose a potential for the profitable creation of jobs and/or food. In addition, Technoserve had to be convinced the local sponsors could eventually become capable of assuming complete management of the operation. The proposed project passed all the tests and so met Technoserve's criteria for participation.

The prospects of success for this six thousand acre cattle ranch seemed positive. With its unbelievably lush grass, the estimated support ratio of land to cattle would seem unbelievable to any U.S. cattle rancher. It enjoyed the same conditions that prevailed a few miles north in the fabulous Choke game park, which supported the teeming herds of elephants, cape buffalo, numerous varieties of antelope and other denizens by the tens of thousands.

The land was flat, dotted with the typically African flat-topped acacias. The equatorial climate at 3,000 feet was further ameliorated by Lake Victoria—27,000 square miles of water.

To complement the excellent physical circumstances, all sorts of development assistance programs could be drawn on. In the early seventies, the political situation at that time gave no indication of instability. This was before General Idi Amin, President for Life of Uganda, experienced the infamous dream that resulted in the expulsion of 50,000 Asians from the country with consequent economic and social breakdown. Clearly, the time and circumstances seemed propitious for the launching of a modern cattle ranch.

We obtained a local commercial bank loan of $250,000 which was guaranteed by the World Bank. A Swedish agency furnished cattle dip designs and material for any group of cattle owners who would provide the labor. Another organization furnished heavy equipment for the construction of water ponds and fire trails. The Ugandan government provided a fencing subsidy. Following the completion of preliminary plans and the assistance agencies standing by, this embryonic ranch needed only a skilled manager to organize its development. Technoserve recruited a young couple from the Middle West to spend a year building a foundation and to recruit and train an African manager to succeed them. On the completion of this assignment, the ranch owners would be on their own, with Technoserve available only in an advisory role.

The development steps began to fall into place. First, Bill Gregory, the manager, contracted for the building of the all-important water ponds and the indispensable tick-dip facilities. In time, he completed the perimeter fence and twenty-acre paddocks, as well as the corrals and other buildings. Mechanically, the ranch stood ready to perform its cattle breeding function.

The local Lagos and Ugandan tribes supplied the herders. Although these folks did maintain the usual small African herds of cattle (primarily to convey the wealth and status of the owner and as currency for bride purchasing), they were mostly agrarian.

Had these tribesmen been one of the Maasai[10] ethnic groups or had the ranch been situated near Maasai territory, the project would've been impossible. The Maasai claim ownership of all the cattle in the world—a gift of their god. When they undertake what the victims call raiding, they contend they are merely "collecting" strays. At least, that is one of the legends told of the Maasai. Moreover, their collecting practices are very impressive. It would be the rare owner who could stand up against the short, broad-bladed assuages so expertly handled by those slender, ocher-colored cattle lovers.

10 The *New World Dictionary*, the *New Columbia Encyclopedia* and Joy Adams, in her book, *The Peoples of Kenya*, use the more common spelling Meas.. However, in two books written by Maasai authors, the double "a" is employed: *An Autobiography of a Warrior* by Tepilit oleo Satiate and *The Maasai by S. S. Snaking.* I chose the Maser's own manner of spelling.

Gregory devised working and operating procedures that might amuse a Colorado rancher. For instance, he expressly forbade the herders from milking the cows for their own use. Any milk taken from these humped, boron cattle would be at the direct expense of the calves. Another prohibition, almost impossible to enforce, addressed the disposal of the carcasses of animals that had died from disease or accident. The veterinary department claimed that the shots given a sick animal could result in a concentration of drugs in the liver, rendering the carcass toxic to humans. Accordingly, the meat wouldn't become food for the herder's family or sold in the market. To illustrate the viewpoint of the Africans to this alleged peril, a veterinary officer called to treat a dying animal would often cheerily remind the herders to "save a bit for me."

The same prohibition applied to animals dying from accident, but for a different reason. The herders must not be allowed to look forward to the death of an animal for any reason.

Gregory strained to cope with this problem. He tried burying the carcass, but it would be exhumed. Out of desperation and on the assumption that if the veterinary officer considered it no threat to his own family, and one way or another the meat would be eaten anyway, he became the dispose of the deceased animal. He sold the meat to a market wholesaler. This ploy at least removed the temptation of the herders to instigate a premature death to an animal. It so happened, the successor manager would inevitably follow the same procedure.

Rules can be made. Rules can be broken. Starving and malnourished calves provided stark evidence of infractions of the no milking rule. This surreptitious fringe benefit provided milk for the families, as well as cash from market sales. Being a humanist and believing that desperation drove the herders to this behavior, Gregory increased the wages in the hope that decreased economic needs would alleviate the problem. He found that only physical surveillance could save the calves.

Another minor problem connected with the raising of African cattle is the irresistible urge the neighbors have to just purloin any cattle not adequately protected. Love is often the suspected reason; one lovesick young man cut the fence and stole twenty-five—the usual bride price. He had no chance to get away with the venture, but perhaps he envisioned the maiden's face mirrored in the eyes of a cow and simply couldn't resist the temptation to try. It's a difficult shock for a Third World assistance worker when he first realizes the completely different attitude these delightfully charming people have regarding private ownership rights.

It is interesting to compare the difference in occupational hazards of Western and African cowboys. While the African couldn't conceive of the discomfort of frostbite, nor of being bucked off a cowpony, he does have his special frights. Occasionally, a rogue cape buffalo from the park would wander onto the ranch. These beasts, in a natural herd, are no more dangerous than a herd of Herefords and are inclined to bolt if frightened. But a lone bull, exiled from the herd, is total danger. Such a malevolent creature is known to lie in ambush and will puree the body of a person who doesn't reach a sufficient elevation in a tree. A herder finding even a lone spoor ceases herding until the perceived danger is determined to be past.

Other natural enemies, unique to African ranching, are insects. The tsetse fly is a potential killer to both man and beast, although not currently a threat to humans. Wins ton Churchill describes this terrible epidemic in his visit (about 1905):

But a far more terrible shadow darkens the Uganda Protectorate. In July, 1901 a doctor of the Church Missionary Society Hospital at Kampala noticed eight cases of a mysterious disease.

Six months later he reported that over two hundred natives had died of it... The pestilence swiftly spread through all the districts of the lake shore, and the mortality was appalling.... The disease ran along the coasts and islands of the great lake like fire in a high wind... By the end of 1903 the reported deaths numbered over ninety thousand, and the lake shore people were completely exterminated.... By the end of 1905 considerably more than two hundred thousand persons had perished in the plague-stricken regions, out of a population in those regions which could not have exceeded three hundred thousand.

The other demon insect is the tick that carries the lethal East Coast fever which is deadly to cattle that have not developed some immunity. It requires a certain degree of moisture to exist. The high equatorial area in Kenya and Uganda is just right for its comfort.

Churchill also describes this nemesis:

It came across the German border (Tanganyika) about a year and a half ago. It has been gradually spreading through the protectorate. A diseased cow may take thirty days to die. In the meantime wherever it goes the swarming ticks are infected. They hold their poisons for a year. If, during this time, other cattle pass over the ground, the ticks fasten upon them and inoculate them with the sickness. And each new victim wanders off to spread the curse to new ticks, who cast it to new cattle, and so on till the end of the story.

Where this scourge exists, exotic cattle must be dipped—completely immersed—in a chemical solution at least once a week or the losses can be phenomenal. Half a herd of exotic cattle, lacking the genetic immunity of the native cattle, can die in a week if dipping is neglected. Even the native cattle can suffer a loss of five to ten percent.

Not only must the dipping be regular and meticulous, the solution must be carefully monitored. If it is too diluted, perhaps by the rain, the ticks can develop an immunity or, it may fail to provide protection. It is highly toxic and, if too strong, can kill the cattle.

The management of this chemical is a real problem. Samples are routinely sent to the veterinary department for testing. It is not unusual to get a reading from one department that the solution is too dilute, while a sample from the same batch is determined to be lethal by another department, enough so to cause instant death to an animal going through it. One learns to do one's own testing.

But one way or another, solutions are found and problems lived with. Secondary profit opportunities evolved while the herd expansion program progressed. We purchased the bone-thin Somali and Ethiopian cattle that were herded through the Kenyan northwestern frontier, something akin to the old Chi Trail. These animals could gain weight at a fast clip on the surplus pasture and provide a nice profit when sold later.

We sought expert advice for upgrading the lot of scrub cattle that came with the various land purchases. They constituted a descendant cross-section of the ancient African breeds. Tiny Ankle beasts, adorned with their enormous lyre-shaped horns, made up a good part of the herd. It is claimed the early Egyptians specially bred this species to achieve the elaborate horn structure. The rest of the herd consisted of the many-colored, humped Boron and Subs.. The herd could be likened somewhat to Texas longhorns.

In our initial cattle improvement program, we replaced the scrub bulls with two splendid, upgraded red Boron animals. I hated to see the tiny Ankle bull go, but I couldn't see the need for genes that would produce steaks of such diminutive size.

Ankole cattle

One expert advised crossing the beefy Boron with a milking variety, such as an exotic Holstein, with the hope the calves would prosper from the greater quantities of milk resulting from a "crossed" mother. In view of our difficulties insuring calves got enough milk to grow, let alone thrive, we rejected that suggestion out of hand. We were loath to create a dairy for our herders.

Eventually, the ranch was off and running. It achieved the break-even point and additional breeding stock would classify it as a profitable enterprise. A Canadian agency had agreed to provide a $100,000 grant for that purpose. Various other agencies provided a variety of assistance. Everyone connected to the project felt just fine. The obvious success of the ranch proved the feasibility of African self-help projects to Technoserve—at least, when accompanied with the proper outside aid and one-to-one assistance. In addition, the ranch won a vote held by the veterinary department for the best new Uganda ranch.

The first challenge to this hard-earned smudginess came about when the American ranch manager found an African game hunter on the ranch. A number of varieties of antelope, Uganda water bucks, elands, gazelles and such, as well as numerous wild guinea hen flocks, lived on the ranch. He ordered the hunter off "my ranch." This injudicious use of the possessive pronoun by an American, on African soil, enraged the hunter. After some harsh words on both sides, the hunter left, making threats. After a call from the American ambassador, we learned that our manager had bullied a minister of General Idi Amin.

Actually, we solved the problem fairly easily. Together with the American ambassador and the feeling-hurt hunter, we met with the General in his "command quarters." After apologies for the overzealousness of our impetuous young ranch manager, who was clearly too diligent for his own safety, we offered a solution. He and his wife would be on the next plane out of Uganda. That settled that.

The ranch manager's year was nearly up anyway. The African manager-in-training could take over and the next phase could begin. The apprentice manager happily assumed the responsibility and prestige of his new position. Unfortunately, it soon became evident his joy was in having possession of the ranch's Datsun pickup. He began to log enormous numbers of miles that were in no way related to ranch needs.

To compound the onslaught of enormous travel expenses, other serious problems suggested a breakdown of ranch supervision. Again the poor condition of the calves indicated unrestricted milking. More seriously, mature animals began to die from mysterious causes and as could be expected, in flagrant violation of ranch policy, the meat went home with the herders or showed up in the market. Clearly, the situation necessitated an immediate and radical review of the program. Between the manager and the herders, the ranch was being looted.

I recognized a dilemma. These acts of flagrant and blatant dishonesty were grounds for immediate dismissal. On the other hand, Technoserve had turned over the management responsibility to the sponsors, maintaining only an advisory role. Because of this, I was loath to unilaterally kick the man off the ranch, impound the truck and force a new manager on these sponsors. I called an urgent meeting of the sponsors.

The members of the board were retired civil servants and school teachers, all very well educated and competent. One, a successful men's clothing store owner, was also an adviser in the General's kitchen cabinet staff. Unfortunately, he had to miss this meeting due to a pressing request for advice from the General. I had always worked well with these folks and I expected a speedy resolution of the problem.

I detailed the seriousness of the situation, how the manager was running the truck to Kampala and carrying passengers. I explained he had been operating an intercity transport service at ranch expense. In addition to this expense, I summed up the loss to the ranch from the unsupervised cattle herders. "The man is shamelessly dishonest. The operators are eating your ranch," I concluded.

The minutes of the meeting reveal the following conversation:

"Technoserve admits that it made a mistake in selecting the present manager. We will advertise for an experienced manager to replace the present one. Meanwhile, Technoserve will assume active management again. We suggest this manager be notified immediately. Get the keys away from him."

"Maybe we should sell the truck," was the response.

"Well, yes, to sell the truck would make a big saving. But this man is dishonest. He is allowing the ranch to eat itself up."

Silence...

"Gentlemen, Technoserve admits to having turned over the ranch and its responsibility to your credit union. At the same time, we would feel bad about all our work going for nothing. We hate to see you people lose your money, as you surely will. Furthermore, Technoserve has used its good faith and name to obtain funding and services from many sources, along with our own funds. Our reputation as a developer of sound projects will suffer if this problem remains unsolved. "

I was stunned that they decided to do nothing. Yet, after regrouping, I admitted to myself I had encountered this attitude in both East and West Africa. Citizens permit government officials to embezzle, engage in blatant nepotism, paying little attention to their duties. Unfettered newspapers report such dereliction, but to no avail. I suppose the cliché that it is natural for a person to "eat" if given the opportunity, applied to this episode as well.

As it happened, historic events were removing decision-making prerogatives from all of us. It was during this three-month period when General Amin was busily implementing the details of his dream. The Asians were frantically seeking to comply with his 90-day limit for departing the country. Discipline, social as well as military, had evaporated; any soldier could seek to enrich himself with little fear of retaliation. This involved indiscriminate looting, anad car hijacking which often resulted in death for the driver.

The incredible failure of the board to take action on the erring ranch manager became academic. A group of soldiers moved on to the ranch, killed some herders and sponsors, and simply drove the cattle away for their private use.

This ended my euphoria and pleasure in ranch development and my efforts in trying to provide a source of protein, jobs and profit for the country. My illusion that well-meaning, outside experts can expect a high level of success in a venture (in effect, "lay a program" on the folks) vanished. If the people are not willing to actively cooperate at every step of the program, particularly in the establishment of direction, failure is guaranteed. End of ranch.

Death of a Maize Plantation

Another of my Uganda projects, a maize plantation, also fell victim to marauding soldiers.

James Mugabe earned two master's degrees, agronomy and horticulture, from the University of California at Davis. At the time I met him, he occupied a chair at the University of Makerere in Kampala. He had five children by an English wife and seemed well fixed. Concurrently, he had undertaken to develop his father's five hundred acres of prime land on the shores of Lake Victoria, fifty miles to the east of Kampala. Furthermore, he believed he had found a solution for maintaining his university position and accomplishing his agriculture desires at the same time.

Like most well-connected men on the African continent who have outside interests beyond their job in civil service, government or the private sector, James had a dilemma. He was loath to abdicate his sinecures, but still yearned to pursue some other project. The solution: hire a manager.

My Technoserve predecessor, John Bates, didn't know he was offered such a solution. He had taken James on as a client under circumstances at odds with both Technoserve principles for selecting clients and procedures for project evaluation.

My take on the situation—a field man unilaterally taking on a client in violation of organizational policy—was that John had fallen under the spell of the charming African who was promoting a personal project. Without being too mystical, it appears Africans possess some special gene for creating an image of ambition, trustworthiness and responsibility. When this eminently convincing demeanor comes in contact with the Westerner who is eager to provide assistance to such a person anyway, the Westerner drops all his Western business and economic judgment. He sells himself on the idea that what this deserving man needs is a bit of assistance to succeed in some worthy endeavor. After all, that is the reason he came to Africa. (This scintillating observation has grown out of my personal experience.)

Not only did John violate company policy, he abdicated good sense as well. He advanced personal funds to get the farm started and committed Technoserve to further financing. Beyond that, he naively believed that James would give up his professorship and return home to manage the farm, although James, admittedly, implied as much.

At the time I took over the Uganda responsibility, James had found a manager in his home town who seemed to be working out exceedingly well. Little did anyone suspect that Joseph's (the manager) diligence reflected his intention to profit personally. He had a crop of maize and groundnuts showing good life and prospects. He had spent the money James had advanced for building sheds, drying tables and such, as needed by the crops, giving no suspicion of dishonesty.

Joseph acquired the lumber from a source completely beyond my experience. He had purchased a growing tree, a variety of teak having a density twice that of the teak used for a boat deck. In the absence of anything like a sawmill, I questioned how it was to be rendered into boards. Naturally, these folks had a way. Two men dug a pit near the tree. They felled it in such a way that it laid across the pit. One man took a position in the pit holding the end of a long timber saw. The man on top managed the other end. In this fashion the sawing team produced boards of remarkable symmetry. They called the technique, "pit sawing."

The farming project moved forward so smoothly, I had little to do. James made weekend trips to the farm to look things over. I reported "corn as high as an elephant's eye" to the home office.

Then James suffered a badly damaged arm in a car accident and was still hospitalized when harvest time arrived. Since the manager had performed very well, supporting all expenditures with neatly substantiated documents and the production of a prime crop, there was no reason not to authorize him to handle the harvest. I visited the operation as often as I could, doing what I could considering the language difficulties. But, at the same time, I succumbed to the Westerner's built-in inclination to trust.

I called on James for money to pay the harvesters. Strangely, he had no money. Having authorized the hiring of people, he hadn't made provisions for payday. Or, as it turned out, maybe he had. Technoserve's budget had made no provision for this development. I had no alternative; I paid the workers with my personal funds.

But the devastating moment of truth came when the manager and I tallied the crop output. It turned out to be a disappointing harvest indeed, especially the groundnuts. We checked the vines, nothing missed. The same with the maize.

"Mr. Manager, where is the crop?" I asked. His answer was basically, "Gee whiz, I don't know, maybe the birds got it." Birds indeed! Half the crop went home with the pickers—Joseph's kinfolk. James, at last up and about, made a surprise visit to the now-discredited manager's home. He noticed two large bags of groundnuts in an adjoining room.

In the end, it didn't matter much. The soldiers got wind of the storehouse and carried away whatever remained.

This double disaster to James's farm experiment didn't end his travail, although he took consolation in not having been around when the soldiers took a total levy on the remainder of the crop.

That ended James's and Technoserve's interest in that plantation project. Soon, James's interest in another venture ran afoul of the army's confusing policy on the takeover of Asian businesses. The business James took over may or may not have been acquired during the period when there were no restrictions on personal dealings with Asians. An army court was divided on whether his acquisition of his Asian store had violated the particular regulation. Half the board decided he had acquired the property when it was legal to do so. Others thought differently; they let him know he was doomed whatever clearance he got. Highly educated people are not trusted in African countries, especially when power is in a state of flux.

By that time I had (depending on your viewpoint) fled, slipped out or merely transferred operations to Kenya. James got word to me that he had secured authorization to reside in Australia—he had enemies and was hiding out. He intended to escape with his family using the Lake Victoria freight-passenger boat that made a stop in Kenya. He wanted me to meet the boat and hide him and his family for a while until he could raise funds for passage to Australia.

They didn't show up at the appointed time at the ferry dock. I had no way of knowing where they were. Later that morning, at the post office, I found what I thought was a jammed box. After reporting this to the postal clerk, he grinned at my complaint and told me where I could find the Mugabe family.

Upon joining up with them, I complimented the wife on her cleverness—but where was James?

She explained that after observing a soldier posted near their cabin, they fled. The wife and children managed a ride by car to Kisumu where we lived. James turned up a day or two later.

I arranged for Technoserve to pay the fare to Australia for James and his family. I hope their life is more secure.

Perilous Departure from Uganda

Once the Asian exodus was underway, Amin turned his attention to Europeans (whites). Daily broadcasts warned the populace to watch the Europeans: "Any indication of spying, sabotage or other acts against the government is to be dealt with."

If Amin worried from the beginning about possible Western interference of his Asian adventure, he needn't have been concerned. While the British muttered over the inhumanity of the three-month expulsion allowance, they reflected more concern over absorbing the 15,000 penniless, British, passport-carrying Asians about to be dumped, en masse, on their doorstep.

This hostility toward whites reflected Amin's desire to strike back at the West's lack of sympathy for his housecleaning project and serve as a not-so-subtle reminder that he had a hostage card to play.

The perpetual reinterpretation of laws and regulations generated vast uncertainty in the white community. Work permits were canceled. Various business owners received a 24-hour notice to depart the country or face prosecution for "engaging in acts against the economy."

Most of the Americans had gone by the time I left. The Peace Corps contingent had slipped out during the night, following the shooting of two of their own. The USAID and embassy ranks had been reduced to caretaker staffs. My projects had all died for various reasons, but mostly because my clients could not be found. The phrase "dead or fled" explained missing persons. Then, too, most of the government agencies had shut down. Nothing could be accomplished amid this chaos. It was time for me to join my wife and the daughter remaining with us, in Kenya.

Europeans and Americans had an advantage over the Asians. We could acquire export permits, under very severe restrictions. Asians left with no more belongings than they could carry. The government took the position that anything imported purchased with Ugandan shillings must stay in the country, especially such things as automobiles. Every packing required the attendance of a customs agent, a policeman and a soldier, as a deterrent to anyone removing "treasure" from the country. The owner with cleared goods had some fears, too. He, or an agent, found it a wise policy to accompany the goods to a sealed freight car or the plane.

A French forwarding firm had a monopoly on this packing and shipping trade. The firm exacted a price of twelve dollars per packed cubic foot. Neither my budget or time could afford this inconvenience.

Luckily, two employees of the firm offered to do some moonlighting. Since they had the authority to handle the documentation and arrange the necessary inspections, they could handle all the paperwork required to legally clear my shipment to Nairobi. They also ordered a small wagon (box car) for the particular Sunday afternoon. Furthermore, they agreed to arrange for a policeman and soldier to be on hand for the required inspection prior to my loading the car.

It seemed to me these men had accomplished a lot on their Sunday off. As it developed, their part of the expedition went off without a snag. I gladly paid their fee and enjoyed my relief over escaping all the confusion and paperwork. Supposedly, I could manage from there. I needed only to load the goods on to a truck and reload them into a wagon—no problem. I should have learned by then to be suspicious of situations that appeared too easy.

In Africa, one doesn't look for a rental truck agency when in need of a conveyance. One goes to the market and finds a transportation unit: a truck, driver and standby crew of four to eight men.

I engaged a "transportation unit" and we wheeled up the hill to my apartment. My merry crew made short work of loading files, desks, beds, chairs and everything else that I might have used in office and living quarters, haphazardly on the truck. (Sometimes now when I look for a bottle opener, I recall how this crew decapitated a case of Coke instantly with strong white teeth.)

Now everything seemed straightforward, as legal as anyone could know. The wagon should be waiting at the freight yards with the assorted inspectors. But I had a small worry about a favor I had agreed to do.

An Englishman I knew, who was married to an Asian woman then living in Nairobi, had casually asked if I minded including a few "things" belonging to his in-laws along with mine when I got ready to move to Nairobi. I agreed to stop at their Ugandan house on my way out of the country. He supplied the address and, more as an afterthought, a key in case no one was at home when I called. I would know what things to pick up. A nuisance, but what are friends for?

From the casual manner of the request, I envisaged a suitcase or two. I didn't realize I was agreeing to take on an extremely dangerous errand. During this phase, Asians with bona fide Uganda citizenship were exempted from the Asian expulsion program provided they hadn't "runned away." If they had, their property was automatically forfeited to the state. Many citizens slipped out of the country—too fearful to stay—hoping conditions would change. If so, they would slip back in. But their absence had to remain a secret or their property would be considered abandoned.

I gave the Asian in-laws' address to the driver. He took off, with me following in my car. I hadn't really looked at the address, and so I suffered a major shock when I realized we were charging up Kololo Hill, the location of General Amin's residence and command post.

If possible, people avoided getting within four streets of his house because of the ever-present, weapon-laden army patrol vehicles, alert for any potential or imaginary danger to the General. But there was no way to stop my noisy crew now! By the time I had caught up with them, they had entered the circular drive of a mansion every bit as impressive as Amin's next door but one.

Efficient, this crew of mine. Before I could get parked, they had maneuvered the truck to the doorway with a great deal of shouting. I desperately began searching for the Ugandan words to say, "Cool it, fellows. Let's skip this stop." But I couldn't manage it.

It wasn't until I saw a soldier with a rifle lounging on the porch that I really began to sweat. Best be bold, I thought, since I could see no way to retreat discreetly. A little friendly conversation seemed appropriate. Very casually, I inquired as to who had stationed him here, why and how long had he been so engaged. It seems that he had been hired as a guard by the owners of the house, but he hadn't seen them for about a month.

I had conflicted feelings about this information. First, I was delighted. This tiny soldier, no taller than his rifle, had not been formally stationed on the premises. On the other hand, the absence of the owners concerned me. Sure enough, when I entered the house, it became obvious that nobody lived here anymore. They had "runned away."

Well, it was too late now. I had opened the door expecting to grab a suitcase and get the hell out of there fast. But to my dismay, everything in this huge room was packed, boxed and ready for transport. The largest item was a custom made, twelve-place dining room set, elaborately carved of extremely dense hardwood. The vulnerable edges had been protected with sewn-on material. The chairs appeared to be upholstered in silk. The owners had taken a lot of care with this furniture in a forlorn hope of shipment.

A lacquered Chinese screen and matching chest had been treated equally as tenderly. And well they should, for they looked valuable. All the decorative motifs appeared to be of jade rather than the more common mother-of-pearl. The chest interested me because of its unbelievable weight. What contents could weigh so much? It had no lock, but was heavily strapped. I opened it. The top layer of clothes covered several canvases without frames. Then, the silverware: tureens, platters, pitchers, tableware, a service for twelve I supposed. Whatever else it contained, I didn't take time to inspect. In addition, the large room contained a number of bundles also with sewn-on burlap coverings.

The vulnerability of my position was staggering. There I was, standing inside a mansion that, along with all its contents, had automatically become the property of the Ugandan government. There had been many instances when soldiers had quite willingly obeyed their instructions to shoot enemies of the economy "caught in the act." My present position qualified me for inclusion in that group and more vulnerable than most.

I had visions of a couple of jeeps wheeling in, looking for the cause of all this racket. I could face summary execution for just being there, never mind with a truck and crew ready to load up. But before I could make any decision, my exuberant crew, eager to complete this contract and get paid, began loading everything. Why not continue? I thought. It would take more time, without decreasing the risk, to explain the situation to my crew. Besides, I had convinced the guard of the authorization for this entry. Why wouldn't he be convinced? I had a key, it was broad daylight and I had white skin. I could only rejoice in his naiveté. He must have been fresh from the country.

Shortly after completing the precarious loading, we sped out of the driveway onto the street and began a wild run down Kololo Hill to the railroad yard, whooping and hollering all the way. How we escaped detection from a soldier patrol, I will never know.

Even before I had established that I actually had a wagon, the crew had stripped the load off the truck onto the ground. The driver held out his hand for the money—end of engagement with these wild men. I now had lonely charge of a massive pile of goods, with no shelter, positioned alongside a railroad track on a late Sunday afternoon and wholly dependent on arrangements presumably made for me. I looked around for the policeman and soldier hired for the "inspection."

Much to my elation, I observed a tiny switch engine puffing along in my direction towing a small wagon. At least I would be able to load up the wagon and lock it. I had no desire to face the danger and unpleasantness of guarding this stuff all night.

About then, a policeman ambled over and claimed he had been engaged to inspect my goods for "contraband" (they used that word a lot). He poked around a little and tried to open up some drawers; when I failed to produce a key, he didn't press the issue. After asking a few questions, he gave the opinion there didn't appear to be any contraband and turned to leave.

"What about the soldier?" I asked.

"Oh, don't worry about him. He's drinking up your money."

I enlisted some help to load the car. The switchman closed the door and immobilized the latch with some heavy gauge wire. Project completed. I stopped sweating. I boarded a Nairobi plane and joined my family.

Two days later, I learned that my wagon had arrived from Uganda. I called the number for the person in Nairobi who would be interested in the "few household items" I had agreed to bring out with me. My friend's wife came on the line. Her reaction puzzled me. She gave nothing away, no questions or pleasantries. Just silence on the line—waiting. I wondered if she had been apprised of what I had been doing on her behalf. I ended the one-sided conversation by telling her to meet me at a particular siding. And "bring a truck." That electrified her. I could feel the release of pent-up emotion that came through with her acknowledgment. She informed me I could recognize her by her long hair.

Surely, the pretty young Asian woman waiting for me had waist-long hair, for there was no mistaking that identifying feature. But this sari-clad lady had no welcoming smile. In fact, her face reflected a combination of apprehension, hope and a flicker of suspicion, justified I suppose. She could have feared my anger, knowing I had been virtually trapped into committing a capital offense. She could also have been wondering what part of the treasure I had decided to keep. It would have been justified if I had helped myself, I mused later.

Certainly, I more than qualified for a salvage percentage.

Together, we watched a workman cut the heavy wire seal. As soon as he slid the door open, she scrambled up into the car. She unstrapped the chest, opened it, felt around inside for a while and seemed pleased. She next inspected the furniture, lovingly caressing each piece. I assumed she was looking for damage. Then she began to cry —tears and sobs.

This shocked me. I had been building up a case of hurt feelings over this woman's cool reaction ever since I spoke to her on the phone. I had been anticipating a bit of enthusiasm, perhaps a little praise or even some word of concern for my safety. After all, I only knew her husband slightly, and I had operated in an area of extreme danger, admittedly inadvertent, but nonetheless, I could have reduced my risk by running like hell when I found out what a hole I was in.

My outburst was rather explosive, "Good God, lady. I risked getting shot by pulling your stuff out from under the nose of Amin's army. And your people might just possibly have engaged in a bit of trickery to get me into the venture in the first place. What did I do wrong? Is something broken?"

"Nothing is wrong," she replied. "Nothing is broken. You were perfect. I am so glad no harm came to you. I am crying because I am so happy. You can't know how much this means to my family. My parents are now in England. I am taking this down to the airport for shipment to them."

"The whole carload?" I expostulated.

"Everything. Yes. Thank you," she said.

As she was about to enter the truck, I shouted after her: "Where's your husband?" She may not have heard me. Anyway, I never encountered either one of them again. (I did later receive a letter of thanks from her folks in England.)

PRINLAND LIMITED
Directors: A.H. Nathu A.C.I.S. T.A. Nathu
Service Station, Garage, Body Repairs, Car and Motor Cycle Sales
23-25 HIGHFIELD STREET
LEICESTER LE2 1AB Regd. Office
Tel. (0533) 58973 Registered in England No. 1075207

27th Feb. 1973

Dear Mr. Casto,

I write on behalf of my parents and wish to apologise for the delay in replying to your letter. So many different matters need one's attention when one begins a new beginning.

My parents and we all would like to sincerely thank you and your wife for all that you have done for us at such risk to yourselves.

We have indeed received safely the furniture you so kindly salvaged for us and my wife is very grateful to you for making it possible for her to have few of the things which were of so much sentimental value.

It would be a pleasure to meet you if you are ever in England and please do call on us should you be visiting this part of the world.

Mohammed is in Vancouver and still in the process of finding his feet! Begining a new life is a challenge but I believe that an acceptance of that challenge is half the battle.

With kind regards from the whole family.

Yours sincerely,

Dear Mr. Casto:
I write on behalf of my parents. My parents and we all would like to sincerely thank you for all that you have done for us at such risk to yourself. We have indeed received gratefully the furniture you so kindly salvaged for us and my wife is very grateful to you for making it possible for us to have the few things of sentimental value.
Muhammad is in Vancouver and still in the process of finding his feet. Beginning a new life is a challenge but I believe that an acceptance of that challenge is half the battle.
Many regards from the whole family.

Excerpts from the original letter.

President of Uganda, Yoweri Museveni

When I left Uganda in late 1972, the "pearl of Africa" more closely resembled a charnel house. And it got worse. Although I have visited Kenya a few more times over the years, a Uganda visit was not attractive. Too many friends had fallen into the category of "address unknowns." Some ex-Uganda Asian friends are doing very well in Canada and Australia. At any rate, why return to mourn over a period of wasted experience in prime time?

In 1979, the return of Milton Obote, Amin's *bete noire,* under the sponsorship of his Tanzanian buddy, Nyerere, did constitute an end to the eight years of Amin's sadistic savagery; but it only brought about a different reign of terror, with different victims. In the first place, the victorious Tanzanian troops that sent President for Life Idi Amin fleeing into the desert (to Libya or Saudi Arabia, it was presumed) found they were expected to live off the land.

In addition to this plague, it was payback time for Obote. Bill Berkeley reports the slaughtering of thousands of civilians in Amin's West Nile by invading Tanzanian troops under the command of Major General Tito Okello's command. In his article, "An African Success Story?" (Foreign Affairs, September 1994, page 22), he estimates hundreds of thousands were slaughtered in the area where guerrilla leader Yoweri Museveni's insurgency was based. Ultimately, Berkeley reports, "Okello turned on Obote." The six months of Okello's tenure as head of state were the most chaotic in Uganda's history; Kampala disintegrated into Beirut-like fiefs controlled by warlords and roamed by murderous gangs.

> *Through this period of rape, pillage and murder, the present Marxist leader, Yoweri Museveni, fought his way into power by 1986. (Okello, in turn, fled into what Leslie Crawford called "self-exile.") In an interview with Berkeley, Museveni described his* goal: . . . to *bring Uganda back from the dead. Uganda occupies a singular place among the horror-plagued countries of post-independence Africa. In the 1970s and early 1980s Idi Amin, and the less notorious but no less wanton Milton Obote,*

plunged Uganda into a nightmare as dark and sinister as the one that has unfolded just across its southern border in Rwanda. Perhaps a million Ugandans died in two decades of sheer terror.

Museveni regards his economic program as a key to stability. He shed his Marxist ideology and embraced a free-market economy. Berkeley describes it as "a virtual textbook adaptation" of the IMF's "structural adjustment program: [characterized by] free markets, a convertible currency, an independent central bank, the selling of state-owned companies, tight budgets and downsizing the civil service and the army."

Museveni has sought to establish the rule of law Amin and Obote had destroyed. He virtually scrapped the discredited police force and hired and trained a new one. He worked to diversify and professionalize the army. But most astonishingly, he opened the way for the return of the Asians, rendered valid by at least some program of restitution for confiscated Asian property.

Berkeley finds Uganda in 1994 a peaceful and stable country, contrasting to the horrors in Rwanda, Zaire and Sudan. In Uganda, there are "no road blocks; streets are safe at night." Crawford is also complimentary and summarized how well she thinks Museveni has succeeded with his program: A country once synonymous with tyranny and economic disaster is undergoing a transformation. Tourists are returning to Uganda's game parks. Asians expelled by Idi Amin are returning to reclaim homes and businesses. . . . Uganda has made remarkable progress in overcoming as grim a legacy as an African government has known.

Return of the Asians

I was astonished to learn the Uganda government is vigorously pursuing a policy of inviting the Asians to return and to reclaim their property that was confiscated in 1971 or to be compensated. (During that 90-day period of expulsion, when they sought refuge in any country in the world that would take them, I wonder if any one harbored a thought of some day being urged to return.)

I called some ex-Uganda Asian friends in Canada and Australia for more information about this extraordinary development. As a consequence of my efforts, Nazlin Rahemtulla, who works for a major financial institution in Vancouver, B.C., Canada, sent some pertinent clippings. She reminded me that many Asians had hidden Ugandan currency in the event they would be allowed to return, only to find the the government has changed the currency. She was entirely conversant with the situation and, at the invitation of the government, had enlisted in Uganda's reconstruction program to the extent of leading a team of potential investors to Uganda. The visit was preceded by a delegation of Nazlin-hosted, high-ranking, Ugandan officials, who had come to Vancouver seeking potential investors.

Initially, Nazlin returned to Uganda with a plan either to sell the family-owned carbon-dioxide and soft-drink plants situated in Jinja, an industrial town located on Lake Victoria at the source of the Nile, or to remain in the country as an emigree to operate the business. While there, she stayed at the estate of her family's close friends, the Madhvanis, who treated her to a tour of their huge sugar plantation. Torn between the strong ties of the land of her birth, where she had friends and relatives, and the good life she had constructed in Vancouver, she pondered her decision a long time. She finally decided to sell the business and return to her Canadian home, resuming her work at the financial institution in Canada she had enjoyed for fifteen years.

My feelings were mixed. I had witnessed the sorrow and desolation of 50,000 people as they were summarily and brutally pushed out of their homeland with hardly a change of clothes. One could expect them to harbor a hatred of Uganda until their dying days.

Very strange, people's feelings. In an interview, Azim Shariff, a man of twenty at the time of the exodus, now content and doing well in Canada, agreed to read the Uganda section of my manuscript. I wondered how he would take my observations on the disrespect and discrimination the Asians had visited on Ugandan Africans during their daily life.

"I have no arguments with the Asian attitudes described," he said. "There is perhaps an explanation for the Asian attitude in East Africa (explanation *not* excuse). The Asian community came to East Africa while the British ruled. The British are class conscious. To them, the Asians were coolies: greedy, hard working, subservient, reliable agents to use as middle-men to accomplish the task of building Her Majesty's Great Empire."

Referring to the expulsion of Asians, Azim mentioned another reason: "Amin had wanted to rebuild his army into a formidable force befitting the most powerful general in Africa! He had asked the British for aid in this regard, but the British had refused. Accordingly, it was to spite the British that he first decided to expel Asians with British passports."

He went on to confess that the Asians themselves are strong adherents/victims of the caste system. "Therefore, in East Africa, the master (the British) treated the Asians as a low class. They, in turn, treated each other as low or high as warranted. Finally, the community, as a collective, regarded the African as belonging to the lowest class—and treated him accordingly."[13]

Nothing new about those discriminatory concepts, I thought. But I had never heard it spelled out so succinctly. Furthermore, I was not ready for his denouement. "It was a real eye-opener for the expelled Asians who came to North America to find that the white people (whom they always thought to be a superior race) were actually treating them as equals." He went on to say, "Many have mentioned that if they went back, they would do things differently, especially treat the black Ugandans with more respect."

As early as 1908, while traveling in East Africa, Winston Churchill recorded his philosophical musings. He dismissed the black man as no competition for the white man. "It is the brown man who is the rival." He listed the middle-class professions to which whites were entitled—traders, merchants, bankers and farmers which would be threatened. He continued:

13 I was friendly with a Kenyan Asian who had grown up under British rule and was not the least tolerant of class relationships. He bitterly recalled the seating sections in a theater; whites occupied the best section, Asians the next best and then the blacks.

And here strikes in the Asiatic. In every single employment of this class, his power of subsisting upon a few shillings a month, his industry, his thrift, his sharp business aptitudes give him the economic superiority, and if economic superiority is to be the final rule—as it has never been and never will be in the history of the world—there is not a single employment of this middle class, from which he will not, to a very large extent, clear the white man, as surely and as remorselessly as the brown rat extirpated the black from British soil.

Since I wasted six months of prime time twenty-three years ago in my efforts to help improve the Ugandan economy, I am quite interested in their program now, particularly in the government's good sense in recognizing the Asian resource. The explorations made by expatriate Nazlin Rahemtulla in the country that, only two decades ago, had become a killing field for black citizens and pure hell for Asians, certainly provide credence to the seriousness of the government's policy—as much credence as an African policy could have, in my mind.

Only a small number of Asians, about 1,000 families, were in the initial group accepting the government's invitation to return. Several thousands more have arrived in Uganda since then. In his article "Bittersweet Homecoming" in *Asia, Inc.* (June 1994), Barry Shlachter summarized the motivations of these Asians: "Some return to sell property, some come to live and some just want to have a look around. Whatever their reasons, Asians are returning to Uganda—the country that threw them out 22 years ago."

Shlachter reproduced a World Bank report that showed the effects of President Amin's expulsion of Asians in carrying out his Africanization policy:

Ninety percent of the companies, crippled by managerial inexperience and embezzlement, have been operating at less than 20 percent capacity. The expulsion and expropriation, added to the reckless policies of Amin, all but killed the once promising Ugandan economy.

Shlachter also described disparate feelings among the Ugandans. Many citizens welcome the Asians; they remember when there were jobs and commerce. Others feel black businesses will be injured and urban dwellers will lose their homes. Some Asians have returned to find high government officials occupying their homes, rent free. The blacks over the years have acquired a vested interest in businesses and property they could be expected to be exceedingly unwilling to walk away from.

These roadblocks, plus natural inertia, would understandably slow the program, which they did. It was taking one year to process an Asian reclamation of property application. The World Bank became involved in speeding up the process. It threatened to hold back a $125 million structural adjustment loan and placed an American adviser on the Departed Asians' Property custodian Board. This leverage reduced the wait from one year to one month.

Forbes magazine (July 18, 1994) provides information on the restructuring of the big Mehta and Madhvani Group:

> ***Rising out of the ashes is the Madhvani Group, Uganda's largest industrial group, with annual turnover of over $100 million up from nothing in 1989, when the Madhvani family, with roots in India, began in earnest to rehabilitate businesses that had been expropriated by Idi Amin in 1971.***

The article explains "up from nothing." The Madhvanis, among the first families to return to Uganda, found most of the 22,000-acre sugar plantation had returned to the bush. With help from the World Bank and other lenders, they undertook a $55 million rehabilitation effort. It paid off. "The Madhvani's Ugandan enterprises now employ capital of around $200 million and account for about 9 percent of the country's GNP." The pre-Amin levels of 70,000 tons of sugar production should be accomplished by 1995, with the volume rising to 130,000 tons by 1998.

The *Forbes* reference to the Madhvani Group "rising out of the ashes" can apply equally well to the whole country of Uganda.

The Nile River

Murchison Falls, Uganda

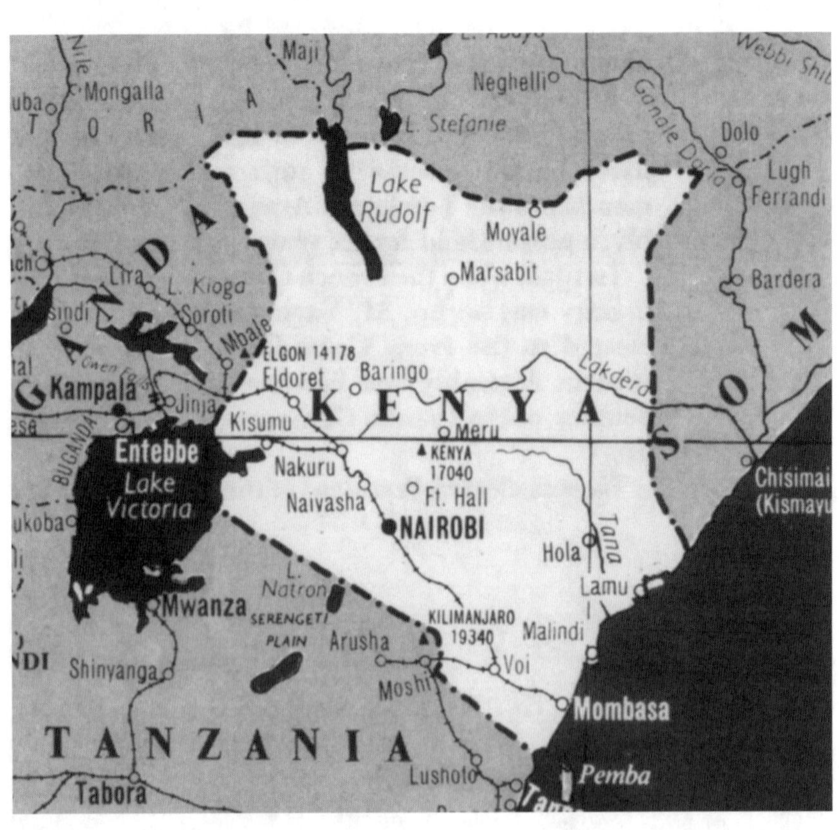
Maji
Mongalla
Neghelli
L. Stefanie
Dolo
Lugh Ferrandi
Lake Rudolf
Moyale
Marsabit
Bardera
L. Kioga
Lira
Soroti
Mbale
ELGON 14178
Eldoret
Baringo
Kampala
Jinja
Kisumu
K E N Y A
Meru
Entebbe
Lake Victoria
Nakuru
KENYA 17040
Naivasha
Ft. Hall
NAIROBI
Chisimai (Kismayu)
Hola
Tana
Lamu
L. Natron
Mwanza
SERENGETI PLAIN
KILIMANJARO 19340
Arusha
Malindi
Shinyanga
Voi
Moshi
Mombasa
T A N Z A N I A
Lushoto
Pemba
Tabora
BUGANDA

KENYA

At the time of our departure from Uganda, we hadn't known too much about Kenya, outside of names associated with game hunting, such as Ernest Hemingway and Theodore Roosevelt. While the Mau Mau terror was little more than a name, Jomo Kenyatta was a world figure, associated with Kenya's independence. What history we did have of the development of the colony, the English involvement and other matters stirred us to learn more.

Accordingly, we took a crash course in Kenyan history.

The Colonization of Kenya

Those who harbor the viewpoint that African colonization was launched from a platform of greed, a desire to plunder the "wealth" of the dark continent, have not studied its history—at least not of the African east coast. There were basically two contributing factors. One was that Napoleon's occupation of Egypt and his aspirations to challenge Britain's power in India triggered a major event that finally led to England's colonization of Kenya. The other was England's dedication to stopping the slave trade in the Indian Ocean.[1]

Without these factors, it is highly unlikely that England would have had any interest in East Africa. Until the last two decades of the nineteenth century, Imperial thinking was that territorial expansion, inland from the east coast of that awful *terra incognito,* was tanta-

1 The historical material on the colonization of Kenya is based on information in Charles Miller's *Lunatic Express* (New York: Macmillan, 1971).

mount to madness. In spite of this, Kenya became, first, a protectorate by diplomatic accident, and later on, a reluctant colony.

European activity in the Indian Ocean started with the Portuguese Vasco da Gama's historic voyage around Cape of Good Hope to India in 1497. He recognized the value of the island of Zanzibar and the coastal town of Mombassa as provisioning stations for caravels traveling to India. Tribute could be exacted from the local Persian, Arab and Swahili inhabitants as well. Other than Fort Jesus, which still stands in Mombassa, the Portuguese left no trace of their 200-year savage rule. The Omani Arabs finally broke the Portuguese hold in East Africa in 1729. Britain's activity in the Indian Ocean, relating both to blocking the slave trade and Napoleon's move to dominate India as well as Egypt, was linked to these Arabs by treaty.

Vasco da Gama

England devised two major strategic policies to prevent Napoleon's ships from reaching India. In 1795, she wrested control of the Dutch settlement at the Cape of Good Hope and created a barrier to keep French ships from rounding the African continent into the Indian Ocean. A little later, in 1800, the British intercepted a French letter to the Imam of Oman, Seyidd Sultan, requesting a treaty. Having thus learned of Napoleon's intention, Britain negotiated her own treaty with the Imam, beating the French to the punch.

This effectively ended Napoleon's plan for a staging base at the Oman capital of Muscat, from which he could have launched a back-door invasion of India. The treaty also allowed England to make use of the Oman-controlled island of Zanzibar and the town of Mombassa as sentry posts for guarding the southern route to India and bases for their crusade to suppress the Arab slave trade. The mutually antagonistic objectives of the parties undermined the British program. The Omani Arabs had an entrenched profitable traffic in slaves, which they had built up over a thousand years and had no intention of relinquishing. On the other hand, England had an extremely powerful missionary population rabidly opposed to the practice of slavery.

The British found a way to manage this dichotomy of aims. To maintain their Omani-Anglo treaty and still appear to be doing some harm to the slave trade, they fashioned anti-slave treaties with enough loopholes to avoid any perceived threat to the trade. At the same time, they allowed the Royal Navy ships to dash about as if they were doing some good.

Such juggling of objectives failed in a most unexpected fashion. Through a foolhardy administrative blunder, the Omani leaders themselves set the stage for disharmony in their political relationships by selecting as their absentee administrator in Mombassa the ferocious aristocratic Mazuri family. It was an astounding decision, especially in view of the Mazuri clan's age-old conviction they were the rightful rulers of Mombassa. With such obvious conflicts of beliefs and values, continuous strife could be expected. The irate Imam's tax collector would sometimes prevail and at other times, fail. Actually, the Imam had hoped the treaty providing for the British presence in the area would help keep the Mazuri in check, but that hope went unfulfilled.

In 1824, entering into this political feud was the Royal Navy's Captain William Fitz William Wentworth Owen. Commanding two ships, the Captain was peacefully charting the East African coast. Who could have predicted that a man engaged in such a limited responsibility would take a unilateral course of action that would lead to an international political uproar?

What Captain Owen did was to provide a British protectorate over the Mazuri in Mombassa against the Imam of Oman himself. The action was not frivolous. In exchange, he required a promise that the Mazuri cease slave trading. Of course, the gleeful Mazuri complied—for the moment. To give all possible credit to Owen and his perspective, he seized an unexpected opportunity to strike a substantial blow against the Arabian slave trade. At the same time, the Mazuri clan was ecstatic over its success in manipulating Owen into this pro tem protection by the British.

Owen, of course, must have been ignorant of the extent and importance of English involvements in the area. He was obviously unaware Mombassa was a part of Seyidd Sultan's domain and for twenty years, England had been pursuing a delicately balanced policy of anti-slave trade and Napoleon containment under a treaty with this very Seyidd Sultan. By his impetuous decision, Owen had committed a breathtaking act of insubordination amounting to open defiance of the Imam of Oman, the Lords of the Admiralty, the Foreign Office, the Directors of the East Indian Company, as well as breaching the Omani-Anglo treaty. Eventually, the damage was repaired.

Taking the long view, Owen's action was seventy years too soon. In 1895, England, no longer fearing the French challenge to India and having become deeply drawn into the slave-trade conflict, at last bowed to the inevitable and made East Africa a protectorate. She annexed Kenya as a colony in 1920 (Kenya won independence in 1963).

The Settling of Kenya

Emergence of this British protectorate from a wilderness began at the turn of the century, commencing with the building of the Mombassa to Uganda railroad. The main reason for constructing the railroad was the perceived strategic need to control the Ugandan source of the Nile. Also, by opening up the interior to settlers for the first time, the railroad was a spur to Sir Charles Eliot, Her Majesty's commissioner, to increase the commercial value of the land and thus encourage more settlement.

One of the more interesting programs to encourage immigration involved recruitment efforts in South Africa. Shortly after the defeat of the Afrikaners in the Boer War, one could have expected some antipathy to a British project. Such was not the case. 1908 probably saw the peak of settlement when, on 11 July, 250 Boers arrived at

Mombassa. Their leader, Jansen Van Rensberg, had chartered the S.S. *Windhoek'* to bring in twenty-seven Boer families including his own... The Boers imported complete farms, unassembled houses, seventy-two horses, forty-two wagons and a variety-of stock and were destined to create their own small township, Eldoret.[2]

Jews were another potential source of settlers. A survey was made to determine the feasibility of creating a homeland in Kenya. This idea was developed by Dr. Theodore Herzl, a Jewish leader; who dreamed of founding a Jewish nation where the dispersed wanderers bonded by their religion could build their own nation. His objective corresponded with the aims of Joseph Chamberlain, Secretary of State for Colonies, who made a tour of Kenya in 1902. Recognizing that the Uganda railroad was losing vast sums of money, Chamberlain undertook to assist Sir Charles Eliot, the commissioner, father of the white settlement, who was still frantically searching for more settlers.

A fortuitous circumstance helped to round out the plan. At this time, Jewish refugees were flooding into England to escape some gruesome Russian pogroms. Chamberlain saw the opportunity to use the huge empty tracts of land to benefit the protectorate and at the same time, give asylum to the Russian Jews. As a threat to English trade unionists, they were not wanted in England anyway. It had the appearance of a great idea—given the needs and the time.[3]

A Zionist Commission was formed to explore the Uasin Plateau and to determine its suitability for a Jewish homeland. "In July 1905, the 7th Zionist Congress met in Basle, at which the commission recommended that 'the proffered land was not sufficient in extent or the resources for colonization on a large scale.'...With this resolution the Jewish East African project came to an end and the search for a Jewish homeland shifted from Africa to Australia."[4] One can only wonder how the Kenyan government of independence would

2 Errol Trzebinski, *The Kenya Pioneers* (New York: W. W. Norton & Co., 1986), p. 110, 133-34.

3 Trzebinski, p. 48-50.

4 Trzebinski, p. 111.

have dealt with a full-scale settlement of Jews when the winds of Africanization swept the continent. The Jews had nowhere to go home to.

Asians were another sizable group attracted to the land. Many who had been imported to work on the railroad stayed on. Others came for the expected commercial opportunities that a railroad would provide. Unlike the British, however, who never gave up their attachments to England, the Asians came to stay forever. While this commitment to the colony-nation-to-be could have been regarded as a worthwhile trait, it proved not to be. In fact, it came to be seen as an "Asian Problem." And after Uganda's "final solution," there was apprehension and resignation in the Kenyan Asian community: "It could also happen here."

Expelling Asians didn't happen in a wholesale manner as occurred in Uganda. Kenya pursued a more methodical, more cautious, policy. The Kenyanization program, formalized with the Trade Licensing Act of 1967, provided for reserving commodities and areas for Kenyan citizens exclusively. The need for the act, it was explained, was that a major part of the economy was owned and operated by expatriates: Asians and British. Specifically, it was claimed, the act addressed the problem of the 180,000 Asians. The term "expatriates" was inappropriately applied to the Asians, since nearly all of them were born in Kenya and had no allegiance anywhere else, although sixty percent had failed to qualify for citizenship in the two-year post-independence grace period. They apparently didn't feel that Kenyan citizenship would guarantee an African future.

Again, for the third time, our development assistance efforts had to contend with the effects of government programs that displaced people with skills and with commercial and professional capital. How much better off would these nations have been if they had accepted these proven elements as an irreplaceable resource and built a long-term program designed to involve the black citizens in the existing commercial structure. Non-blacks would have been overjoyed to assist such a program in exchange for a sense of permanence in the land of their birth.

Jomo Kenyatta (1893-1978)

Jomo Kenyatta,
President for Life,
Father of the Country

Studying the life of Jomo Kenyatta, President for Life, Father of the Country, Mzee (Swahili meaning "grand old man"), was mandatory, since he had fashioned the modern political environment. As an early nationalist leader, he campaigned for land reform and political rights for Africans, often taking his grievances to London. (At the time he lived in England he became a co-founder, with Kwame Nkrumah, of the Pan-African Federation.)

His agitation finally became too much for the British. After a four-month trial in a colonial court, Kenyatta was convicted of managing the Mau Mau terror (Movement of Unity). A curious aside (or perhaps not so curious) is he had the fervent emotional support of English citizens, similar to that given by international well-wishers to South Africa's Nelson Mandella during his trial. Kenyatta was imprisoned in 1953 and later exiled to a remote desert outpost.

After Kenyatta's release from prison in 1961, he participated with the British in creating a new constitution for Kenya as a prelude to independence, which was conferred in 1963. In 1964, he became president and held that position until his death in 1978. (His remains rest in a mausoleum in a downtown Nairobi park protected 24 hours a day by an honor guard.)

The Mau Mau movement, which Kenyatta was imprisoned for leading, is described in one dictionary as a "secret society of Kikuyu tribesmen in Kenya, organized in 1951 to fight against white rule: both the movement and its suppression were marked by terrorism and violence." Another source holds that the "Mau Mau Emergency," led by the Kikuyu tribesmen, was partially a revolt against the British and an attempt to return to pre-European ways.

These descriptions are only vaguely right at best. While its original objective was to rebel against the colonial whites and, more specifically, to gain civil rights, it degenerated into an orgy of black-on-black murder, probably because of obsessive demands for loyalty to the movement. Those who broke their oath to the Mau Maus were apt to be tracked down and murdered. It was not a black movement led by Kikuyus, as implied. Rather, it was solely a Kikuyu affair; none of the other tribes could be induced to join. The final death toll of forty thousand tribesmen cannot be blamed on the British but on fighting among the Kikuyus; only about one hundred whites and Asians were killed.

In the end, the Mau Mau rebellion did not hasten independence from Britain. Twenty years later, a Mau Mau veteran could trade on his earlier involvement. In the legislature, for example, a representative would sometimes denigrate an opponent with the challenge: "Where were you when we were fighting for independence?"

Swahili in Kenya

Millions of assorted East Africans employ Swahili as a *lingua franca*, but the Arabic word—meaning "coast people"—also serves as the name for eleven million descendants of black African, Arab and other traders who evolved from a distinct ethnicity and now bear the Swahili appellation. These non-cohesive ethnic groups are loosely united by common economic pursuits (especially trade), cultural traditions (Islamic) and use of the language. Their resident areas are chiefly Kenya, Tanzania, Somalia, the Mozambique coast, Uganda and eastern Zaire.

In Mombassa, Kenya, the Swahilis are distinguished by their Moslem dress and brown complexion, all reflecting their Arab background. Women wear the standard black gown with their face partially covered. Men sport a white robe slung over their body, with a twisted cloth arrangement fixed on their head or a small embroidered, brimless hat.

The evolution of Swahili—both the language and ethnicity—began in Persia when a schism in the Moslem religion produced the Shias and Suuni factions. Large groups of Suuni migrated south, becoming part of the gene pool in East Africa—along with the Arabic, English, Portuguese and others—that intermingled with the Bantu-speaking Africans. This merger produced the Swahili ethnic group and, with the mixture of their various languages, a *lingua franca* for eastern Africa.

Charles Miller, in *Lunatic Express,* describes the mixing process that gave rise to Swahili:

> ***For thousands of years, Persians, Indians, Mediterraneans and Arabs in their dhows have taken advantage of the seasonal winds breathing back and forth across the Indian Ocean with metronome regularity. Between October and April the winds blow from the northeast. They then veer 180 degrees and retrace an invisible path for the next six months.***[5]

Over a period of thousands of years, one could think of the monsoons as a sort of meteorological paving machine that converted the Indian Ocean into a boulevard for whatever maritime nations chose to ply it. Merchant sailors, particularly, used the monsoons for trade with a number of city-states that sprang up along the 2,000-mile littoral of East Africa that now delineates the basic Swahili territory. With this genesis, Swahili can be seen as a "participator" language, reflecting a variety of ethnic contributions geared to the needs of trade.

Remnants of this thousand-year Arabic trade can still be seen in Mombassa harbor. The cumbersome, lateen-rigged sailing vessels have changed little from the early days when slaves and ivory were the most likely cargo. Nowadays the vessels load tidewater mangrove logs destined for wood-starved Arabia and use diesel motors to assist the power of the wind.

5 Charles Miller, *Lunatic Express,* page 11, The Macmillan Co. 1971

The lateen-rigged sailing vessels have changed little from the slave-trading days

This old drawing shows how the slaves were packed into these old sailing vessels

Swahili's degree of sophistication is measured by its adoption as the official language of Kenya and Tanzania, albeit employed more solidly in Tanzania. The differences in use relates to their respective previous colonial rulers. In Tanzania, the haughty German administrators regarded their mother tongue as being too good for the natives as well as substantially beyond their general capability to learn it. In contrast, the British in Kenya had no reluctance about imposing English as the common voice of the land and they were amazingly successful. With English learned in every school, few were not conversant in the language.

The prevailing use of English in Kenya irritated Jomo Kenyatta, the revered Father of the Country, who decided it was unseemly for a newly independent government to conduct its formal affairs in the language of the previous colonial master. He issued the dictum, "Hereafter, Swahili will be the language of the National Assembly," effectively silencing many of the previously most vocal assembly members.

The Swahili language was provided with an important role by the missionary, Johann Ludwig Krapf. Born in 1810 Germany, Krapf learned the language as a consequence of being sent to East Africa by England's Church Missionary. He settled in Mombassa where he learned the language and subsequently translated the *New Testament* into Swahili. By 1850 he had completed his classic *Outline of the Elements of the Kiswahili Language.* This feat of having removed the language barrier earned him the accolade of having made the greatest contribution to the white men who followed him. It was to become a standard text for many missionaries, explorers, administrators, traders and settlers.

When it used the Arabic alphabet, Swahili was a vehicle for noteworthy literature from the beginning of the eighteenth century. After the missionaries introduced the Roman alphabet in the second half of the nineteenth century, Swahili writing has continued to flourish, producing some native authors of distinction.

Kenya Cattle-Raising Scheme

In the early seventies, the World Bank, with the participation of USAID and the British government, launched a massive social-engineering project. The intent? To settle a nomadic Kenyan cattle-raising people on fixed modern ranches. Through this radical reordering of lives, they sought to improve the existence of an entire ethnical group. Another objective was to increase beef production substantially by improving ranching methods and cattle ranges and by upgrading the varieties of cattle raised. The project objectives were clearly perceived to be needed and the technology applications so obvious, the budgeting of $50 million must not have presented a problem. It posed no harmful environmental threat.

Certainly, on the face of it, the proposed lifestyle changes offered enormous benefits for these wanderers who, in their everlasting need to search for grass and water for their cattle, could enjoy only minimal possessions and little of life's comforts. They had lived this closed, self-sufficient existence for centuries and might well have continued in this way except for two aspects of their lives that made them susceptible to outside attention.

First, their incompatibility with the central government of Kenya made them particularly vulnerable. Since these folk lived off the milk and blood of their cattle, they needed little money. Consequently, the government experienced chronic frustration over its inability to levy and collect taxes. A second threat to their nomadic way of life was the international horror that these nomad children were unable to obtain a formal education. The tribal perception of this problem ranked with the lack of opportunity to learn astronomy. The children were carefully instructed in tribal lore, history and the rest of learning applicable to their life, especially cattle care.

All in all, the modern humanists' response to this challenge to improve a primitive way of life was perhaps akin to the early African missionaries answering the call "to save the heathens."

The consortium, headed by the World Bank, did discuss its plan with the black government; understandably, this body could not object to the importation of $50 million, particularly with a quasi-Kenyan corporate agency charged to handle the money. Furthermore, the government had no reluctance in assuming the authority to speak for the nomadic people, who were a thorn in the nation's side anyway. The government's position held if these "wild men" could be induced to stay put, it would be all the better for control purposes.

The government's accedence to a program involving its own citizens apparently certified the project's legitimacy. An undertaking intending such an extreme effect on the lives of a people should have included those people in the planning. On the other hand, perhaps the planners couldn't conceive of the rejection of a program loaded with such wondrous benefits.

One does have to appreciate the pristine beauty of the development opportunity. The Maasai owned thousands of square miles in Kenya and Tanzania subject to the project. It needed only an application of proper technology to the land, grasses, water potential and an upgrading of the scrawny cattle,[6] and it could become Texas South. What people wouldn't jump at the chance to improve their wandering, nomadic lives? Without the always-on-the-move bondage to their cattle, they could join up with the rest of the population and at last send their kids to school. The logic was impeccable.

Here, the deadly virus of "lack of empathy" is released, for the project planners ignored the subjective nature of values. Consequently, they never ascertained whether or not the cattle people actually wanted their lives to be arbitrarily changed by outside "helpers," however well-meaning. Perhaps the cattle people didn't want to stay home all the time. And for sure, these cinnamon-colored Hamitic people didn't fancy becoming part of the predominantly black Bantu population.

While those in charge disregarded out of hand such personal considerations, they did attempt to consider almost all other important details. They indulged the bureaucratic penchant for employing consultants. Some thirty different specialists, related to all aspects of cattle raising and ranching as practiced in the West, fed their knowledge into the plan. This involved the study of diseases, grasses,

6 Scrawny or low grade may seem appropriate adjectives to apply to these Maasai cattle without realizing the probable evolutionary process which adapted them to their environment. The situation can be likened to that of the small western mustangs prior to the mingling of their genes with domesticated upgraded horses.

climate, water and many other details. In addition, sociologists and anthropologists were on the team. (One cannot help but wonder why local culture experts were either not included or not listened to.)

Two conditions governed the rationale for ranch design: the size of the Maasai clan and the potential cattle-carrying capacity of the particular property. A ranch of 250,000 acres, for instance, could feed enough cattle to support 300 members, while a mix of fewer people on higher quality land could get by with 10,000 acres.

The program began—and ended, for that matter—with a layout of thirty ranches located near the Tsavo Game Park, midway between Nairobi and Mombassa. Technoserve was invited to participate after the results of the first phase of the project had been revealed as a colossal failure. The World Bank officials had returned to Kenya to set up the second phase, only to find nothing had been accomplished, and the allocated money had been dissipated. The intended beneficiaries had indifferently gone off with their cattle as they had long been accustomed to doing.

To understand how this debacle actually happened—and worse, remained a secret—requires an understanding of the Western aid-givers' philosophy. The World Bank followed the conventional sociological wisdom of insisting trust be bestowed if trust is to be learned. The same logic applies to teaching responsibility. Accordingly, the first-phase funds were turned over to the inexperienced Kenyan officers, whose responsibility was to make preparations for the second-phase of the stocking program. This involved constructing roads, fire trails, water tanks and fencing.

It is strange the World Bank project planners could not have foreseen the inability of local corporation officers to handle such a program. The task was difficult. The local people had to hang on to the money and at the same time resist the pressure of powerful politicians bent on acquiring these subsidized ranch properties.[7]

7 My knowledge of the details of this project and what had happened up to that date, came from a verbal briefing by the working World Bank administrators and their Kenyan counterparts. I make this disclaimer because of the World Bank's refusal to provide documentary details of the plan's objectives and history.

Technoserve made a proposal to the English-Kenyan citizen who had been appointed as the new head of the corporation in charge of the project. It provided that Technoserve lend a company man as administrative manager of a new corporation whose shares were to be owned by the ranches. This manager would control the money and maintain scrupulous records for all the ranches; he would undertake the necessary purchase of heavy machinery and supervise the construction of roads and ponds on the ranches. In addition, he would organize a central facility to provide veterinary care, maintain stud bulls and furnish additional general help if needed. The harassed English project manager and World Bank officials regarded this as a splendid plan that might not only salvage this thirty-ranch program but could be applied worldwide.

By now, though, the program had lost its original objective of helping nomadic people, as a myriad of non-nomadic people had taken over the ownership of most of the ranches. Some ended up in the hands of politicians; an English company with Kenyan citizenship status acquired one; diverse interests became owners of others. It seemed to be a project worth salvaging and we put the plan into operation. The objective now became one of salvaging whatever possible the program had to offer.

A few ranches acquired cattle and had some initial success. But the project petered out. Had the cattle tribes been consulted in the first place, the designers would have known that adequate supplies of water for fixed ranches could never be counted on for even a short ten-year period. Basically, it was a bad idea, even if the resources had been adequate.

It is strange that none of the brains seeking to fashion a major transformation of the lives of a group of people could have failed to consider the tribal point of view. Had they done so, they might have learned these cattle people would have considered as absolutely outrageous a life devoted to the production of cows for a slaughter-house. To these Maa-speakers, cattle are family. Each animal is familiar to its owner. The number of cattle—not their quality—denotes the man's worth. He buys wives with cattle. Cattle-stealing furnishes an excuse for raids on other tribes. Milk and blood from cattle is their primary source of food.

So the question remains: How could these international experts have fashioned a project that failed so miserably—not only politically and socially, but in its first objective to produce more and better meat? One must conclude the experts, burdened with Western intellectual conditioning, planned according to abstractions; realism never had a chance. Only a task force of anthropologists, with knowledge of the language and culture and the time to study the conditions, perhaps five years, might have designed a successful program or alternatively, killed the idea at conception.

After suggesting that it was a bad idea from almost every standpoint, a review of the history of the plan supports the view that such faulty administration would have doomed the best program. The psychological, or perhaps philosophical, justification for turning over responsibility for the first phase to the corporation contained some specious reasoning at the very least. The project was, after all, designed for the Kenyan nation. The citizens should have the right to participate in accordance with the self-help principle of aid giving.

An added element of their philosophy is the contention their particular operating procedures teach virtues. Thus, positioning a group of administrators of limited experience at the head of a complex program and failing to provide adequate assistance or supervision is called a "learning experience." Moreover, entrusting them with unbelievable amounts of cash is supposed "to teach trust." Such practices, instead of teaching virtues and trust, only encourage corruption and waste.

The Maasai

The Maasai have long remained the ideal mental conceptualization of the Western European idea of an African "noble savage." Tall, elegant, handsome... seemingly proud and indifferent to all but the most necessary external influences.[8]

An African tribe that has undergone missionary salvation at home and received encouragement for state development from overseas could hardly fit the designation "savage," whether or not "noble." The Maasai have successfully resisted both types of intrusion into their culture. At least, they had to my amateur anthropological viewpoint at the time.

I had not read this book about the Maasai by S. S. Sankan when I gained my first sight of a trio striding along a downtown Nairobi street. But if I had and recalled the "noble savage" concept, I could have applied it to these folks. I was more struck by their similarity to pictures of old-time U.S. Indians. For a member of these groups to be injected into a European- or American-dressed population would provide a startling contrast. Imagine a band of Sioux on patrol in the

8 S.S. Ole Sankan, *The Maasai* (Dar es Salaam, Tanzania: East African Literature Bureau, n.d.), p. vii.

Chicago Loop, dressed in porcupine-quill-decorated buckskins, sporting an eagle feather in their head bands and moccasins on their feet.

Then picture the Maasai: ochre-colored blankets casually draped over one shoulder, falling a bit below the buttocks, shod in bull-hide sandals and heads held high with carefully structured hair arrangements fixed in place with ochre-colored grease. The visiting Maasai I saw carried no weapons, but on the range they are seldom far from their short lance-like spears; they often carry a bayonet-sized knife or sword as well.

To complement the alienness of dress when compared to the general European styles, is the body configuration. The complexion, a cinnamon color not too dissimilar from the brown-red of the American Indian, compared to the black pigmentation of the majority of the Kenyan people, definitely set them apart.

The slender body configuration, lighter skin color and other physical characteristics of the Maasai reflect their origins independently from the black sub-Saharan African. While they are generally considered to be Nilo-Hamitic from the north, there are other speculations about their roots. The most exotic theory identifies them as descendants of the lost legions of Mark Antony's Egyptian campaign, whose troops marched off into the desert and never returned. Did they produce a new ethnic group—a new tribe?

Supporting this explanation is the similarity of their weapons: the Maasai's short-handled, long-bladed lance is claimed to be patterned after the lance used by the Roman legions. In addition, the Maasai's style of fighting is thought to emulate Roman field tactics. In any event, their fighting style differs from the spear-throwing approach of the blacks. Maasai customs, as well, differ substantially from those blacks in the region, particularly in their earlier commitment to incessant warfare.

Although the Maasai recognize the black governments of Kenya and Tanzania, they stay as aloof from these bodies as they can. They travel in great circles in their vast territories with their cattle. They live primarily off the blood and milk of their cattle and meat of their goats. They still sporadically raid for cattle, but no longer collect women.

Their proud imperious bearing seemed to support the alleged Maasai practice of assigning degrees of worthiness to the various races. First in the eyes of the Maasai is, of course, the Maa-speakers: the Samburo and others whose primary love in life is cattle. To the dismay of those Westerners who become outraged at any value judgment based on skin color, especially if whites rate higher, the Maasai qualify whites as second in worth. In any event, blacks rank last on the Maasai quality chart.

Whether or not this legendary quality assessment is a basic cultural attitude, it has justification from their standpoint. In the early days, they struck terror into the hearts of black tribesmen with raids. The whites, on the other hand, gained stature, for after all, they conquered and ruled the land and, of considerable importance to the Maasai, they successfully cared for their cattle.

Now, the continuing low regard of the Maasai for blacks (and vice versa) is rooted in the incompatibility of lifestyles and cultures. The Maasai never experienced much confrontation with the English during the colonial period, but did endure a persistent harassment from the governments of Kenya and Tanzania, who don't hide their disgust over the tribe's perceived barbarism. The Maasai's unchanging lifestyle rankles many black leaders. One representative in the Tanzanian parliament proposed the Maasai be forced to wear decent clothing. He was jeered down by those wanting to know why the sight of bare buttocks on the range affronted him. The Maasai are an anomaly in modern East Africa.

The blacks justify their contempt for the cattle-grounded way of life by the consequences of that lifestyle. Because the Maasai are so often on the move, their belongings are few, their housing is simple and temporary, their clothing is meager—a blanket for the men and little more than beads for the women. They resist change and have little interest in the modern world.

The Maasai way of life is now assailed from another direction. Both black and white social engineers react with horror at the way the Maasai children are deprived of a formal education by the nomadic life. They are pressured to leave their children behind so they won't grow up as ignorant savages. The Maasai, however, fail to understand how an education obtained in a black-run school, teaching the remnants of a colonial curriculum, can help train their children for cattle care.

NOTE: People in Australia concerned with the welfare of aboriginal children living in a life style providing little or no opportunity for education or modern cultural development, created a major social scheme to rectify the situation, at least for those of a mixed race. From its inception in 1910 until 1970, 100,000 children were permanently separated from their parents and transplanted into the modern world.

The 1998 Europa World Fact book (1998, page 450) along with other sources record the hullabaloo and horror of the citizens upon their access to a two-year study made of the program. Apparently, no fruits of the program had been given any attention, although the program has produced lawyers, teachers and other achievers. Still, judging from the epithets reflecting the attitude of citizens to the scheme—racists, genocide, kidnapping and the like—no benefit could be worth the atrocity. There are demands, both for governmental apology and reparations. this has not happened yet, although most of the states have issued apologies.

Therefore the predictive costs to Maasai could be the same: automatic orphanhood and the demise of the Maasai ethnicity.

More than that, the Maasai have a close-knit family orientation. To be separated from their children is quite intolerable for both parents and children. The immersion in an alien culture for years on end is certain to wean the children from their heritage. Accordingly, such an "education" is not only useless to the Maasai, but it would alienate the children from their family, tribe and tradition. What life would these pseudo-orphans lead? What would they do?

There are many more general, seemingly insurmountable problems between the two ethnicities. The rapidly expanding populations of blacks covet the vast tracts of Maasai tribal land, arid though it is, and the Maasai bitterly resent this intrusion. They believe land should be dedicated to pasture and not farmed.

They contend plowing hurts the land and they are so right. In one instance, the Nairobi brewery inveigled a piece of land from a clan as a source of barley. After three years, the mined land was abandoned only to become a weed patch.

While the Maasai have sound reasoning for resisting agricultural uses of their pasture land, they are not keen either about the government attempt to take control of their territory for other uses. For example, when the government undertook construction of Amboseli game park, it ordered the Maasai cattle out of the area. The Maasai reaction was: if you insist on this policy, by morning every rhino will be dead. Legend? Well, Maasai cattle were still grazing, as were antelopes, rhino, zebras the last time I was there.

The cattle-dependent way of life is doomed. Eventually, the Maasai will be forced to yield to black pressure for a reduction of pasture land. This will break up the seasonal shifting of the range, a migratory program that allows their cattle to find fodder and water throughout the year. Is there any hope of achieving a compatibility between cattle-raising methods and farming? Developing fixed cattle ranches would seem to be the only possibility. But, as has been shown, one such gigantic $50 million ranch program—undertaken by the World Bank and American and English assistance agencies—failed. (see p. 154-156).

Even if the Maasai could control their present land tenure and modify their cattle-based existence, will the impact of social pressure doom them? What will be the outcome of an increasingly extensive schooling program, for instance? Will the grown-up, educated children scorn the lives of their parents and fail to replace them in the cattle life? Even if these lifestyle changes could be worked out, Mother Nature has her own way of solving problems. The claimed Maasai birthrate presages a declining population.

Can a reasonable projection of the Maasai future have any resemblance to the story of the American Indians' way of life? Will Maasai tribal remnants eventually be rounded up and relocated on the reservations? Some day we may observe these one-time cattle raiders standing around tourist areas, in full regalia, posing for tourist cameras.

If these threats to the Maasai way of life are not enough to overcome them, I witnessed a portent of another insidious danger that could debauch their proud independence: the beguilement of civilization. One day at about 9:00 a.m. I stopped in one of the few towns in Maasai territory at a cafe-bar for a bit of breakfast. I was astonished to see a couple dozen Maasai men in their Sunday best and sporting freshened coiffures, chatting and drinking beer. I was puzzled because I believed it was out of character. I wondered where they got the money for what was promising to be a long day of drinking. This type of drinking could raise some cash flow problems. Did they sell some of their treasured cattle? Perhaps they leased some land. They certainly did not deign to take jobs.

I had a nagging, uneasy feeling about the tableau, though I had never seen a drunken Maasai. Nevertheless, I remembered the character destruction of American Indians who had taken up alcohol. Primitive people do not seem to cope well with alcohol—we cannot give civilized people too high a mark either, for that matter. But I fear that if the Maasai got to liking alcohol, they could easily lose their model status in S. S. Sankan's vision of the "noble savage."

Daniel Arap Moi: Democracy Destroyer

"Kenya offers a sad story and a scenario too often repeated in many African countries. Kenya used to be highly respected by other African nations. It was one of the rare African edifices of prosperity, order, and stability—an enviable exception to the

cupidity, mismanagement, and violence that have afflicted much of the continent."[9]

Ayittey refers to the robust 6 percent economic growth in the 1960s and 1970s, as the envy of Africa. But he is fearful this progress is in danger of being aborted, not so much, he says, "because of defective economic policies but because of the increasing paranoia of the Daniel Arap Moi regime and a rapidly deteriorating political situation."

President Daniel Arap Moi

Moi's appointment as vice president (he was not elected) had a purpose other than actual succession to Kenya's first president, Jomo Kenyatta. The ruling Kikuyu clique—Kenyatta, the attorney general, and a few other ministers—sought a symbolic non-Kikuyu member to soften the solid Kikuyu image. Moreover, any political risk was abated by the constitutional restriction on the vice president's tenure to 90 days; at least this scenario reflected the political wisdom at the time.

If it was assumed this man from the small Kalenjin tribe in the highlands, with limited political standing and ambition (so it was thought), could be easily manipulated. It was a grave error. Following Kenyatta's death in 1978, ending his fourteen-year reign, vice president Moi undertook his acting-president responsibility with relish, marking the end of his passive compliance. By executive order, *sans* election, Moi simply declared himself president. He followed this boldness with the promulgation of the Preservation Act, again under the guise of an existing emergency, which resulted in hundreds of political dissidents—professors, students, journalists—being jailed. It

9 George B.N. Ayittey, *Africa Betrayed*, (New York: St. Martin's Press) 1992, p. 182.

was obvious Moi had been preparing this plan and list of enemies for some time, but where did the strength of his supporters come from?

Reporter Leslie Crawford, writing about Kenya in the *Financial Times Survey,* has satisfied my curiosity about Moi's political power grab from Kenya's largest ethnic group and traditional power holder, the Kikuyus. "Since 1978 president Moi has governed with a coalition of minority Rift Valley tribes, who resented Kikuyu domination under Jomo Kenyatta... and fear a continuation of Kikuyu power." As Crawford explains: "Of course, the greater number of Kikuyu voters underlies Moi's abhorrence of democratic voting procedures. From his standpoint, domination by the largest tribe is a consequence and not an ideological improvement over one-party rule."[10]

Ayittey details the next steps Moi took to buttress the security of his position. On June 17, 1982, Charles Mugane Njonjo, long-time friend of Moi's, engineered the adoption of a one-party-state through an amendment to the constitution—again, or still, citing threats to the security of the nation. The Kenyan African National Union (KANU) became the sole legal party. Only party members in good standing could vote or work for the government. KANU undertook to control all aspects of life and sought to curtail civil rights. Various professional and trade unions were banned, strikes were brutally suppressed and detention without trial became the norm ongoing policy.

Moi broke up a coup of disaffected soldiers; he court-marshaled 1,000 men and meted out long-term prison sentences to hundreds. Many more hundreds were detained without trial. Political arrests imprisoned university students and professors, former parliament members, even newspaper vendors. People from all walks of life feared for their safety. During the 1980s, much of the paranoia and hysteria that prevailed stemmed from the activities of an underground movement, the Union of Nationalists to Liberate Kenya. Moi

10 Leslie Crawford, "An African Test Case for Good Government," *Financial Times Survey. Kenya,* May 10, 1994.

regarded it as a fanatical socialist organization and anyone connected with it was arrested.

Ayittey gives an encyclopedic listing of atrocities resultant to Moi's obsessive search for total security. Individuals, churches, schools, universities fell under his administration's scrutiny; printed matter, even personal diaries were examined. All were subject to punishment. The courts and parliament "followed closely in his foot-steps." Voting was a farce, rigged to reveal each voter's preference. Any ballot cast other than the "correct" way would result in punishment: loss of a job, harassment or other measures of chastisement.

Ayittey reports how an Amnesty study found the "percentage of Kenyans imprisoned has come to be the highest in the world... Kenyan prisons are overcrowded and have deplorable facilities. In May 1986, contaminated water killed five inmates at Kodiaga Prison."

By 1990, important people summoned the courage to publicly call for change. Two former cabinet members, Kenneth Matiba and Charles Rubia, issued a statement: "We believe our single-party system is the single major contributory factor and almost solely the root cause of the political, economic and social woes we now face."[11]

These resolute men paid for their audacity. They were under surveillance, the wife and daughter of one of the men was beaten and both men were subsequently arrested. Nothing enraged Moi more than the mere mention of a multi-party political system. Nevertheless, his administration had begun feeding on itself. Change was inevitable.

Finally, it was outside forces who were responsible for instigating change. The donor organizations finally realized they were subsidizing some of the world's most vicious dictators and financial aid was being wasted on non-productive economies. They began looking for signs of democratic activity in other African donee countries. Tanzania escaped such scrutiny. It had a far more efficient public relations system than Kenya's brutal, single-party, "who cares" administration,

11 *Washington Times*, May 11, 1990, p. A8.

that utilized unfair voting procedures, the abolishment of civil rights and many other methods destructive of the citizens' social and political freedom.

Kenya's long-time friendship with the United States became strained consequent to U.S. nagging over the single-party government and detention without trial, torture and other attributes of its dictatorship. In 1991, Michael A. Hiltzik of the *Los Angeles Times* wrote of Kenya's disgruntlement. He explained how U.S. Ambassador Hempstone "appears to be a stand-in for what is really bugging the government of President Daniel Arap Moi: American officials' increasing criticism of Kenya's human rights record and a congressional move to freeze American aid to the country for the same reasons."[12]

Ambassador Hempstone agreed with this characterization, revealing "the embassy gave shelter to a prominent dissident, arranged for his departure from the country and issued pointed complaints about the Moi regime's general treatment of its political opponents." He pointed to examples: "Three leading dissidents have been in jail, without being charged, since July [1990]; their main offense appears to have been calling for an end to the 10-year, one-party rule of KANU." Hempstone warned the U.S. Congress was "increasingly inclined to expect recipients of foreign aid to make progress toward democracy, a criterion the Moi government was failing to meet."

Hiltzik reported Moi had considered a request for Hempstone's recall. Herman Cohen, U.S. Assistant for African Affairs, scotched that wish on a visit to Nairobi, and warning Moi that Hempstone's views fully reflected those of the American government. The Moi government's defense was it regarded its "human-rights record as superior to those of such neighbors as Ethiopia, Sudan and Uganda." But the U.S. State Department was unmoved by the argument.

In August 1992, Keith B. Richburg of the *Washington Post* wrote about "Kenya's Moi: Reluctant Candidate, Now Tough Foe." He told how Moi "saw the light," as it were, following the World Bank's

12 Michael A. Hiltzik, *Los Angeles* Times, March 19, 1991, p. A12. The following discussion and Hempstone quotes are from this article.

suspension of aid "pending Kenyan steps to curb widespread corruption and to revive trampled political liberties and human rights."

"Moi has ruled for 14 years. He only recently, and reluctantly, embraced multi-party politics, and he still has not set a date for the elections," Richburg wrote. "Moi's reluctance is emphasized by his activities; only nine months ago when it was politics as usual, Moi was staunchly defending his one-party rule with the usual crushing of opponents, 'like rats."' Despite the continued acts of oppression, Richburg noted, the World Bank's action got Moi's attention. "He has done an about-face, calling for an end to his party's constitutional monopoly on power, declaring he was ready to take on the opposition at the ballot box." [13]

Reporter Leslie Crawford also discussed the withholding of donee funds pending some improvement in democratic functions. "Kenya is being held as a test case for new donor policies linking aid to good government." Since November 1991, "the World Bank, IMF and other governments decided to withhold hundreds of millions of dollars of financial assistance as a protest against mounting corruption and against Kenya's political and economic failing."[14]

Moi's belated willingness to take on the opposition in an election was not an act of bravado. He must have been privy to the extent of dissension in his challengers' organizations. Officers of the largest opposition party, the Forum for the Restoration of Democracy, announced their intention to compete even though the party was in disarray, split into rival factions engaged in bitter name-calling and party squabbles.

On December 29, 1992, an election was held. The Associated Press reported: "More than 60 percent of the 7.6 million registered voters participated in Tuesday's ballot." The Kenyan Television Network gave Moi 1,796,233 votes to Matiba's 1,228,870, with only

13 Keith B. Richburg, "Kenya's Moi: Reluctant Candidate Now Tough Foe," *Washington Post*, reprinted in the *San Francisco Chronicle*, August 8, 1992, p. A10.

14 Leslie Crawford, "An African Test Case for Good Government," *Financial Times Survey, Kenya*, May 10, 1994.

19 out of 188 parliamentary districts not yet accounted for. The AP described the campaign as being "marred by widespread political violence and charges of gerrymandering and vote buying. Dozens were killed, thousands were displaced from their homes, candidates were stoned and party offices were burned." The international observers, although noting widespread problems, had yet to rule on the fairness of the election. From this AP report, the event resembled more a revolution than an election, except the "power" side won most votes, whatever the extent of the fraud. Predictably, the opposition leaders told reporters they rejected the results.[15]

In February 1993, the *Christian Science Monitor's* Robert M. Press wrote a follow-up story, "Kenyans are learning a lesson being forced on many Africans: the gains by political opposition groups through elections are no guarantee of change or peace." He went on to explain: "More than a month after Kenya's historical multiparty elections, in which opposition parties won 44 percent of the parliamentary seats, President Daniel Arap Moi is showing no sign of even recognizing there is an opposition."

As Press reported, Moi closed the new multi-party parliament after it met for one day. A director of political affairs could not give any date whatever as to when it might re-open. Disappointment was widespread among those who had high hopes for the benefits of a multi-party government. Press commented: "The message being sent [to the opposition] is: 'Your votes don't count.' 'That is a slap at the electorate.' 'Some Kenyans want to change the Constitution to strip the president of the power to open and close Parliament.'"[16]

In a procedural one-man-one-vote election, which was demanded of him, President Daniel Arap Moi won a five-year term. The expectation of the magic of a multiparty voting system failed to improve civil rights. What now?

15 Associated Press dispatch, *San Francisco Chronicle*, January 2, 1993.

16 Robert M. Press, "Kenyan Opposition Stymied Despite Election Success," *Christian Science Monitor,* February 1993.

Richard Haass, director of Foreign Policy Studies, Booking Institutions, editor of *Economic Sanction and America Diplomacy* argues in a November 1998 speech that economic sanctions have become the de facto recourse of the American government when trying to influence foreign countries in the Post-Cold War era. He lists a number of objectives. The U.S. involvement with Kenya is certainly one of them. While this course certainly indicates displeasure over non-compliance, it invariably causes economic damage, with more severe destitution among poorer citizens and only cosmetic improvements in the targeted government's activities.

In this instance, the equivalent of sanctions was to withhold designated funds from Kenya pending a unilateral determination of compliance with the ordered program. Makau wa Mutua, Projects Director for the Harvard Law School Human Rights Program, expressed his opinion in the restricting of funds: "Donor countries should not resume aid to Kenya on the basis of fraudulent elections. The West must not reward Moi for heightened government repression and disrespect for democracy and human rights."[17]

Stephen D. Hayes of the *Christian Science Monitor* also made these observations on the curtailment of funds: "The State Department is waiting for 'signals.' ...In a 24-month period Washington suspended much of its foreign military and economic assistance to Kenya and changed the 'rules of the game.'"

Hayes outlined other plans to withhold funds pending a series of additional economic and "good governance" reforms on Kenya's part. Congress, not to be outdone, expanded to five the criteria of Moi's required compliance list. Herman Cohen, Assistant Secretary of State, added another dimension. Finally, in October 1992, Congress passed yet another change in the steps Kenya must take before security assistance could be resumed. Nairobi expressed its frustration about such game playing: "The challenge of trying to 'satisfy'

17 Makua Wa Mutua, "Stung by Opposition Gains, Kenya Regime Returns to Politics of Intimidation," *Christian Science Monitor,* January 26, 1993, p. 19.

Uncle Sam is like playing football with the goal line moved farther back after each series of downs."[18]

The United States was merely flexing its muscles. If Moi is to be allowed to remain as head of the government, he should be given a coherent program. Also, after fourteen years, his administration has built up a complete system of vested interests and systems. Is he to replace all this as if he were redesigning a Harvard University model? Nevertheless, he is stuck with continued aggravation because he wasn't supposed to win his "cave in" multi-party election. And the western challenge of vote fraud seems more like donor face saving. What do they expect from an African election? The initial one at that.

One can ponder the selection of Kenya for this equivalence of an invasion. Why her and not Tanzania, Zimbabwe or a number of other single-party countries, equally and much more, guilty of civil right atrocities and semi-useless economic systems? The Kenyan government, bad and corrupt as it is, symbolizes declaration by the government the polls are now open to other parties and is not going to release any political prisoners.

Much had been written about the horrible conditions of the Kenyan prison and judicial systems. But Mary Anne Fitzgerald was more than an observer. Being a writer for a number of papers, *The Sunday Times, The Independent* and others, she foolhardily refused to bow to censorship of her criticism of the Moi regime. In her book, *Nomad*, published in 1994, she recounted her gruesome experience of months of incarceration consequent to enraging Moi, not only of her own experience but of her knowledge of the system—60,000 inmates in prisons designed for 14,000; corruption and breakdown of any form of justice.

An argument to support the position the donors of the world bear some responsibility for the condition of former colonial African countries can be found in a comparison of the conditions before and after European forays into continental Africa. The thousand tribes

18 Stephen D. Hayes, *Christian Science Monitor*, March 4, 1993, p. 18.

had, over the millennium, evolved a stable coexistence. Their traditional chiefs provided all the government they needed; they could feed themselves; they fought with spears rather than mass-killing weapons. Perhaps the most important safety feature they lost by coming into the new age was population stability. No baby survived beyond the tribe's capacity to provide for it. Now, feeding them has become accepted as a donor responsibility.

Would the tribes have been better off had they been allowed to evolve into something other than nations (not the impossibility of a Pan-Africa union)? Did the paternalistic assistance of the West that guided them into the modern age stifle a slower but more suitable evolution?

This speculation has no particular value unless it serves to induce a *mea culpa* attitude in the donor countries—a recognition these African countries, for the most part, are not now able to feed themselves nor create institutions that guarantee civil rights. And because of the two-four percent population growth rate, tied to the loss of the entrepreneurial element, this dependency on donors is likely to be permanent.

In spite of this dire analysis, will the present take-charge activities of the donor faction give these countries a new direction, a new start toward independent nationhood? The World Bank appears to have helped to turn the socio-economy of Ghana around and, according to Crawford, is supporting radical changes in Kenya: "The arithmetic of dwindling aid dollars has made talking with Kenya's distrustful donors an absolute imperative." Decreased aid, tendered by the effects of an enormous financial scandal consequent to irregularities over unsecured loans in the Central Bank, "jolted Kenya's decision makers to their senses. A rapprochement was sought with the World Bank and IMF." A new Central Bank governor, Mr. Micah Cheserem, instituted a reform program within months of his appointment. In January 1993, the newly appointed finance minister, Mr. Musalia Mudavadi, "began work on the most rapid deregulation of an economy Africa has ever seen."[19]

One must agree after careful analysis, the deregulation list is massive and appears to be a complete switch to a free market system.

> *The Kenya shilling was devalued and then floated. Exporters were allowed to keep their foreign exchange earnings. Restrictions on the reparations of profits and dividends were lifted. All price controls, with the exception of petroleum products, were abolished. The government opened to private traders the import and marketing of maize.*[20]

Among the many effects of the new system were increased opportunities in exports and it was no longer necessary to queue up and bribe to obtain import licenses.

If these reforms provide a free market for farmers, the improvement in food production could be immense. The reforms should encompass a private market provision for all the services the government now furnishes so poorly: services for seed, fertilizer, warehousing and mechanical equipment.

Alas, if the agricultural reform program is dependent on farmer trust of government, such development will have to overcome a thirty-year history of betrayal. The only solution for the food problem is for a completely uninvolved government.

With all the hand-wringing over depredation of black civil rights, no concern has been shown over the lack of rights of non-blacks. In many African countries, white, brown and yellow people have often become exiles from the land of their birth, suffering humiliation, losing property and even their lives. This plight has been ignored under the rubric "Africa for Africans."

Asians do have attributes which generate envy: their ostentatious affluence and their bearing. But how can the horrendous cost of racism in a developing country be ignored by donors who are subsidizing this cost?

19 Crawford, *Financial Times Survey,* "Kenya," May 10, 1994.

20 Ibid.

For instance, Kenya's expulsion of Asians started when Kenyatta was president with the passage of the Trade Licensing Act of 1967. Justification for the act pointed out "a major part of the economy was owned and operated by expatriates: Asians and British." The *Wall Street Journal* commented on the significance of the government's policy in Kenya's business world:

> ***Stepping up Kenyanization was the government answer. Although done more gradually and gently than in neighboring Uganda, the procedure still required a certain number of non-citizens to leave their jobs or shops and depart the country. The main targets are Indians, partly because of prejudice and partly because they tend to have the small retail stores the government figures Africans are most capable of running.***[21]

Undoubtedly, Africans were capable and they had a wide open opportunity. In 1973, an article in the *Wall Street Journal* reported that more than 1,500 traders had been told to get out. What the government never understood was the disinterest of blacks to take over the businesses. They did not want to work as hard as the Asians did for small rewards. The *Journal* reported this lapse in judgment had serious consequences: "The large town of Kisumu is on the verge of collapse because Africans aren't continuing the same sort of vital services in vacated Indian shops." Other businesses were more profitable.[22]

The inevitability of this kind of collapse was obvious to me when I lived in Kisumu in 1972. In a large farming area north of the town, I visited a modern, Asian-owned wholesale store. It was well-stocked with everything the small Asian-owned retail stores could need. Without this source close by, retail store-owners would have to travel to Kisumu.

21 "Contrasts in Nairobi: Hot Stocks and Beggars: Stability and Ferment," *Wall Street Journal*, September 26, 1973, p. 30.

22 Ibid.

The Asian wholesale lament was no African could be induced to take over the business: a modern building, fully stocked with tools, building materials and anything else that retailers would need. Actually, it was that no African would take the business over; a successor had been designated. They pointed to a watchmaker working away in a cubicle of the shop, but explained that he took no interest in the functioning of the business. He would never be able to do anything more than locate the cash and sell off everything. "What will these retailers do when we are gone?" was the rhetorical question. "Kisumu is too far to go for some salt, medicine or cloth." The *Wall Street Journal's* answer: "the rural business will 'collapse,' as will businesses in Kisumu."

An Asian-owned exquisitely designed peanut-processing plant was available for the asking, but no inquiries were made when I was there. Technoserve was asked to assist in the management of eight cotton gins, but no managers could be found. British mechanized farms were issued to ministers and their wives, who immediately began looking for managers: no luck. I visited dairies that had failed to dip the cattle and had let the surviving milk cows fend for themselves.

The example of Ugandan president Yoweri Museveni's program of inducing the return of the Asians could have spurred the Kenyan's government to review its thirty years of developmental handicap directly traceable to its Kenyanization policy. Uganda experienced the restoration of the huge sugar industry along with the creation of a healthy number of other job-creating endeavors resulting from this policy. The donor countries might be advised to assist Kenya in facing up to this resource.

EAST AFRICAN REMINISCENCES

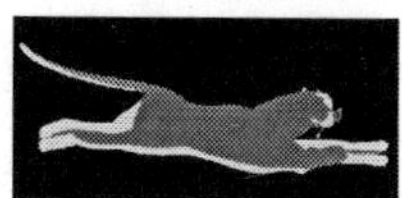

The Mysterious Borehole

The following incident illustrates how good intentions can lead to inappropriate results.

On one of the infrequent occasions I traveled the road through the arid area north of Mombassa, Kenya, I observed a dozen or so Maasai people lounging around a shed located some distance off the road. It appeared to be a family group, that is, not exclusively spear-armed warriors. The group included women with shaved heads, their bodies festooned with elaborate bead arrangements. Contrasted to the bald-headed women, the men make a big thing of their hair, dressing it with a combination of ochre and grease. The whole affair is tricked up in some intricate fashion.

The gathering eventually piqued my curiosity enough to cause me to investigate the reason for the congregation. What attracted them to this shadeless spot? Why weren't they off playing with their cattle?

I had always admired these proud, independent people and knew a few words of the Maa language. I decided to stop by, pat palms, play as much of the greeting game as I could manage and find out what anchored them to this particular spot.

They seemed unduly pleased with my visit. While they are a friendly people, the degree of welcome they showed a stranger exceeded my expectations. I found myself being gently maneuvered inside the shed, where they excitedly directed my attention to a huge diesel-powered pump installed over a borehole.

Well, that is nice, my smile meant to say, in answer to their smiles, which I interpreted as an indication of pride in their magnificent possession. Then, I noticed that it showed no evidence of ever having been turned on. There was no external piping, no watering trough or facility for using any water if any ever came up.

This was puzzling. Did they actually know the purpose of this monster? I mimed, "What is it?" seeking some indication they knew what they had. This caused a cessation of movement, a long silence and soon expressions of puzzlement replaced the smiles. Oh well, I thought, a mime I am not. I had obviously failed to get my question across, perhaps just as well.

Finally one of the men mimed the scene of cattle drinking. Many nodded their heads in agreement. Obviously, someone had explained the capability of this strange device to force the ground to give up water.

In a burst of virtuosity, I pretended an unsuccessful attempt to obtain a drink from the machine. This brought down the house—a real knee-slapping performance. But this hilarity quickly abated. Actually, a feeling of anxiety became pervasive. I no longer felt welcome and departed as gracefully as I could.

It struck me, if they thought this pump capable of producing water for their beloved cattle, it must be sacred. And while my antics were at first comical, they wanted no comedian around who might offend this mysterious thing. Obviously, I was of no practical help. I speculated they had been engaged in trying to work out some magical ritual or incantation to cause this device to perform. Their initial welcome to me could be a belief I might know the secret of this white man's marvel. Anyway, that is the way I worked out my experience, but who can know for sure? I have been baffled many times before over some inexplicable behavior of native African people.

But while I could only surmise the workings of the Maasai mind, I had a much stronger conviction I could guess the genesis of the pump installation. I had seen inoperative machinery standing unused many times on the continent. I understood this situation very well.

This inactive pump most likely was procured through a random act of generosity founded on erroneous assumptions. Some humanitarian group, probably a church, had selected a suitable group of people as a target for an act of benevolence. It may have been as simple as: "Let's provide a borehole and a pump to assist the desert people to water their cattle when there is a drought." Church members could find a project of this nature exciting and exotic.

Following this decision to act, funds are raised, a pump purchased—the best—a contractor is found and given a contract to drill a hole and install the pump. He sends a picture of the installation, surrounded by smiling villagers, back home. All the benefactors can feel warm about the assistance they are bestowing on their brethren overseas. Meanwhile the contractor, having discharged his obligation, departs.

The well-meaning sponsors will never know the outcome of their generosity. How could they have known the villagers would have no means of putting the pump to work? The fate of the gift was to rust and rot—forever useless.

I sought out the district officer. After all, someone had spent a lot of money on this installation, why not get some return? The officer said that a crew from Nairobi had arrived one day with a lorry load of equipment. The men drilled a borehole, installed the machine, built the shed and left.

"Why don't you start the pump and see if it pumps water?" His claim of not being authorized concealed his obvious ignorance of its mechanism and his demeanor indicated his comfort in not knowing.

I wondered how long the Maasai would wait for something to happen before disillusionment set in.

Broken Dreams

The failure of this project illustrates how an assistance giver's deviation from the project director's policies can result in frustration and loss of time. In 1973, Madeline, a young American volunteer, put together a unique program which was geared to salvage presumably unsalvageable, physically defective people. It had a built-in hidden defect—it superseded the plan of the district officer.

Madeline had been recruited to operate an organization called the Handicap Training Center in northern Kenya. An American church group funded the expenses of the endeavor, while the Kenyan government provided the buildings. The project fell under the jurisdiction of the district officer.

Madeline was to train handicapped people for jobs in the fabric printing trade. While the directions were a model of simplicity, she might have inquired what the officer had in mind as to function and detail. On the other hand, her recruiters back home may have told her, in the sweetest way, "It is your program and, although we organized and financed it, its success depends on your skills."

The word *handicapped* is subject to variable interpretation, but the conditions of some of the students she collected were "severe." The thirty individuals mostly suffered from the ravages of polio. Two had grotesque enlargements of body parts caused by elephantiasis.

The skills she sought to teach her students included tie-dying, a method in which the cloth is knotted or tied before dipping. The result can be a rainbow sunburst or other imaginative images. Silk-screen printing (also in the program) was another method. Bolts of cloth are stretched and fastened to long tables. The dye is applied to the cloth through stencils or masks to produce the wanted design on the cloth.

The most saleable products feature traditional African designs that have been passed down through the centuries. It is said each has a particular meaning, perhaps a moral or other message. For instance, the pictograph of two crossed crocodiles joined at the stomach, suggests the foolishness of two individuals fighting over food when they share the same stomach.

The dyed cloth becomes material for shirts, skirts, dresses, blouses, wall hangings and even drapes and furniture coverings. There is a market for good quality, properly selected designs. Tourists and expatriates greatly favor native handicrafts and "African art."

It didn't take Madeline long to realize that her mandate lacked realism. It was training, but to what end? She believed some of the applicants, with training, might become employable, but most had no chance of overcoming their profound handicaps to successfully compete in the job market. Moreover, there was no industry in the area as a source for jobs; only one poorly-managed factory.

Madeline realized the program as devised was a waste of time for everyone. She hadn't come to Africa to waste time nor to engage in some pointless "train the handicapped" program, regardless of the nice job description. She undertook to unilaterally revise her own mandate.

This inspiration kicked her imagination into high gear. Her vision resulted in a plan going far beyond a ceremony of handing out diplomas and then bidding the students goodbye. Her plan included a means of putting the trainees to work with the skills they would acquire. It required the expansion of the industry itself.

This reorientation of objective involved a total reevaluation of the training approach. She no longer intended to turn out as many viable trainees as possible and then dump those who couldn't make the grade. Her plan called for the development of an integrated work force. Each student would be trained to fit in somehow, determined by his physical limitations and trainability. Thus, instead of a random dispersal of a graduating class, this unitary work force would operate a dyeing factory they themselves would own. Thus, Madeline could complete her two-phase program of providing usable skills to all and expanding the industry at the same time.

Only a dedicated, idealistic individual, one with a world of faith in an ability to call down miracles, could believe that each of these folks could be trained to produce an economically useful contribution, especially to the extent the project could eventually become competitive and unsubsidized. But what a grand goal! To the extent this approach might become successful, the participants would gain independence and the pride of making an honest living. This was quite a contrast to the alternative life of a beggar, existing underfoot in the filth of a pedestrian sidewalk, beseeching alms.

It must be admitted Madeline's unilateral decision to revise the program developed for her suggests a bit of paternalism and arrogance. However well-intended, and how much of an improvement would result, she certainly lacked the authority to revise the program so radically. I had a disquieting feeling about her confidence that the success of her revision would absolve her of censure.

But arrogance or excessive independence is perhaps unjustified criticism. The very nature of assistance programs engender these attitudes of independence. The volunteer may have a feeling, unconsciously or even consciously, that he or she must know more than the local folks or they wouldn't need the help. Beyond that, she may have shared my experience: you seldom have contact with those in charge of the department responsible for your work.

True or not, feelings and protocol must be abided. A burst of creativity or change in the local plan can easily be perceived as disrespect, or at least as implied criticism of the originator's designs. Gratitude cannot be taken for granted.

If Madeline did harbor any fear of censure from the district officer, the enthusiasm of her students and the probability of the eventual success of her experiment must have alleviated any apprehensions.

As Madeline's program got underway, the plan did seem to work. Individuals with impaired legs sketched original designs; some supervised a department; some fabricated masks or mixed dyes. It appeared every one of them could contribute in some way, particularly after modifying tools and furniture.

Consider the adaptability of little Jomo, who ran his errands on a skateboard, chuckling and giggling at the consternation of visitors as they became aware of him zooming by their feet. Whether he carried a message or supplies, he certainly had a sense of participation and being part of the operation.

Armless Pete, with his judgment-day mien, could describe techniques for correcting errors and making improvements strictly through articulate explanations. And woe to anyone attempting to pass less than a perfect product past him.

On my periodic visits, strictly as a friend and well-wisher, I observed Madeline's superior training method: using an actual production line for teaching instead of a static, classroom approach. By the end of the year, the factory functioned as smoothly as one manned by "normal" workers—i.e., those concerned mainly with wages and lacking the compensating enthusiasm of the handicapped. The students' confidence in their expected success fueled endless speculation on the amount of money they could make after they owned their own factory.

Madeline felt pleased with her success, as well she should. She had proven her plan and the market. The morale of her class was one of total exuberance. But, in view of her success, she naively failed to anticipate any resistance to her *fait accompli.*

She needed only the district officer's permission to change the classification of her building from training class to experimental factory. If another training building could be built, her specially-designed workplaces and tools could be retained intact. Furthermore, customer confusion could be decreased. She planned to extend her year contract for a couple of months to see that things started right.

"Negative," ruled the district officer. "Since this class is ready to graduate, the students can look for jobs in the market. Now we start another training class."

There was no question that Madeline had grossly departed from the terms of her mandate, at least as far as the district officer was concerned. While she had provided tie-dye training, her eventual plan—to put the entire graduating class into business as a trained unit—was more than the district officer could contend with. How would he sell his superior on such a weird plan as creating a factory with a collection of workers having such terribly malformed bodies?

Particularly, when the original plan mandated training individuals, not synchronized groups.

And what of the graduating class? With their desperate physical disabilities, these people had little chance of finding jobs through the usual channels, even in a large tie-dye industry. They had been given a promise of salvation, only to have the promise smashed. It was the end of the only practicable way of obtaining an economically viable and satisfactory life for these people.

Poor Madeline. She had projected her American sense of values. These values are more apt to be influenced by results than the values of the African bureaucrat, who apparently placed a higher value on consistency with established rules and methods. Still, it wasn't fair. Everyone connected with the project knew of her intentions. Sometime during the course of the program, she could have been reoriented.

Madeline cried for several days. She didn't know how to cope with the shattered expectations and deep despair of her charges, or her own sense of a year wasted, stuck in an environment that had little going for it other than the possibility she could accomplish something good.

I never learned how the lady closed out her dream. She returned to the States. Nor did I find out if someone else took over the training program. It was not in my operating area. I was only an interested observer.

Ivory Harvesting? Poaching?

Reflections on an Impingement of the Ivory Trade

Ivory trafficking didn't appear too threatening to East Africa elephants in the 70s. Herds comprised of many dozen animals were scattered over the vast area. In the natural family mix, numerous members sported fully developed tusks, seemingly large enough to constitute an impediment to the animals' daily life. That is, until it became necessary to dig through the sand for water. Solitary old bulls took their ease in the shade of a tree, unmolested, although their tusks could weigh as much as one hundred pounds each. I remember my fourteen-year-old daughter's surprise when noticing this sign while learning to drive the Land Rover in a game park: "Elephants have the right of way."

On the road from Nairobi to Mombassa lived the pink elephants—named so for their reddish-brown color, which was from the iron oxide content of their dust baths. In our initial elephant experience, being grounded only in tales of elephant ivory collectors being trampled, we found ourselves in the midst of a herd of four or five family groups—little Dumbos, mamas and mature bulls engaged in lunching on tree branches. This close encounter occasioned a startled whimper demanding QUIET. No need. We might have been amidst a herd of sheep for all the attention we got.

Ivory wasn't free for the taking. It had value. A market existed. These countries exercised some control in the form of permits, licenses and the establishment of certain off-limits areas. This confluence of circumstances created a balance between the needs of the tourist trade and the ivory traffic.

I experienced a slice of the ivory trade in my office in downtown Kampala—second floor, capital city, downtown. Periodically, I would hear a racket coming from my Asian neighbor's office next door. It sounded like large chunks of firewood being dropped on the floor; only there was no need for a fireplace in this climate. On the other hand, I couldn't imagine an ordinary business office operation generating a noise that could only be made by a lot of heavy material being moved around.

As I drew near to the door of my noisy neighbor, I caught an odor, also not associated with an office, but more to a slaughter house. The smell was connected with slaughter all right: elephants and rhinos.

Three blacks had lugged about two dozen pairs of tusks up the stairs and dumped them on the floor. They stood waiting for the Asian to estimate the weight and quality to calculate their pay. It was rather ghastly, but not as distressing as the sight of the three rhino horns on top of the desk. While I suppose one animal life is no more precious than another, the rhino is far scarcer and presents no problem to the peasant farmers, as the elephants do.

This daylight, wide-open trafficking seemed awfully blatant. I asked the Asian how he got away with it. "Simple," he said. "I break no Uganda laws. This is ivory poached in Zaire and smuggled into Uganda for sale. I'm clear, but I do need Uganda exit permits (he then made a gesture suggesting bribery). Then it is legal merchandise in the trade."

The elephant herds were regarded as destructive nuisances by the peasant farmers. Their shambas (small farms or gardens) would be periodically wiped out. Forests and orchards were badly damaged. As might be expected, the farmers didn't share the government's interest in the elephants' value as a tourist attraction. In order to maintain some balance, the governments sometimes organized a thinning of the herds. The government of Rwanda hired the total slaughter of its remaining band.

The rhinos live in the arid regions and cause no harm to anyone, except occasionally to a camera-laden tourist maneuvering around to get a shot of the beasts' best side.

But economics became the elephants' undoing, and vanity that of the rhino. Ivory carvers bid up the price of raw ivory to the level where a native poacher could sell a tusk for enough to feed his family for a year. His trader or middleman, too often a minister (or equivalent) in the government, could buy a Mercedes after doing only a small amount of business.

The rhino's imminent demise, albeit connected with economics, has two additional pressures. The first is the belief of some Oriental men that the ingestion of ground rhino horn can gear up their libido to that of a twenty year old. The second comes from the status achieved by some rich Arabian youths, who sport a dagger handle made of rhino horn.

Strange, the rippling effects of somewhat inconsequential decisions. An increasing desire for carved ivory can result in the decimation of the elephant herds thousands of miles away, with a corollary effect of increasing corruption in governments. Perhaps this is a parallel to the old legend that the decision to shorten women's skirts an inch could result in starvation of many Chinese textile workers.

Although new programs for saving the elephant are unlikely, there is an experiment being tried in a South African game park to save the rhino. The animal is dehorned. It amounts to a "give up your horn and live," proposition. One can speculate about the effect on the breeding habits.

The Great Game Park Safari

We were in the heart of the most stupendous system of east African game parks. This system was in a state of flux. Uganda's was under destruction consequent to the exodus of the Asians, who had handled the tourist trade, and the general break-down in government supervision and protection. Kenya and Tanzania were intermittently closing their borders to each other's traffic. It seemed best to get our kids over here—Carol, Lynnanne, Kent and companions—for what might be the last chance for a grand sweep of the Kenya-Tanzanian parks. It certainly appeared that way at the time.

Once they arrived, we loaded the Land Rover and set out with the camping equipment, food and film that we expected to need.

Little Boy Robbers

On the first night of our intended month-long tour of the game parks, we camped on the rim of Ngorongoro crater. The enormous cup of this extinct volcanic crater is home for as large a variety of animals that can be found in Africa. Located in northern Tanzania, it is definitely an important segment in the loops of parks. Two other campers shared our organized campsite.

I broke a cardinal rule about leaving valuables in the car, regardless of the security of the locks. Just before our party settled into sleep, one of our sharpest ears heard a slight rattle by the Rover. Alarm, alarm! We rushed out to find a back door open and a gutted vehicle.

My son and I hopped in the car and charged off in pursuit. Shortly, our lights swept across an area under a tree to reveal a sight that brought us to a screeching halt. There in a pile, were our belongings—cameras, glasses, everything. But there was other loot as well. Obviously, we had stumbled on a staging area, prior to pick-up time. We immediately alerted the other campers, who came to claim their belongings.

The next morning, one of the women from the other camp related her experience during the night while sleeping in her car. She awoke, she said, to find a ten-year-old boy peering in at her.

Before departing, we located an ongoing robber stakeout near the edge of the site. This lair boasted a bench arrangement, there were clothes hanging on branches, beer cans tossed about and a valuable, neatly rolled sleeping bag stashed in the crotch of a tree. We decided against confiscating it.

Dumbo

One of the most unlikely fates to fear, is to be trampled to death by a baby elephant. Well, not actually being trampled under the feet of the little beast itself; but just having the baby alert its mother to consider such a deed.

We had encountered many elephants on our safari, as well as on other occasions. And we saw no reason not to agree with the general wisdom: that ordinarily elephants pose little threat. It came to pass, however, the word "ordinarily" was no safety net. We were cruising through a wooded area in a Tanzanian game park with the kids seated

Dumbo sounding the alarm

on the roof of the Land Rover. Suddenly we came upon a herd of elephants busily lunching on the limbs of trees. No problem; we just relaxed and waited for them to meander across the road. Suddenly, a little Dumbo swung his head in our direction and with ears trained forward and trunk raised, he sounded a juvenile trumpet of alarm. Instantly, the whole herd opened up yards and yards of ears and swung their head in our direction. Alerted, twenty elephants focused on our vehicle. "Reverse and floor it, Dad," was the instruction I heard from topside. However, to not frighten the little sentinel, I eased back slowly.

The herd opened up yards of ears

At that moment, a story I'd heard came to mind. The incident supposedly occurred when a Volkswagen van tour impatiently honked at an elephant blocking the road. The beast ambled over to the bus, hooked his trunk under a fender and rolled the vehicle over, passengers—and all.

The Month-Long Safari Ends

Virtually any pleasure is subject to satiation. Thus, after daily sighting most of the African animals we had ever heard of, and some we had not, we began to feel we had seen them all—over and over again. Yet, the Samburo National Reserve was different and presented several mysteries.

For instance, we had long been familiar with the thousands of common, wide-striped zebra, those with the elongated horse-like ears. But, in this park, we encountered the Grevy, a narrow-striped zebra with comical, Mickey Mouse-like ears.

Despite the bark-like sound zebras make (so unlike the neigh of the horse), these animals are cousins to the horse. Both varieties can mate with horses. The mating of a Grevy with a horse produces "zebroids." If a wide-striped zebra mates with a horse it results in a "zedonk," the African equivalent of the donkey.

A gerenuk

In the Samburo Reserve even the giraffe has changed his coat. The color arrangement of most giraffes is orange-brown to black irregular spots splattered on a yellowish tan background. Here, these animals' skin design has given them the elegant designation of "reticulated giraffes." Their color pattern has narrow white lines separating a larger spot positioned on a dark background.

The gerenuk, a quite different antelope, makes his home in Samburo. This antelope has evolved to have an extraordinarily elongated neck, which enables him to reach high into a tree to lunch on leaves while standing on his long hind legs.

During this month of travel through Tanzania and Kenya game parks, we experienced many encounters with the African animal kingdom. We saw lions lying on the large, lower limbs of trees, taking their ease in the cooler air. Once we had observed a leopard napping on a limb halfway up a tree; not unusual, except this cat had the carcass of a full-grown Thompson's gazelle wedged in a fork of the tree above his resting place. How it managed to maneuver an animal as large and heavy as the gazelle high into a tree staggers the imagination.

The leopard in the tree

After accompanying hundreds of thousands of antelope, zebras and buffalo on their annual migration route out of Tanzania, across the Serengeti Plain to Maasai Mara in Kenya, I mentioned the last park on our itinerary. The response of this jaded group was, "Enough, Dad! No more animals! Please. Let's get back to Nairobi." And that is what we did.

Kenya's Two Remote Lakes

Lakes Baringo and Rudolf (now Turkana) are two Kenyan geographical landmarks that appeared on my "Must-Visit" list. Both lakes are due north of ofNairobi on the same north/south fault: Baringo 125 miles away and Rudolf 125 beyond that. Lake Baringo gained historical importance by being the most northern stopover in Kenya for caravans seeking food provisions and rest before continuing on through the forbidding country to the north.

We read that an expedition led by Count Samuel Teleki von Szek and Ludwig von Höhnel had stopped at Baringo for last-minute provisions before marching off on their search for Lake Rudolf somewhere in the unknown. The record of the hardships of their trip—fighting hostile tribesmen, unbearable thirst and often near starvation—leading to their final triumphant discovery was a story I hoped to read more about.

I was sure we would manage a visit to Lake Rudolf some day, but this particular Christmas morning, my wife and I climbed into the Land Rover and departed Nairobi—Lake Baringo our destination. We soon arrived at an inn that was now located hundreds of yards from a receding lake shore.

The inn, we discovered, was closed to drop-in trade because of planned Christmas festivities. The lady who owned the inn explained it was primarily a family affair with a few regular guests. Fortunately, she graciously invited us to stay the night and enjoy the holiday with them. We accepted with pleasure.

After everyone had arrived, we noticed the family part of the guest list appeared to be two almost identical sets of children: each set was of mixed gender and had similar age groups ranging from those attending elementary school to the upper teens. My wife noticed a genetic similarity between the groups as well. It was curious enough to ask about.

There was nothing remarkable about the explanation: the two sets of children had the same father, but different mothers. Our charming hostess was one of the mothers—the only one present.

Polygamy is legal in Kenya, although one usually relates this permissiveness to the customs of the black citizens.

Another set of guests was a chartered plane load of Italians who apparently made this trip an annual event. The adults stayed with us on shore, while their kids occupied a lodge to themselves on an island in the lake. A modern safari leader—cameras, not guns—was also a guest, and put together a marvelous trip which I couldn't manage to find a way to join.

Another guest was a Leakey brother, who owned a venomous snake ranch down the road. He invited us to visit and we did just that the following morning. A black handler entertained us by "handling" those deadly poisonous creatures, including a horned viper. I inquired about the cause of a shortened pinky finger. He was pleased I had noticed the mutilated finger and smiled as if I had complimented him in some way.

"I chopped it off with a machete after this old fellow bit me," he said.

"You manufacture anti-venom serum here. Why didn't you run into the lab and give yourself a shot?" I asked.

Another smile. "You don't understand. You get bitten by this old fellow," he said, "you drop dead before you run twenty steps." This friendly snake handler busted the supposed given that Africans have an inordinate fear of snakes. But I had more admiration for his lightning recognition of the need to sacrifice a finger.

It turned out that most of the people at the lodge were "birders." Following the visit to the snake farm, nothing would do until we visited some cliffs up a ways, the home of a rare species. With one of the hands as a driver-guide, we set out. I don't remember much about the birds, but I do have a vivid memory of a stop we made at a Potok village.

The Potoks are a semi-nomadic, cattle-loving people, probably Maa-speakers. They have a distinctly different skin color and different origins from the majority of Bantu-speaking blacks. The women adorn their bodies with beads heavily enough to serve as clothing. The men shunned clothes as well, although some sported an over-

Potok woman in all her finery

the-shoulder blanket. Nakedness aside, these people's customs and environment brought on a strong itch in my camera shutter-finger. But I knew how risky picture-taking can be when these cinnamon-colored cattle-loving people are the target. Actually, it's legally prohibited to "shoot" their Maasai cousins.

So, with a certain amount of trepidation, I instructed our guide to inquire politely if I could capture on film a particularly photogenic young woman's perfect body. My offer, of course, included a model's fee. Our guide-interpreter exhibited more than a little hesitance in broaching such a request. But he managed and returned with her reply.

"You can't offer me enough money to allow you to take my picture. If you do it anyway, my brother," she pointed to a man lounging against a wall watching, "will do something to you."

The interpreter was too nervous to provide the specifics of the threat and he was on the verge of leaving without us. No matter, I could read the message in this young woman's eyes. And since these cattle people sleep with their spears, I decided to drop it.

The story of this incident might have ended there except that something the driver said later set me to thinking. "These Potoks were formerly known as 'Suks,'" he explained. This information tied in with an event recorded by von Höhnel about the Lake Rudolf expedition. He wrote that following their first departure from Baringo, the rumor of an impending attack by the Suks forced them back to Baringo for protection. Later, by conducting a raid on the ancestors of these same Suks, the exhausted, starving expedition obtained enough food to complete their return march from Lake Rudolf.

❖ ❖ ❖

Some time following this visit to Lake Baringo, a pending special astronomical event prompted our seeking out the second "Must Visit" lake. In 1974, Kenya anticipated a total eclipse of the sun. Nairobi served as a staging point for an influx of scientists from around the world eager to witness and study a rare natural phenomenon: a solar eclipse featuring five planets visible at one time.

Arrangements had been made to transport the scientists and their loads of highly specialized equipment to an island in the middle of Lake Turkana (formerly called Rudolf). That specific location was on the latitudinal line where the sun would be obscured by the shadow of the moon for a theoretical maximum of seven minutes and forty seconds. At the same time, such an isolated encampment would help the scientists avoid problems that large groups of bystanders might pose.

My young daughter, Lynnanne, and I decided we must experience this once-in-a-lifetime phenomenon—at Lake Turkana. (We never did see any of the scientists.)

❖ ❖ ❖

I had gained some respect for the terrain we were to travel from reading about the harrowing, near-fatal experience of the Teleki/von Höhnel expedition. Furthermore, remembering Alistair Graham's description of this "most remote spot on earth," I felt reassured to be part of a caravan of two Land Rovers in addition to our own.

> ***[Lake Rudolf is] awkward to get to, uncomfortable when reached, and dangerous if meddled with. It lies in the Great Rift Valley just south of the Ethiopian highlands. . .a 180-mile-long trough, six to 30 miles wide, of slippery green water, brackish enough to make one vomit and vindictive enough to make one hate.***[1]

1 Alistair Graham, *Eyelids of Morning*, illus. by Peter Beard, A. & W Visual Library (New York: Nework Graphic Society Ltd., 1973), p. 19.

(The lake's color prompted another writer to give it the romantic name the "Jade Sea"[2].)

An encyclopedia gives a more objective description of this desolate area "in northwest Kenya and southeast Ethiopia at an altitude of 1,200 feet. Surrounded as it is by barren volcanic mountains, the lake is the focus of interior drainage and, with no outlet, is becoming increasingly saline."

⊠ ⊠ ⊠

My passenger manifest included a Chinese Peace Corps fellow, who was forever demonstrating the martial art stance of a contemporary Chinese screen personality. He also delighted in acting the part of a Chinese immigrant stereotype. Additionally, there were two young women, barely twenty-one, who had come to Kenya as Canadian Peace Corps volunteers with assignments to teach at a national girls' school. Upon their arrival, one of the girls had been assigned as head mistress of this 150-student school. By their own admission, both were "blazing feminists." Whatever the importance of that statement was, they found no need to call on we men for help with the Coleman stove or anything else on the trip.

Loaded with fuel, water, food and camping equipment, we set out. The first night, we stopped over at a Catholic mission. I feel confident the priest gave me all the heavenly points about our trip ahead in return for the pineapple I left with him.

Following this stop, we entered the area that could have been the inspiration for the term "trackless waste." It was a truly desolate landscape, totally arid, bearing only a few scattered acacia trees and no observable human habitation. A game park it was not. There were misleading tracks to sort out; certainly no signs. Luckily, one driver had been over the route before and guessed right in choosing directions.

2 John Hillaby, *Journey to the Jade Sea* (London: Constable and Co. Ltd., 1964).

Actually, it seemed he had been everywhere before. By his travel history and way of handling his six-cylinder machine, one might conclude he had been a mad biker in his youth. My four-cylinder steed was taxed even with its double transmission, which gave it strength (figuratively) to climb a tree, admittedly at about the speed of a snail.

We encountered no other traffic or humans, though a partially buried Rover in a dry creek bed provided evidence of past travel. We learned it had been caught in mid-channel by a sudden roaring flash flood of water from an up-country cloudburst. Were the driver and passengers of the destroyed vehicle buried under the sand? Or did he—they—have companions to rescue them from this lonely, desolate area? We learned to gun our Rovers across other such locations and took comfort in our companions.

Near the end of the journey, we came to a small settlement called Lodwar. It had distinguished itself by being the site of Jomo Kenyatta's exile. More immediately important to us was the repair shop mechanic who boasted he could repair any Land Rover. Luckily, we had no need to challenge his claim and drove on to the western shore of Lake Rudolf. There we set up a campsite and waited for the heavenly spectacle. Meanwhile, we had the opportunity to explore the lake and our surroundings.

The El Molo, a very primitive and dying tribe, whose natural livelihood depended on fishing and crocodile killing, were living on the eastern side of the lake. The few people on our side were dropouts from the cattle-loving, semi-nomadic, warrior people known as the Turkans. (Following Kenya's independence from Britain, the Lake's European name of Rudolf was changed to Lake Turkana, reflecting its location in Turkanaland.) But the few Turkanas we saw were, in no respect, warlike; having been disowned by their own people, they were thoroughly demoralized and reduced to living on fish, counter to their culture.

A missionary station had been built nearby, a testament that every soul, however lowly, deserves to be saved. A casual observer might wonder about the number in need in that small field. The only other non-native establishment was a fishing lodge. It has much to offer sportsmen. The lake is a natural fish and crocodile nursery. There are catfish, flatfish and giant perch weighing up to 200 pounds; the leviathan crocks, which can be 20 feet long, are a world phenomenon.

We needed to acclimate ourselves to the 120-degree dry heat. Lynnanne solved a problem of breaking hair caused by the heat by lacing her braids with canned margarine and then covering her greased coiffure with a scarf.

One startling characteristic of this wilderness was the total lack of artificial light at night. At 10:00 p.m., when the generator light shut down at the missionary house on the hill, the only light came from the stars, with occasional streakers adding variety, lending reality to Homer's "light of heaven."

As is true of women the world over, I suppose, the Turkana ladies, whose sole apparent possessions were the beads on their bodies, still managed to create some trade goods. Centimeter-sized drilled discs of ostrich egg shells, meticulously strung, created a solid ivory-colored necklace. Another novelty was a necklace fabricated from the vertebra of the large lake fish. They made some sales to the extent one had coins. Paper money would move no merchandise.

When time for raising the curtain on this show came closer, we checked our dark glasses and the settings on our cameras. We had been told that camera settings could not be seen during the blackout. True. As the countdown began to proceed, our anticipation increased proportionately. Subconsciously, we developed an urge to get the show started and began to feel like an audience kept waiting too long. Perhaps we should have expressed our impatience and clapped our hands in unison.

The anticipated attraction began—on time. There was no possibility of disappointment. On cue, as if controlled by a rheostat, the light dimmed to the point of darkness equivalent to a moonlight-filled night. The birds flew in from the lake to roost and fell silent. Curiously, the waves dropped in height from around three feet to inches. The stars came out in full array. A band of sunlight, brightened by contrast to the darkness, encircled the horizon. The Baily's beads, caused by the sun's rays breaking through the irregularities on the moon's surface, appeared to dance as they continuously changed in size and location during the sliding of the mask across the sun. The "prominences" caused by flaming gas eruptions contrasting with the face of the black moon disc added variety to the phenomenon.

As awe-inspiring as an eclipse is to a sophisticated person prepared for such an event, the phenomenon of steadily decreasing sunlight to near-total darkness in the middle of the day must be absolutely terrifying to a person unable to understand what is happening.

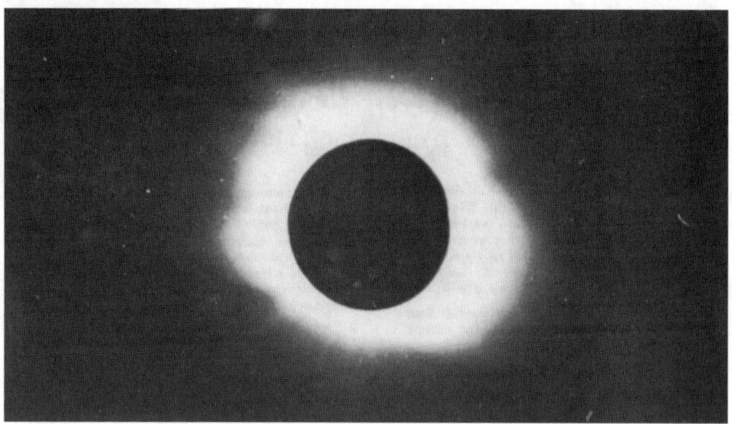

The awe-inspiring total eclipse

The Kenyan government had announced a program of enlightenment to educate the primitive people living on the projected narrow path of darkness along the earth's surface. Specifically, it sought to warn against the danger to the eyesight from gazing at the strange thing happening to the sun. But we saw no evidence of these government efforts and we had no chance to observe the reactions of the locals—since by the conclusion of the show, they had all vanished from our vicinity.

Nairobi's partial eclipse, far outside the exact pathway, would have been a non-event to us. At that distance, the sky loses no more light than would occur from a heavy cloud cover. Observers there could not experience the eerie effect of blackness, the stars and a blazing corona encircling the face of the moon. We rejoiced at our having visited the spot where we could witness this glorious event.

⌘ ⌘ ⌘

Ludwig von Höhnel

We might ask why an Austrian count, Teleki von Szek, and a young navy lieutenant, Ludwig von Höhnel, with connections in Austrian society, would broaden the scope of a hunting safari to explore the unknown lands north of Lake Baringo, with the goal of locating a legendary great lake.

Count Teleki

Explorer Joseph Thomson's book *Through Maasai Land,* published in 1885, revealed the original impetus that started Teleki organizing the safari. Thomson described the myriad game animals, especially rhino, elephant, buffalo and lion (the big four) running wild in the area around the Baringo and Victoria lakes. With the blessing of his friend Crown Prince Rudolf of Austria, Teleki had completed his plans by the end of 1886, following the publication of the book.

Rudolf's help may not have ended with the big-game hunting project. Did Rudolf lure Teleki away from his original plans with the siren song of "exploration"? Did he drop a suggestion such as, "Since you're already organized, why don't you run up north and check out Thomson's story about an inland sea or lake somewhere north of Baringo? It's no-man's country and needs some exploration anyway. To add legitimacy to the expedition, I can introduce you to a chap named von Höhnel to be your geographer and recorder."

In retrospect, if this scenario is valid, seldom has a friend urged a more disastrous program change on anyone. Teleki gave up—or at least put on hold—his plans for a hunting safari in the most salubrious geographical area on the continent, where an infinite number and variety of big game animals roamed. In exchange for what? As it turned out, he had chosen a thirteen-month-long journey of hardship and deprivation through a vast no-man's land whose aridity and ruggedness could not have been imagined. But the journey did have a reward: he did at last reach the Jade Sea.

The idea may have taken little persuasion. Under the circumstances in which Teleki found himself, he could well have rejoiced at the opportunity to conduct some worthwhile exploration because in the late 1880s, there was little left to discover on the continent. Speke had located the source of the Nile in 1861. By the time Livingstone died in 1873, he had walked alone the full width of the continent and back again. Stanley had completed his great 1874-77 transcontinental journey tracing the huge Congo from its source to the Atlantic. And here, Teleki had the opportunity to explore the unknown northern section of Kenya, hitherto closed to European penetration by savage tribes. What a goal: a mysterious lake! It had to be discovered.

The list of provisions for the expedition reveals another explanation for the ease with which Teleki signed on for his foray into the unknown. The mixture of supplies indicates a joint-purpose campaign. In addition to basic materials that could be expected for an exploratory trip, he brought in wine and all the comforts considered necessary for a lavish hunting safari. And of course, he spared no expense in obtaining first-rate firearms; he had an assortment of five rifles produced by the world's best craftsmen. In view of the copious amounts of ammunition usually expended on hunts, his supply must have loaded up a number of porters.

Richard Burton, the eminent explorer, provided what turned out to be the most valuable advice Teleki received. He urged the recruiting of Somalis as personal escorts. Following Burton's suggestion, Teleki signed on eight Somalis, headed by Dualla Idris. It is hard to

Richard Burton

believe that this young Somali, with an illustrious resumé even then, was only twenty-six years old. For six years, he had been one of Stanley's most trusted and faithful followers in the Congo. He had once guided an expedition to Somalia, which was rough duty in itself.

Dualla Idris rose to a position of undisputed authority with Teleki, who heartily acknowledged his worth: "Every day we learnt to value Dualla more; he was such a sympathetic fellow, so thoroughly to be relied upon." This praise was surely deserved. He was connected in some way to the solution of every desperate problem that arose. One can easily credit him with having saved the expedition.

Dualla Idris

Dualla later received recognition as a key man in the success of Lord Lugard's expedition into Uganda with this accolade: "He [Dualla] was the most energetic, valuable native I have ever met, thoroughly trustworthy and very conscientious and willing."[3]

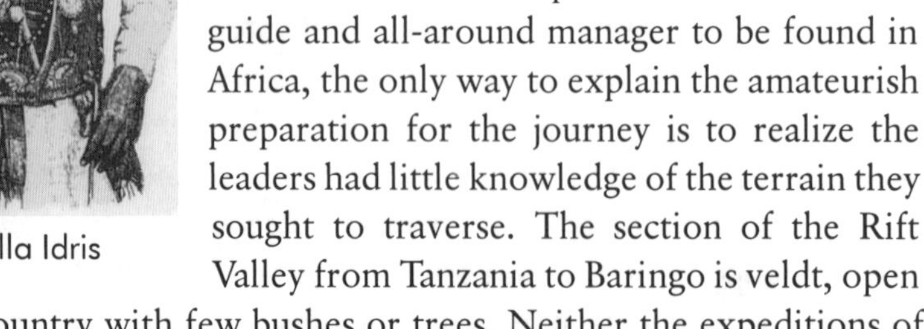

Since Teleki's expedition had the best guide and all-around manager to be found in Africa, the only way to explain the amateurish preparation for the journey is to realize the leaders had little knowledge of the terrain they sought to traverse. The section of the Rift Valley from Tanzania to Baringo is veldt, open grassy country with few bushes or trees. Neither the expeditions of Burton-Speke or Teleki's mentor, Thomson, had encountered any geographical difficulty in leading their head-loaded porter trains the length of their respective trips. Otherwise, how could Teleki have

3 Nigel Pavitt, *Kenya, The First Explorers*, p. 143, St. Martin's Press, 1989

dreamt of transporting thirty-five tons of stock, including a disassembled iron boat in six sections and a canvas boat in two. This inventory involved 470 head loads of goods of every conceivable type. As expected, the number of porters necessary to move this enormous load could not be assembled. In the never-ending quest for new recruits, the head count changed daily, the results of recruitment, desertions and deaths.

However well equipped, on January 23, 1887, the Austrian Count Samuel Teleki von Szek and naval officer Ludwig van Höhnel, as second in command, set out from Zanzibar, leading a force of 283 people to seek the legendary "great lake" in northern Kenya. They had charted Lake Baringo, approximately 500 miles away, as their last food supply stop.

They made do with donkeys as far as possible. The first attempt proved to be hilariously impossible. The herd they acquired was untrained and resisted whenever anything was placed on their backs. This episode elicited a rueful comment from von Höhnel: "I soon gave up the idea that one can wander about Africa in a light-hearted way." Vast quantities of goods had to be left behind, perhaps to be picked up later but most likely abandoned. The iron boat was the first item to be abandoned. By the time the expedition entered Maasai land, at the southern border of Kenya, the group numbered 265 men.

The account of the expedition's good relations with the dreaded Maasai, who had sealed their territory until the penetration by Thomson, was in stark contrast to his trip four years earlier. The expedition leaders would later contrast this friendly relationship with their treatment by the Kikuyus (unfavorable for the Kikuyus), whose territory they were to enter upon reaching the Ngong Hills staging area (the site of present-day Nairobi).

They were now midway between the Taveta supply point, near Kilimanjaro and Baringo, their last station. To reach Baringo they should have retraced Thomson's direct route through the center of the country. However, they made a sixty-mile detour eastward to Mt. Kenya. Teleki loved to assault mountains. He had climbed to within 2,000 feet of the summit of Kilimanjaro and was to climb up to

13,600 feet on Mt. Kenya, most likely becoming the first white man to climb to the snow line.

A view of Mt Kenya

The expedition soon experienced the difference in the hospitality quotient between tribes. The expected eight-day journey through Kikuyu territory to Baringo turned into a nightmarish six weeks, with the loss of eight men. They were harassed, treated to overbearing insolence, endured losses by theft and were always just barely successful in defusing explosive situations. The men were forever marching in the midst of thousands of semi-hostile warriors, never knowing when aggression would increase.

Finally, Dualla lost his temper over some particularly belligerent act. He opened fire, thus signaling a general assault on the pugnacious warriors. Thus aroused, the expedition men went on to set fire to several villages and to confiscate a herd of 1,300 sheep and goats and ninety cows. This provided enough food to reach Baringo.

The expedition met with great disappointment when they finally arrived at Lake Baringo. The area was beset with the same drought and food shortages to be encountered on the balance of the journey. Ready to explore the great unknown, they had little food and no great opportunities for acquiring any.

In spite of their fights with the Kikuyu tribes, Dualla, with 117 men, was sent back in a partially successful attempt to trade for food. While desperate measures were being taken to acquire food, von Höhnel was fighting to stave off death from dysentery.

In August, the expedition, now down to only 238 men, decided to forge onward, with only enough food for about two weeks. They began a series of grueling marches and sought food along the route in a land afflicted with famine. To add to their woes, water was chronically inadequate in quantity and of a vile quality. It was often impossible to find. To exacerbate this problem, few of the men had calabashes for storing water. Several times sickness threatened to abort the expedition. Von Höhnel had a relapse of his dysentery and suffered malaria at another time. These bouts required him to be carried on a litter.

(Coincidentally, at about the same latitude to the east Thomson had nearly died. It was reported he was inspired to fight off death because the Maasai allowed hyena to act as their morticians; they believed the burial of corpses poisoned the soil. The Maasai revere the soil because it produces the grass that sustains their beloved cattle. Could any present-day environmentalists match this dedication?)

Just when they had reached the limits of their endurance, the expedition came upon some friendly people who gave them food and a place to rest. Here, they also learned their goal, Basso Narok, the legendary "Black Lake," was only a few days' march to the northwest. Although the distance was short and they had enough food, they encountered the worst terrain to date. As von Höhnel described it:

The scenery became more and more dreary as we advanced. The barren ground was strewn with gleaming, chiefly red and green volcanic debris, pumice stone, huge blocks of blistered lava... . There was no regular path and we had to pick our way carefully amongst the scoriae, some of which were as sharp as knives.

Finally, half-starved, thirsty and completely worn-out the party came to the lake.

The void down in the depths became filled as if by magic with picturesque mountains and rugged slopes, with a medley of ravines and valleys, which appeared to be closing up from every side to form a fitting frame for the dark green gleaming surface of the lake stretching away beyond as far as the eye could reach... gratefully remembering the gracious interest in our plans from the first by his Royal and Imperial Highness, Prince Rudolf of Austria, Count Teleki named the sheet of water, set like a pearl of great price in the wonderful landscape beneath us, Lake Rudolf.

The date was March 5, 1888. After journeying thirteen punishing months in search of this rather dubious objective, their dream of discovery was at last a reality. Suddenly the world appeared more rosy.

Von Höhnel described their experience of actually reaching the water after having been near death from thirst so much of the journey: "Although utterly exhausted we felt our spirits rise... rushed down shouting into the lake... clear as crystal... and, bitter disappointment; the water was brackish."

Still, the men were undaunted. They had achieved their goal. They needed now only to collect the facts relating to the length and breadth of the lake and plot the course of its shores. This seemed simple enough after all they had gone through. Teleki, made an improbable and exceedingly unwise decision to take a detour that brought all hands of the expedition as close to death as any other event on the trip.

While tracing the eastern shore of the lake, they encountered a projecting mountain section. Hoping to find an easier way than the rock-strewn shore, they plunged inland into the same dried-up, foodless, wind-swept, desolate world that had almost killed them on their incoming journey. At one point, most of the porters were strung out along the route. Von Höhnel painted a desperate scene:

> ***The men were lying about staring vacantly before them; loads and animals were in the most hopeless confusion; donkeys and sheep wandering aimlessly about, not an Askan or a donkey boy to be seen anywhere. All discipline was at an end and the men were utterly demoralized.***

Then, the advance scouts found a trickle of water.

Late in the evening and during the night the stragglers came in and flung themselves like wild vultures upon the water. Each one was eager to be first, so that the dark ravine was soon the scene of bitter struggle. Not until after the help of the Somal mercilessly wielding their whips were the combatants separated and something like order restored.

After barely surviving this detour from the lake shore, the company entered an area alive with all sorts of game. Since Teleki and von Höhnel had come to Africa to hunt, they did just that. More accurately, according to their records, they engaged in an orgy of slaughter. Even three elephants were counted in the carnage.

One must remember the era of the early African "big game hunters" precedes the emergence of sportsmanship concepts and the protection of endangered species. A picture of Henri de Rothschild shows him astride a hippo carcass. Big game? This animal is indifferent to humans and climbs naturally out of the river to graze. The caption read, "This hippo was added to his 536 bag," suggesting that these hunters killed anything that moved for as long as the light held. So the Teleki party did what came naturally.

The caption under the executed hippo picture illustrates the scoring practices connected with the hunting engagements. As could be expected, the same scoring procedures were followed in the Teleki camp. In the bag score von Höhnel kept for one hunt, he reported: two elephants, twenty-five buffalo and various other game types. One month, Teleki hunted every day. The score for rhino reached one hundred animals by trip's end. Although many elephants were killed, there was no mention of ivory salvage; ivory trading and hunting was rife at the time.

Without his animal kills, the caravan would have starved; their normal food (corn or sorghum, some goat and cattle meat) was scarce for most of the trip. The kills reported, however, involved much more meat than could be justified as "pot" killing. Curiously, von Höhnel did not write of the animals "bagged" in an exultant tone of "now we can eat"; it was more "the count had good luck on his hunt today." In this connection, the journals record that, only days after leaving the lake, they were again desperately searching for food. Why had they not dried the meat from the game they shot or the fish and crocodile so abundant in the lake area?

I would have expected some discussion regarding the reaction of the porters to the introduction of rhino, cape buffalo and elephant meat to the larder. In my experience, the Kenyan tribal people are light meat eaters. Such a change in diet could represent a hardship, particularly since they regard wild animals as food with about the same enthusiasm as Westerners feel about dog meat. To them, goats and cattle were put on earth to feed humans. Certainly the Maasai would not eat game, but for that matter, neither would they ever be found in a caravan.

Von Höhnel did muse about the exquisite pleasure a large plate of fat would provide. The group regarded goats and cattle as choice food in contrast to game meat, which contains little fat. The Chisholm Trail cowboys had a similar lament over the long periods when they had little more than the meat of the lean cattle they were driving, although for them it was primarily grain products that occupied their food dreams.

During the exploration of the lake, the expedition made a mysterious discovery. Described by von Höhnel, it seemed quite out of place in the "valley of the moon" setting and is still unexplained as far as I know:

> *We came upon a regular heap of camel's bones. There must have been the remains of some two hundred animals in one pile, and although the bones were already bleaching in the sun, there was still as odor of putrid flesh upon them . . . the natural position in which the skeletons lay proved that they had not been carried here, but had lain as they fell.*

How did they succumb *en masse*? From where did they come and to where were they going? What happened to the loads they were carrying, whatever it was?

Graham reports another mystery:

> *In these bleak surroundings are many ancient rock paintings, some of them exceedingly beautiful, created by Stone Age artists. . . . There is an elephant whose outline is exactly that of a mammoth; there are graceful giraffe, and greater kudu with fantastic spiraling horns; there are rhino, oryx and goats—a mystical exhibition in a tumbled gallery of fractured boulders.*

Unfortunately at these sites, no people today possess any knowledge of these early rock painters.

One wonders if the early painters of African animals, whose depictions appear in such locations as Lake Rudolf, the Sahara and Southwest Africa, all attended the same drawing school. Why the concentration on animals? Why no self-portraits? Since modern experts can identify the work of modern artists by brush stroke and such, perhaps they could undertake a study of these diverse rock artists, identifying them by time frame and the type of subjects.

Teleki passed right through Koobi Fora, the area that would become the world's richest known treasure-trove of early man fossils. It was here the team of Dr. Richard Leakey found a skull of *Homo habilis* more than a million years old.

The intrepid Teleki/von Höhnel expedition had been living daily, for a year and a half, with the terrors of starvation, thirst, isolation and sickness. After the boundaries of the lake were established, they still had to retrace their steps south to Zanzibar. Graham describes the scarred terrain they traversed at the southern end of the lake:

> *Monstrous upheavals had torn up the stark land leaving a jumble of mountains, cliffs, deep gorges, and jagged boulders. Coal-black lava had been spewed about everywhere over the older red-brown rocks. By day the region was a sun-fired furnace through which howled a searing wind. . . . All was desolation, lifeless and deserted.*

Desperate to acquire food for their return journey, they entered Turkanaland. These wild warriors were anything but hospitable. The Teleki outfit negotiated long and hard, but acquired neither sympathy nor food. The Turkana, moreover, played a trick to destroy the caravan by informing Teleki that the expedition "would find a large herd of cattle and wild animals as numerous as the grains of sand on the Turkwell River eighty miles to the northeast." This fruitless detour to the promised land lengthened the trek to Baringo by 130 miles. Von Höhnel wrote in despair:

> *Our position was now pretty well desperate. Our men had supported life with the greatest difficulty for weeks; many had succumbed to their privations*
>
> *...Now at the very threshold of the promised land, we were face to face with the fact that it too contained nothing for the support of the caravan.*

The men foraged for food in the wood, "ravenously devouring fledglings from weaver bird nests." They were starving while the local natives had fat cattle—not for sale. Von Höhnel recognized the temptations of the men: "We felt the time was approaching when our caravan would be converted into a mere horde of reckless plunderers."

The leaders controlled their urge to plunder for a time, but not after they moved into Suk country. Scattered about were cattle and goats so desperately needed, but the Suks refused to trade. "Our powers of self-denial were exhausted at last," wrote von Höhnel. "We had to save the lives of our two hundred men at whatever cost to ourselves and others.... We must take the cattle we needed from the natives by force."

The caravan then divided into two parts. The strongest of the men, nineteen in all, were left in the camp with Dualla (as was usual for these salvation exercises). He was to lead a raid upon the natives while the rest of the caravan moved on with the Count. Dualla attacked the *manyattas* under cover of darkness and drove away the herds of cattle, sheep and goats. Two hundred ferocious attacking Suks were driven off by the "fire spears."

It was August 1888, nineteen months into the expedition and the caravan was free of hunger at last. Both the Maasai and Kikuyu were now friendly and readily traded food. Game was plentiful. But the relief came too late for many; the expedition's death rate was tragically high. Teleki had lost a hundred pounds; von Höhnel had contracted malaria and was again carried on a stretcher.

The expedition straggled into Mombasa on October 24, 1888, a mere handful of survivors. They got to Zanzibar forty-eight hours later by boat. Their journey had lasted one year and nine months; they had walked nearly two thousand miles.

Nigel Pavitt summarizes this expedition:

They had completed one of the last great African expeditions of travel and adventure, enabling geographers to add significantly to their knowledge of Mount Kenya and the lacustrine chain of the Great Rift Valley. Cartographers were delighted with von Höhnel's most detailed and painstaking observations which almost completed the map of East Africa, while scientists were fascinated by their comprehensive collection of flora and fauna they had brought with them. Among the many items new to science were three chameleons, sixty beetles, fifteen butterflies and moths as well as locust, spiders, mosses, lichens and flowers.[4]

The more subjective observers would applaud their perseverance and survival against tremendous odds. They followed through on their determination to locate a rumored geographical landmark in one of the most remote areas on earth. Special value can be placed on their dogged dedication despite the loss of many men and the constant threat of death for the whole expedition.

While the Teleki/von Höhnel discoveryof Lake Rudolf in 1888 ranks low when compared to the memorable accomplishments of Livingstone, Stanley or Speke, the desperate hardships endured by the expedition during the year-and-nine-month adventure exceeded the suffering of the more famous explorers recorded in the century. Perhaps their unique claim to fame rests on their having endured the hellish 2,000-mile walk.

The survival of the expedition was clearly due to the dedication and skill of Dualla Idris, their guide and to the porters and other personnel who remained loyal to the end despite their dwindling number.

It is interesting that both the Teleki/von Höhnel expedition and the Samuel White Bakers (Sir Samuel and Lady Baker) met challenges of pure endurance and each achieved credit for discovering a lake. The Bakers suffered mightily while slogging up the length of the Nile River, convinced the river's source must eventually be revealed. They were far better equipped; each day's march wasn't a constant battle to stay alive.

The Teleki/von Höhnel conquest, on the other hand, never experienced the heart-breaking disappointment of the Bakers, who finally arrived at the source of the Nile only to find Speke had already achieved that triumph. Still, the Bakers did get credit later for locating Lake Albert, through which the Nile flows, proving it is also a source of the river.

4 Sir Samuel Baker, *The Albert N'yanza, Great Basin of the Nile*. horizon Press (1962 2 Vol.).

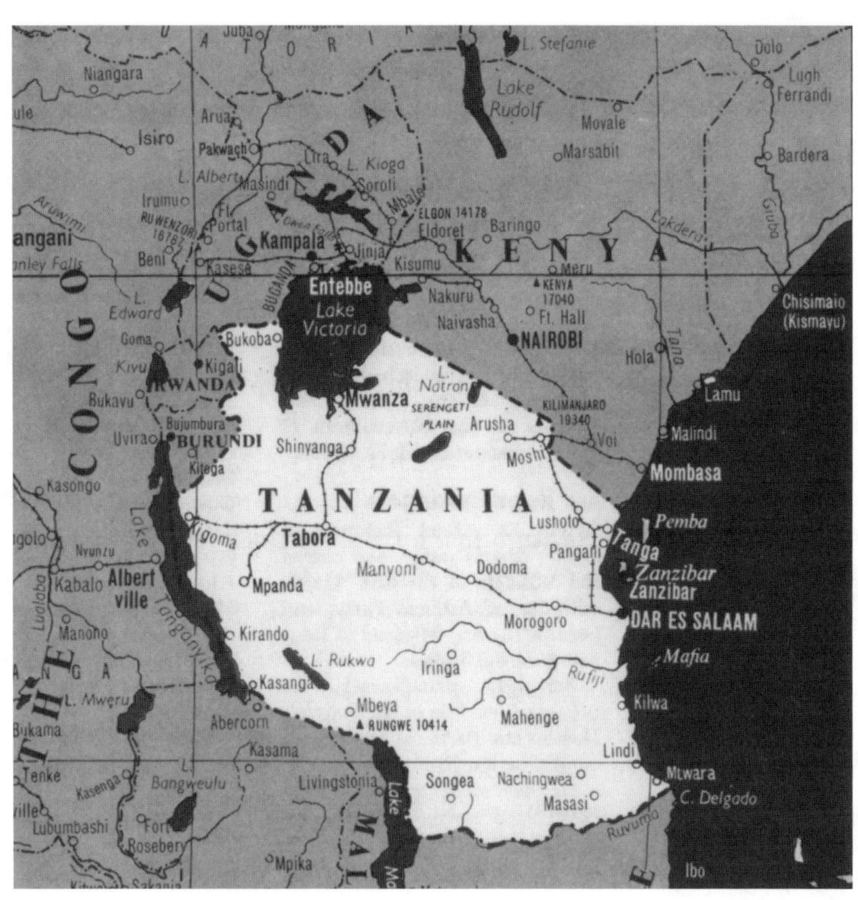

TANZANIA
KENYA
UGANDA
CONGO
RWANDA
BURUNDI
Lake Victoria
Entebbe
Kampala
NAIROBI
Mwanza
Tabora
Dodoma
DAR ES SALAAM
Zanzibar
Pemba
Tanga
Mombasa
Arusha
Moshi
KILIMANJARO 19340
SERENGETI PLAIN
L. Natron
Shinyanga
Bukoba
Kigoma
Mpanda
Manyoni
Morogoro
Iringa
Mbeya
RUNGWE 10414
Mahenge
Songea
Nachingwea
Masasi
Lindi
Mtwara
C. Delgado
Kilwa
Mafia
Rufiji
Lushoto
Pangani
L. Rukwa
Kirando
Kasanga
Abercorn
Kasama
Lake Tanganyika
Albert ville
Kabalo
Nyunzu
Kasongo
Uvira
Bujumbura
Kitega
Bukavu
Kigali
Goma
Kivu
L. Edward
Kasese
Beni
Fort Portal
RUWENZORI 16787
L. Albert
Masindi
Irumu
Isiro
Niangara
Arua
Pakwach
Lira
L. Kioga
Soroti
Mbale
ELGON 14178
Eldoret
Kisumu
Jinja
BUGANDA
Nakuru
Naivasha
Baringo
Meru
KENYA 17040
Ft. Hall
Lake Rudolf
L. Stefanie
Moyale
Marsabit
Dolo
Lugh Ferrandi
Bardera
Giuba
Lakdera
Tana
Hola
Lamu
Malindi
Voi
Chisimaio (Kismayu)
Aruwimi
Lualaba
Manono
L. Mweru
Bukama
Tenke
Kasenga
Lubumbashi
L. Bangweulu
Fort Rosebery
Livingstonia
Mpika
Ruvuma
Ibo

TANZANIA

"Once the Slave-Trade center of Africa, this little island, Zanzibar, long treated strangers like the plague, but it now has come out of the closet. Recently there were 8000 visitors on the island," reported David Lamb in 1978 in the *Los Angeles Times*. This change in attitude was incident to the 1964 merging of Zanzibar's single political party with that of Tanganyika on the mainland, twenty miles to the west, to form the United Republic of Tanzania.

This merger formalized the integration between the mainland and the island, but "local officials on Zanzibar were quick to point out they were not about to surrender any of the local autonomy the 400,000 people here enjoy." Another reason for each area to maintain its own system was Zanzibar is wealthy and its people have no desire "to share their wealth with the 15 million mainland Tanzanians who have "to struggle to even feed themselves."[1]

Although both governments espouse socialism, Zanzibar's revolution is one of the few economically successful in Africa. The slave trade driven prosperity has long since been replaced with a world monopoly in cloves. This crop has allowed the government to build up $100 million in cash reserves. The importance of the government's interest in maintaining this monopoly was evident in the regular Nairobi newspaper reports of the execution of smugglers attempting to do their own merchandising.[2] Rigorous as the government was, it began losing sales after "several Asian countries, among

1 David Lamb, "Zanzibar Talks of Opening the Closet Door," *Los Angeles Times* (1976).

2 Ghana followed the same procedures in protecting the profits of the sales of cocoa for itself, although it never legislated smuggling as a capital offense.

them Vietnam, discovered that cloves are an easy and profitable commodity to produce."[3]

Compared to Zanzibar, progress on the mainland was a different story. Shiva Naipaul described President Julius Nyerere's post-independent "massive resettlement" as paternal socialism." Nyerere's description is more original. He believes it reflects—or recreates—all the virtues of traditional African culture. The theory requires people be moved into villages organized on a cooperative basis." This was less acquiescence than it appeared since it "involved the burning of crops and homesteads to encourage the reluctant."

One supposes Nyerere thought he was improving on the East European collective farming system by assembling all rural people in housing projects. George B.N. Ayittey, with less respect than Naipaul, described the process:

> ***Peasants were loaded into trucks, often forcibly, and moved to new locations. Many lost their lives in the process.... By 1976 some 13 million peasants had been forced into 8,000 cooperative villages, and by the end of the 1970s, about 91 percent of the entire rural population had been moved into government villages.***[4]

The U.S. State Department wrote of the program in more glowing terms: "Under President Nyerere's leadership, Tanzania is seeking to achieve political and economic development within an egalitarian framework appropriate to the rural character and African traditions of its people."[5] This attitude makes understandable USAID's lavish monetary support.)

In 1967, Nyerere used the word *ujamaa* (familyhood) in connection with the "cooperative villages." The substance of this idealism

3 Lamb, "Zanzibar Talks of Opening the Closet Door."

4 George B. N. Ayittey, *Africa Betrayed* (New York: St. Martin's Press, 1992), p. 106.

5 "Tanzania: Long Road to Socialism," *Africa News* (State Dept. Publication 8097), vol. xiv, no. 20 (May 19, 1980), p. 3.

was expressed in the *Tanzanian Socialism and Self-Reliance* handbook published in mid-1967:

> ***To build a society in which all members have rights and equal opportunities; in which all can live at peace with their neighbors without suffering or imposing injustice, being exploited, or exploiting; and in which all have a gradually increasing basic level of material welfare before any individual lives in luxury.***[6]

President
Julius Nyerere

Tanzanian goals were set forth in more conventionally socialist terms in the Arusha Declaration of February 1967. It listed virtually every commercial endeavor in the nation expected to come under government ownership or control.

Since the Arusha Declaration, the official policy of Tanzania's leadership has been to build a socialist state. Received with much enthusiasm by supporters, at home and abroad, the policies laid down that year included nationalization of key economic sectors, a struggle against inequality, priority to rural development.[7]

This article failed to do justice to the enormity of the "enthusiasm by supporters." The *Christian Science Monitor,* in an article headed "Tanzania: Socialist 'Paradise' Can't Pay Its Bills" (March 24, 1982), reported that in his own country, Nyerere was called "nwalimu, Swahili for teacher"; this appellation found favor in student and left-wing circles outside the country as well.

As The Heritage Foundation's *Backgrounder* observed: "The Tanzanian government has 'vanquished' capitalism, which it branded

6 "Tanzanian Socialism and Self-Reliance" (1967), printed in *Africa Insight,* vol. 13, no. 2 (1983).

7 "Tanzania: Long Road to Socialism," *Africa News,* p. 3.

as colonial-era evil." News of a feat of such magnitude, could be expected to spread in some circles, and it did. "Nyerere's African socialism was applauded by leftists around the world. Western governments lionized Nyerere as a visionary and poured over $10 billion of aid into Tanzania between 1967 and 1986."[8]

Julius Nyerere may have revealed some psychological motivations for his extreme deviations from extant ideologies, both capitalism and socialism, in a speech he delivered years ago in Nigeria: "Injustice, even tyranny, reigns supreme in Africa. Despite the atrocities we have seen in Africa, I still maintain it is better to be ruled tyrannically as a free nation than to form part of a colonial empire, however mild its rule."

A recent *National Review* describes the Western intelligentsia's enthrallment over the emergence in 1967 of this non-capitalistic society in Tanzania, whose principles of "self-reliance (i.e., protectionism)," the arrest of "capitalists (i.e., Asians)," the formation of a repressive one-party state, the creation of a "classless society," and the other economic and social breakthroughs in human-based ways of living were analyzed. Most especially enthralled, the article points out, was Robert McNamara, who had just resigned in 1967 from the Johnson Administration to run the World Bank. It also cited a recent internal report of the World Bank which revealed "from 1967 until at least 1980, the Bank viewed Tanzania 'as coming close to being a model development country.'"[9]

Robert McNamara

8 "Tanzania's Travail: Lessons in Improving American Aid to the Third World," The Heritage Foundation *Backgrounder*, no. 866 (Nov. 14, 1991), p. 5; hereafter cited as *Backgrounder*.

9 *National Review*, August 29, 1994, p. 12.

Clearly, the Bank was wrong. It took over twenty-five years, well into the 1990s, and hundreds of millions of dollars in wasted aid before the initial euphoria could atrophy. When Nyerere was forced to step down in 1985, "Tanzanian incomes [were] less than half of what they were in 1980." The nation was forced to rely on foreign donors for 50 percent of her budget (the largest contributor being the World Bank). Finally, the Bank's own report, as the *National Review* points out the "charges that its ...'uncritical support for government policies' helped sustain a 'poorly thought out socialist experiment.'"[10] In a television interview at the time of his resignation from the Bank, McNamara wept—actual tears—as he lamented that so much development aid was left undone due to lack of funds. Obviously, McNamara did not attempt to equate good intentions with actual results.

By 1985, economic conditions forced Nyerere to relinquish the presidency to Ali Hassan Mwinyi, who commissioned "a study of possible multi-party political reform." A year later, in 1986, he signed a series of financial agreements with Western donors, the World Bank and the IMF. These agreements financed the Economic Recovery and Social Action programs of 1986-89 and 1990-92, and ostensibly committed the government to institute a market economy.

"Curiously, Tanzania is being touted by the international development community as a 'success story.'" One assumes they just decided to "declare victory" for they had to overlook many evidences of failures. Tanzania's debt was over $5 billion, and it is the largest per capita recipient of foreign aid and is receiving increasingly generous U.S. and Western assistance—just to eat. After taking such information into account, consider that Tanzania has an annual population increase of 3.6 percent, of which 44 percent is under age 15 (according to *Africa at a Glance,* 1992), providing an adequate supply of mothers to support this 3.6 figure for years to come.

10 Ibid.

To round out the dismal picture, the country is ruled by one party (even though opposition parties are legal), has a state-controlled press and holds many political prisoners. (In one interview, two former prisoners estimated the total number was 4,000.)

In spite of contradictory facts, the *Backgrounder* notes that "Tanzania is being hailed by AID, the U. S., the World Bank, and the IMF as one of the African countries making the fastest strides toward market economic reform." Again, this appraisal constitutes an incredible view of the half-hearted efforts made in that direction. A 1990-91 budget still contained generous and unaffordable expenditures and subsidies. Even more important, the budget report revealed the continued existence of 400 uneconomical and inefficient parastatals certain to be an undermining factor in successful economic reformation; it also indicated that 80 percent of Tanzanian wage laborers still worked for the state.

"The relocation of Tanzanian farmers directly disrupted and reduced Tanzanian agricultural production [these farmers had to spend as much or more of their time commuting as they did hoeing], requiring Tanzania to spend its scarce foreign exchange on food imports, starving its agricultural, manufacturing and transport sectors of essential manufactured imports." This mass relocation of rural people—lazy farmers, non-farmers and whatever other types—must have included the Chagga tribe, reputedly the best farmers in tribal Africa. At any rate, as the *Backgrounder* explained, "The demise of Tanzanian agriculture sealed Tanzania's economic doom."

Tanzania suffered the same results as other African governments that decide the state can more efficiently organize agriculture, while, at the same time, it can redirect the product toward social objectives. The results that invariably follow a government's replacement of the free market system with government control of plantations have been visible deterioration. It begins quickly. Equipment begins to fail from poor maintenance and mishandling or is abandoned from lack of skilled operators. In Tanzania even the *shambas* (small farms) were taken over. "By the late 1970s, Tanzania was importing 78,000 tons of grain annually." An Associated Press release (November 16, 1978) reported the signing of an agreement whereby Tanzania would receive, free of charge, 50,000 tons of American corn over the next two years worth more than $5 million.

A list of extravagances and monuments in which these developing countries were allowed to indulge—on U.S. taxpayer money—almost always included conference halls, international airports, an airline, modern freeways and other works of splendor. The *Christian Science Monitor* (March 24, 1982) reported on Tanzania's new capital being built "of considerable grandeur and cost in the bush at Dodoma. But Dodoma may wind up as a monument to failure." (in 1997, Dar es Salaam continues to be the capital.)

Tanzania also built an international airport to facilitate easy access to her famed game parks. I regarded this airport to be about as attractive as an airport could be: it had nice architecture (for just sitting there on the veldt), no clutter or traffic obstructions—no traffic, for that matter. I arrived solo each of the few times I used it.

The airport would also serve the new international conference center, which had been converted from the headquarters facility for the former East African Community (EAC) after that organization broke up in early 1977. The *Christian Science Monitor* (ibid.) explained the break up of the EAC as caused by the conflict that developed between Tanzania and Kenya when Nyerere turned his back on private enterprise in 1967. Kenya, a proponent of capitalism, could not accommodate his system.

The State Department chose not to pinpoint economic ideology as the basis for Tanzania's conflict with Kenya: "With the break up of the East African Community (EAC) early in 1977, Tanzania has faced the requirement of diverting substantial human and capital resources into institutions and infrastructure to operate and maintain port, rail and air transportation services previously run as common services by the EAC."[11]

11 "Tanzania: Long Road to Socialism," *Africa News*, p. 4.

In retrospect, Julius Nyerere could be considered an African version of Stalin, albeit with a fantastic ability for image making. He drove citizens from their homes. Business owners were jailed or merely deprived. He imprisoned any citizen who dared to object. He eliminated both the democracy he inherited as well as an effective market-based economy. He loaded a debt of $5 billion on a debt-free economy. He reduced a country that could feed itself to one that would starve without begging food from the rest of the world. All of this vicious social engineering, as well as the weird economics, was accepted by the world as a justifiable cost for achieving some sort of rainbow land.

Even by the end of Nyerere's first decade in the late 1970s, reversal of these lunatic policies—herding farmers into makeshift villages, destroying the commercial sector and the rest of the ravagement—would have been impossible to fully reverse. In spite of the patently obvious evidence the experiment had failed, both socially and economically, the donors of the world perpetuated this artificial structure with infusions of money. Who could blame Nyerere for not admitting to failure and thus continuing the flow of donations? (Curiously, it is reported he did confess to misjudgment at the time he turned over power.)

Since 1967, as a result of his actions, vested interests have become hopelessly entrenched, dependent for their very nourishment on this funding. Meanwhile, the brain capital of skilled workers and entrepreneurs have either left the country or atrophied. What happens when the donors come to realize they have been propping up a failed social system—a basket case? Will the international donor community accept the realization they have made a ward of Tanzania? The World Bank finally did. A *mea culpa* is not enough. Can they make amends?

TANZANIA'S FREEDOM RAILROAD

In retrospect, it seems preposterous that western nations, especially along with the Chinese, would dump up to a billion dollars over a period of some seven years (during the Rhodesian closure of the rail shipping route up to its reopening) on a project whose primary purpose was to satisfy Dr. Kenneth Kaunda, president of the newly independent country of Zambia, who was reluctant to deal with the "white dominated south." There was no identifiable economic derivation. The project met no commercial standards of viability of Germany, Russia, Holland, Sweden, nor the U.S. The Chinese, for their own reasons, financed and built it. The other countries furnished millions for operating funds long after the project was an obvious failure. The project: an alternate railroad for the shipment of copper from the mines of Zambia north to the Tanzanian port of Dar es Salaam on the Indian Ocean.

The reason for this alternate route can be understood only by one immersed in the values and political attitudes of the times. The white minority governments, along with being under worldwide sanctions, were bitterly hated, especially by black neighboring countries. A. A. Jorgensen, in his article, "Rail Transport in Southern Africa," published in *Africa Insight Bulletin,* no. 1 1983, provided a thorough background on the story of Zambian copper shipment and the events leading to the Chinese building of the Freedom Road.

By 1910 copper could be shipped by rail transport from the Copperbelt to Cape Town (3,500 km) or channeled via Rhodesia and Mozambique through the port of Beira on the Indian Ocean. Prior to 1965 nearly all Zambia's exports had traditionally been shipped on that line as well as much of her imports. But by 1961, transport rationalism was beginning to be replaced by political considerations. The Central African Federation was broken up. Subsequent political activity had resulted in dissolution of the unitary administration of the railway serving Rhodesia and Zambia. By 1970 Zambia was seeking new rail transport links to the north in order to reduce reliance on the "white dominated south." An actual study with

Tanzania was conducted to investigate the feasibility of a new railway to link the Copperbelt with the port of Dar es Salaam.

The Zambian proposal was known at various times by different names: Uhuru Railway, Tanzam or Tazara Railway. Informally it was referred to as the Freedom Railroad. England, Germany, Russia and the U.S. were approached as prospective builders. Each turned down the offer. Still, in 1987, the U.S. Agency for International Development helped the Zambian and Tanzanian governments reconstruct and pave more than 250 miles of road. Mainline China, perceiving reasons of her own, undertook to build the railroad, signing a contract with both Zambia and Tanzania.

President Kaunda, although emotionally reluctant to be dependent on the white Rhodesian regime, wasn't prepared for the 1973 Rhodesian closure of the Zambian-Rhodesian border, consequent to a conflict between the two countries. As a result, Zambia immediately gave up or lost, fifty percent of her export and most of her import transport availability. One option was to haul copper by trucks , some 250 miles on the unpaved Great North Road, known as the "Hell Run," through Tanzania to Dar es Salaam. Other means was to increase usage of other routes. The Atlantic coast-Lobito run was increased from 20 to 50 percent. Some copper found a way through Malawi to the port of Beira. The Dar road now carried 35 percent of the copper.

Through all this Kaunda held firm to his independent position against his hated neighbor, even though the Rhodesian government did allow vital supplies such as food and seed to pass. *Allowed* is the operative word. Did this indicate a softening of Rhodesia policy? Or more likely, Zambia desperately opted to contract for this particular tonnage. More confusion relates to the succinct phrase, "Rhodesia's closure of its border to Zambian railway traffic." What were the circumstances backing this pat phrase used in so much of the writing of the era? No explanation seems needed. The implication, one can suppose, was everyone supportive of these post independent countries accepted the label of white government ruthlessness without explanation. (That's the way they treat the blacks.) It is true Zambia joined Great Britain in its sanction program against Rhodesia. But that couldn't be a reason for such a Rhodesian government to arbitrarily decide to give up all that Zambian freight revenue. A. A. Jorgensen refers to the Rhodesian "blackmail" as a reason Zambia sought to expedite the completion of the Tanzan railway.

The current wisdom for the reason of this closure, at the time I was in the area, was related to the refusal of Zambia to take responsibility for the act of one of her security guards, who shot two Rhodesian tourists under the railroad border bridge. The main discussion centered on whether or not the guard's perception of a possible sabotage threat was valid. In any event, the conclusion was that the closure had a specific cause—to force compliance. *The New Columbian Encyclopedia,* did render an oblique opinion. "Altogether Zambia suffered considerably from the action taken against Rhodesia." The reality of loss was true.

This 1,116-mile long railroad designed to link landlocked Zambia with the Tanzanian port of Dar es Salaam was destined to fail. Although it opened in a blaze of publicity, it was grossly under designed. It had insufficient locomotive power. The gauge was known only to the Chinese, restricting purchase of spares and other equipment to that country. Managerial mistakes were chronic. For a variety of reasons the line proved unequal to the task of moving Zambian copper to the coast.

The chapter ended with the independence of Zimbabwe in 1980 when traffic, of course, resumed on the traditional routes through Zimbabwe and South Africa.

The magnitude of waste of this emotional politically-founded project can be understood by a listing of the salient elements: the product of 13,500 Chinese laborers, a $412 million loan by the Chinese (later to be canceled), plus millions from other donors. The recognition of the line's commercial failure was masked for many months by the infusion of donor money.

A program of monumental waste, with no chance of success, based strictly on emotion and symbolism was concocted over a relatively minor event. The U.N. could easily have settled the quarrel if it had had a mind to, providing my take on the matter is correct—that Zimbabwe realized she acted injudiciously. Zambia would have been deprived of her banner of victimization, thus avoiding so much turmoil and waste of resources. The U.N. could have interceded, in accordance with its charter. But it could not appear to be aiding a white government under sanctions.

Parting Note

A Chinese passenger plane landed at the Dar es Salaam airport one morning in 1974. Hundreds of small men debarked, lined up and then marched off. They were all dressed in Mao uniforms—a blouse and trousers, topped off with a hat. They were part of the 13,500 contingent of railroad labor. Talking with a local shopkeeper, he explained the nature of these workers as customers waving an arm at his ravaged shelves. Their wages were paid in shillings the Chinese government had been able to buy for pennies in Switzerland. With these shillings, the customers became the equivalent of locusts, depleting the shops of all imported articles. Replacement of the imported stock with this money of no international value was of course impossible. "That is why " he said, "you can sell the shirt off your back for three times what you paid for it." I had seen the same thing in Uganda when the departing population took their foreign exchange with them.

Section IV

AFTER THOUGHTS

Samburu—most expensive photo taken in Africa

One of the men offered to barter for my daughter

BLACK SKIN ATTITUDES

During these years in Africa, I was alert for the alleged psychological similarities between black Africans and African-Americans that would justify the oft-expressed concept of a cultural brotherhood among all blacks. Actually, there appears to be more of an inborn hostility among the internal African tribes than any feeling of racial kinship. And after finding no evidence of harmony anywhere, I speculated on reasons why none exists.

I have come to believe that African-Americans, in their search for identity, have been tempted by fallacious assumptions about Africa and its people. Their error is they (African-Americans) view their own position through the eyes of a social minority, while the African people, in a world markedly different from America, live *their* lives as the majority group. Whether or not this is harmful to American blacks or a beneficial source of comfort is not part of this study.

For me, growing up in southern Utah was a white-skin experience, except for red Indians and one black person. The lone black man's name was Mose; either his mother named him or perhaps he thought whites expected a black person to be called Mose. His style of living protected him from discrimination: his house outside of town, his junk salvaging business and his not seeking status as an elder in the Mormon church. Although the color of his skin was an oddity, children loved his friendly personality.

The next blacks I met were a couple of lionized student athletes in junior college. By then, however, I had already formed a sense of compassion for Negroes through reading the history of slavery and Harriet Beecher Stowe's vivid depiction of the atrocious treatment of blacks in *Uncle Tom's Cabin*. This literature, along with contemporary news accounts of southern lynch mobs, contributed to my image of a helpless, abused people.

With these attitudes firmly ingrained, it was natural for me to join several organizations at the University of California dedicated to improving the lot of the down-trodden, discriminated-against minions of our citizenry. These movements eventually led to enormous political and legal changes in the lives of blacks.

The salient point I discovered that determines attitudes toward black skins, by anyone, relates to the ratio of blacks to those with substantially less melanin. A rare or infrequent sight of such a startling contrast in skin color, touches off special emotions and behavioral patterns in the viewer. Depending on basic attitudes, it may be hateful and discriminatory or one of compulsive protectiveness that can easily verge on patronization. Neither emotion is beneficial to anyone in my opinion.

Carrying this concept of minority a step further, a phenomenon developed, or perhaps it is one I gradually became aware of relating to the significance members of this minority black population personally attaches to his own genetic skin color. Its importance ranges from complete obliviousness to an all-consuming passion. Such esoteric pondering never entered my mind during the heat of the civil rights crusade.

The emotion-fueled civil rights campaigns succeeded in insuring all legal rights and full benefits of citizenship for African-Americans. Perhaps the movement should have retired at that point, with congratulations all around on victory achieved, but that was not to be. The humanists, or socio-political activists, had multiple objectives. The image of black powerlessness sparked the continuation of a program of protection and paternalism that had no completion, no end. While this nurturing attitude has effected the creation of a hothouse (or protective envelope) deemed necessary for establishing catch-up and special race programs, it may also have had a preemptive effect on the blacks' own development goal as well as encouraging dependence on whites.

This concept of the need of whites to guide blacks into the mainstream may have been reflected in a statement made by a black student that, at the time, confounded us emotionally charged people who felt ourselves involved in a near holy crusade. He said: "You liberals are more of a detriment to the black future than the Georgia rednecks are. We know where we stand with them." Although the meaning of his charge escaped us then, he must have been aware of the confusion of our well-meant racial or ethnic development efforts.

For a long time, the aim was the amalgamation of blacks into the melting pot of the general citizenry, seeing them as individuals. "See me as a man not a color" was the theme so eloquently expressed by Martin Luther King. Jr., in his "Dream" speech. Historian John Hope Franklin recorded a common idealistic dream of of black people in modern America: "The effect of the acculturation of the Negro on the U.S. has been so marked that today he is as truly American as any member of any other ethnic group that make up the population of America."[1]

Both King and Franklin misread the spirit, and certainly the direction, that black attitude development was to take on its own, albeit concurrently with environmental changes over which they had little control. For even after the triumphs of the great civil rights battles in the sixties and the massive media blitz that awakened the nation to the presence of the blacks, to be "legally" American, with full civil rights, was not enough. Although African-Americans had been in America longer than any of the waves of immigrants—Irish, Italians and others—they still felt alienated.

Essentially, blacks lacked an identity, and their search for one led to the construction of some unique, innovative, as well as unrealistic attempts to fill the void. First, they had to establish their origin (find their roots) to develop a basis for nationalism. Nationalism, however, requires a nation for its base. For American blacks unwilling to accept their home country in that role, there could be no "nation" as such,

1 Franklin, John Hope, *From Slavery to Freedom: A History of the Negro American* (Alfred A. Knopf, Inc., 5th Ed.), 1979.

just some unknown portion of a huge continent. So they compensated by adopting the whole of continental Africa as their seat of origin. After they accepted this abstract foundation, their zeal for Mother Africa seemed undiminishable. A carefully printed graffiti high on the wall of a men's room at the University of California adamantly expressed this sentiment: "The 'country' of Africa belongs to the blacks."

The adoption of Africa as the blacks' spiritual home provides a sense of belonging, but it also relates to their preoccupation with color. By being connected by color to nearly a half billion Africans, they become part of one of the world's largest races, thus temporarily ameliorating their hated minority status—at least on a planetary basis.

Other aspects of the search for belonging and for a direction for racial evolvement have led American blacks to become reconciled with their color in two regards. First, they have embraced the mark of Cain, the primary evidence that sets them apart, and have imbued it with intrinsic worth. They have gloried in it. As Claude Brown says in his *Manchild in the Promised Land*: "Wow, man, it's a beautiful thing to be colored. Look at us. Aren't we beautiful?"[2]

The importance of color and the emphasis on this attribute have increased to the extent that a black American is not merely an entertainer, writer or politician—he is a black entertainer, black writer or black politician. A collection of black politicians forms a black caucus, not merely a caucus. In addition, the word *black*, usually used as an adjective, has become a noun identifying the race. Thus "black" replaces the hundreds-of-years-old racial designations of "Niger" (Latin) and "Negro" (Portuguese), both terms, in their original languages, merely refer to the chief physical characteristic of blackness.

The second aspect some American blacks entertain is a belief that a uniqueness of purpose, a brotherhood or soul-mate relationship, is

2 Claude Brown, *Manchild in the Promised Land,* (New York: MacMillan Company), 1965.

existent strictly on the basis of their skin coloring. This mysterious element is believed to serve as a carrier of racial recognition. As nearly as can be understood, the generating factor in this unique bond is the common heritage of oppression. The late Leanita McClain, writing for a Chicago paper, lamented in an article her inability to convince non-blacks of the existence of this racial quality. She claimed it was a characteristic of all the blacks in the world—aborigines, Micronesians, all.

Former U.N. Ambassador Andrew Young must also be imbued with these convictions. How else to explain his actions when he flashed about Africa, formulating policy, providing interpretations of the desires, political aspirations and needs of "Africans," assuming an ambassadorship for virtually the whole continent? The answer: He has the fraternal skin and just instinctively knows about black people or so he would have us think.

The fact that Ambassador Young's ancestry is at least six generations removed from some small village in an unknown part of Africa is ignored. He was just going home to see the folks and he hesitated not at all in assuming the role of spokesman. As spokesman for continental Africa, over three times the size of the United States, containing over 400 million people in over fifty political divisions, composed of a thousand diverse tribes speaking almost as many different languages, his task was monumental indeed. It would be impossible, one would suppose, without the gist of genetic memory and a special affinity to other blacks (perhaps comparable to that trait attributed to identical twins).

This overriding preoccupation with color is perhaps strangest in the political arena. For a long time the black people have found it beneficial to vote as a block directed toward a political payoff in terms of specifically favorable laws and conditions. While this coalescence is deeply embedded in political history, the process comes with a sacrifice of individual voter choice.

Another politician, former black caucus Congressman William Clay, had strong ideas about the way black citizens should conduct themselves. When asked in *Ebony Magazine* whether blacks should celebrate the bicentennial, he replied: "Certainly, there is no intelligent reason to celebrate our own second classness, our condition of de facto servitude ...consensus to celebrate gives tacit approval of our foreign policy in Africa ...." Congressman Clay didn't hesitate to instruct his black constituents, but his geography was confusing: Africa was not part of his congressional district.

Historian Franklin does make some concessions to differences among blacks when he speaks of "diversity of physical environment"; yet he said all blacks have "similar racial characteristics." Colin M. Turnbull in his *Man in Africa*[3] also attempts to prove no significant difference in the continental African people:

He takes Franklin's concept of "diversity" to the limit. Although acknowledging wide and equally obvious variations in skin and hair color, he contends that geneticists now find basic unity linking Bushmen to Pygmies and them to the vast bulk of continental Africans; Bantu speakers or not.

However comforting this construct might be, it is strange that no speculation focuses on the nature of this contended racial characteristic. How does it play out and what are the geneticists looking at when they locate this mysterious unity?

These are surely monumental generalizations about Africa, both in Franklin's book, which is purportedly a history of Negro Americans and their ancestors, and especially in Turnbull's.

Prior to my own African experience, I had no reason to question or object to whatever myth, construction or assumption black Americans accepted. What's the harm if it is comforting and has a beneficial effect on self-esteem? A posture of black hands across the seas inducing friendships is not all that common.

Even if they wish to build a fraternal nation within a nation—wherein membership qualifications are based exclusively on color—the Constitution probably would not be violated, although it may seem a bit vainglorious to consider this particular order to have overseas expansion proclivities.

3 Colin M. Turnbull, *Man in Africa* Acre/Doubleday 1976

But, in this desire to expand lies the potential harm. As long as the soulmate attitude remains on a high plane of abstraction, it is the African-American's own business. And in most respects it does just that.

Whether the mystique the African-American feels for the African people is harmful or not, it is self-delusional. The African counterpart does not exist. In every way, the African feels at home in his specific country of birth. He can identify directly with his ancestral roots, traditions, cultural background and the tribal affiliations that the black American so sorely misses.

The Made-in-America consideration of color provides no basis on which the African-American can identify with African continental nationalism. Consider just the basic environmental differences: most African-Americans live in a sea of white faces, or at least see them frequently on television, in the movies or in cruising police cars. From early in his life, the black minority child is reminded daily of the startling contrast of his skin with that of the majority whites. Furthermore, he soon learns that his skin color can he a handicap in various circumstances.

Such experiences are not part of the consciousness of blacks living in a majority situation, as in sub-Sahara Africa. There, a black child from the day of his birth sees only black. He is no more particularly aware of his skin color than he is of having two legs. A black living in an environment of one color could be as unconscious of color as a Swede growing up in Sweden would be unaware of his lack of color.

To the black African child, a white person is a freak, an aberration, with no special threat to or impact on his life. He grows into a culture that evaluates people from an entirely different viewpoint or set of conditions to that of the black American. The African's primary kinship is within the clan and tribe. Not only is one abstract racial membership of no consequence to these allegiances, but even the sharing of a common political citizenship does little to weaken the elemental fidelity to personal family.

In contrast, the African-American, however much he deplores it, is stuck with his own history. He has, in effect, a Made-in-America culture and background. The shipload of slaves, collected from many parts of the vast-Saharan part of Africa, formed a new society in America, compelled by circumstances to learn a common tongue, accept the prevailing religion and adapt to the conditions found in the new land. Each succeeding arrival merged into the existing black population.

While modern African leaders, educated and semi-detribalized, can fill the political leadership role in a nation, they show little inclination to sacrifice any of their extended family interest in deference to some racial or political affiliation. In incidents where whites have dominant power, black freedom fighters will fight under a banner of black against white, but they do so essentially as a means of identification and to correspond with the viewpoints of their humanist western sponsors, who view causes as white-evil against black-good.

Basically, however, the focus of black Africans is on the power locus, not the color of the power holder. Overwhelming evidence for this assertion is found in the way anti-apartheid blacks break into hostile competitive groups when the white-held power becomes vulnerable.

In short, not only has the African black no reciprocity with the African-American, but he is most likely to regard the American black simply as a rich foreigner—certainly not as a soulmate or brother. To repeat, the consideration exists the U.S. program of paternalism and protection may well have been regarded as more hurtful than helpful. This may have led American blacks to seek an unrealistic connection with African blacks to bolster their need to establish their own community in America. Still the attempt to create a mother-Africa-north, negates what should be seen as their basic American citizenship. But whatever value they acquire from this attitude, it can eventually put them at a competitive disadvantage in a sea of new immigrants, who will find it hard to recognize the earlier forced immigration of the black constitutes justification for a special citizenship class.

SUMMARY

Some lifestyle! Our two-year Ghana stint stretched to four years with the added contract in Uganda and Kenya. We had not planned that much of an extension. Certainly, it was an entrance into a life "dimly seen." Working and living in these countries that are located in a broad stretch along the equator provided experiences and knowledge of a cross section of post-independent politics. We observed the economic and social approach to nation building, and caught a glimpse of what is meant by the generic words *culture*and *different values*. Most importantly, we came to realize there are few valid solutions to African problems.

This last statement is more profound and amazing than it may seem. From the humanistic viewpoint of the West, a transfer of technology, money and good will was deemed sufficient to help these newly-independent nations-in-making, gain the requirements for entering the world of U.N. representation. Based on this simplistic notion, donor and loan programs were provided mostly according to the donee country's request; there was little consideration of how appropriate or cost effective that request might be. To ask the struggling country for an accounting of the funds, or a careful analysis, was perceived to be demeaning and counterproductive to the development of trust and responsibility in the newly-formed government.

Misdirected leadership goals, wasted resources, incentives to corruption and other damages were the result of this plethora of free-flowing cash. But an even more lasting handicap to nation building lay in the way the donor/loan programs distracted attention from the problems created by the inappropriate switch from a colonial market system to one of "Scientific Socialism." This shift in policy required central planning, price fixing and all sorts of regulations far exceeding the capability of the new and inexperienced administrators.

Unfortunately, the very program on which we had been hired to work turned out to be an unadulterated catastrophe. The Ghanaization or Africanization, policy not only became an impediment to growth but also promoted continuing stagnation. The pseudomorality of the slogan "Africa for the Africans" sounded positive and worthwhile, but it obscured any realistic projection of the results of such a policy.

The mind-set that inexperienced and completely unsophisticated black citizens could step into the shoes of business families with years of practice, trained administrators and skilled laborers became a *de rigueur* policy in most African countries. The disastrous effects in each country differed only in degree: from mere stagnation to a return to the stone age (as occurred in Uganda).

A retrospective look is in order. What if we had stayed at home? When measuring the paucity of good we provided to a few African countries, we must also contemplate how we personally fared. What did we enjoy or begrudge as a result of our four-year expedition?

Our monetary loss from an expenses-only income was dedicated at the outset. For the children, the break in their academic education program was somewhat difficult, but we hoped the cliché of "travel is broadening" was accurate and made up for the loss. Our girls had a chance to assess their value as wives (in terms of goats and cattle), which was a unique experience.

The children returned, one by one, to California schools.

Myrtle and I hung on, wishing to be with them, yet endeavoring to complete agreements and on-going projects in Kenya, which we did. As adults, we had an interest in the historical demise of the African colonial system and the emergence of dozens of new nations. That interest was fulfilled, but the revelation that humanist-liberal verities relating to nation building were naive at the least, and often clearly uninformed, was eye-opening.

INDEX

A

B

C

D

E

F

Index

W

Z

ABOUT THE AUTHOR

L. DALTON CASTO has worked as a business and economic consultant for the Ghanaian government, assisted business entrepreneurs and tribes in East Africa, Kenya and Uganda, and consulted on other Sub-Saharan African government work. He completed post-graduate work at the University of California at Berkeley, School of Business and Economics, and has a business background in finance, promotion and management.

Mr. Casto has traveled and researched extensively throughout Africa and his first book, *The Dilemmas of Africanization,* which describes the political and social dangers threatening Sub-Saharan Africa, was published in 1998. He makes his home in Northern California.

Order Form

Mail direct orders to:

African Ways Publications
33 Hansen Court
Moraga, CA 94556
Phone: (925) 631-0630
Fax: (925) 376-1926

	Quantity	Amount
African Embrace ISBN: 0-9659830-1-3 **$15.95**	______	______
The Dilemmas of Africanization ISBN: 0-9659830-0-5 **$27.50**	______	______
Priority mail $4.50 first book ($1.00 each additional)		______
California Addresses please add 8.25% sales tax		______
Total amount enclosed (U.S. funds)		______

Company name______________________________

Name______________________________

Address______________________________

City____________________ State_____ Zip________

Telephone (_____)____________________

Order Form

Mail direct orders to:

African Ways Publications
33 Hansen Court
Moraga, CA 94556
Phone: (925) 631-0630
Fax: (925) 376-1926

	Quantity	Amount
African Embrace ISBN: 0-9659830-1-3 **$15.95**	______	______
The Dilemmas of Africanization ISBN: 0-9659830-0-5 **$27.50**	______	______
Priority mail $4.50 first book ($1.00 each additional)		______
California Addresses please add 8.25% sales tax		______
Total amount enclosed (U.S. funds)		______

Company name______________________________

Name______________________________

Address______________________________

City____________________ State_____ Zip________

Telephone (_____)____________________